Up, From The Majestic Hills

UP, FROM THE MAJESTIC HILLS

A Veteran Educator Reflects
On His Travels
And
Life Experiences

Gilfred K. Morris

ISBN:978-0-557-47920-7

Contents

Foreword

Gilfred Keith (G. K.) Morris has generously shared memories of various aspects of his childhood and adult life which also relate to important milestones in Jamaica's modern history. Born in the "Majestic Hills" of North-West Manchester in 1930, Morris'journey to adulthood coincided with watersheds in the island's development: the rise of nationalism and the search for a new identity, the granting of universal adult suffrage, the flowering of community self help projects led by Jamaica Welfare, the growth of modern party politics with noble ideals of nation building that were later undermined by bitter sectarian divide of the 1970s, the experiment with the ill fated West Indies Federation, the granting of Independence, and most importantly, the broadening of opportunity for people of humble background to access secondary and tertiary education. Also, G. K. Morris' overseas sojourns, first to Canada (1969-1974), where he was Principal of a school for Native Canadians in Manitoba, and then to Freeport in the Bahamas (1979 - 1987), underscore the expansion of the Jamaican Diaspora to include middle class professionals seeking economic security and professional development.

We learn that G. K. Morris' family roots are firmly planted in Maidstone, a free village pioneered by Moravian missionaries in 1840 and which attracted the settlement of former enslaved families, including his ancestors. His story underscores the pivotal role of the church and school, quite often inseparable, in rural communities and which profoundly fashioned the fabric of Jamaica's society in its post slavery development. Further, the story of G. K. Morris' childhood presents us with another variant of child rearing in rural Jamaica, for after his mother married and relocated from Maidstone, his grandfather, Samuel Morris, "fathered" and "mothered" him. Samuel Morris, who had a profound influence on G. K. Morris, embodied the values of the freed people who consolidated their triumph over their roots in enslavement and transitioned a foundation for the later rise of the black middle class. Grandfather Morris was a carpenter, as well as a planter of provisions and tree crops such as pimento and coffee, and he also produced honey. Further, literate and widely read, he was the "village lawyer" and the Registrar of Births and Deaths for his district. He was fiercely independent and loyal to the Victorian values of thrift, honesty and diligence that were the staple of his only exposure to formal education in the church school in Maidstone in the 19th century. Not surprisingly, he was the Chairman of the first Peoples National Party (PNP) group that was formed in his area of Northern Manchester. Significantly, while the Jamaica Labour Party swept the polls in the first elections under Adult Suffrage in 1944, Northern Manchester was among the only 4 successful seats for PNP candidates.

Nourished by his grandfather's values and commitment to family and to community, G. K. Morris was exposed early to reading and through books to a larger world and developed a curiosity to see it. Indeed, his passionate pursuit of educational opportunity at the secondary and tertiary levels in the 1940s, 1950s and 1960s is testimony to his upbringing and driving ambition to succeed against insurmountable odds. When financial constraints jettisoned his formal secondary school career after only two years at St. Simons's College in Kingston, self study and success in the Jamaica Local Examinations prepared him for entrance to the Mico College in 1951, then the "Black University of Jamaica" which enabled the sons of the "respectable poor" to contribute to national development by way of education of their less fortunate compatriots.

G. K. Morris graduated in 1954 and while teaching he undertook further study to acquire Ordinary Level and Advanced Level subjects to qualify for entrance to the then University College of the West Indies in 1961. There, he read history and held his own with the best and the brightest from the region and developed a wider regional identity at the time of the ill fated West Indian Federation. After graduation he accepted a History teaching post at St. Georges College where between 1964 and 1968, I and several others were fortunate to have had Gilfred Keith Morris as our history teacher. And now having read his story 40 years later, I have a better appreciation of this calm and highly assured black Jamaican whose confidence and dedicated professionalism have inspired students at the primary, secondary and tertiary levels in Jamaica, Canada and the Bahamas over a period spanning nearly 50 years.

I commend this work which provides a welcome window into various aspects of the social history of modern Jamaica and underscores how important it is for others to write their memoirs. Then, by pooling these experiences we can better construct a broader profile of Jamaica's collective story as the island approaches fifty years of independence in 2012. Indeed, G. K. Morris' memoirs provide plenty to admire and to ponder as we grapple with present day challenges which have their genesis in our past of progress mingled with missed opportunities.

Swithin Wilmot, D. Phil (Oxon)
Dean
Faculty of Humanities and Education
University of the West Indies,
Mona, Jamaica.

Acknowledgements

Very early after my retirement in the late 1990's I began to feel the urge to write and could not for long deny the fact that I had a story to tell. It is a story of my generation and presented to the next generations, marking the rocky road my generation traveled and the foundation and groundwork laid for the improved road surface on which we now tread.

I owe a great debt to my grandfather, Samuel M. Morris, who, as the reader will realise, played such a mighty role in my upbringing, in the moulding of my character, instilling right values and encouraging a healthy view of the world and our fellow men. I treasure the memory of this good man.

My thanks go out to Mrs. Shirley Maynier Burke who took time to read through the manuscript and gave her encouragement. To my good friend and counselor, Dr. Ena Campbell, I owe deep gratitude for her reading through the draft manuscript, for her suggestions, well informed comments and insights and her never-failing encouragement. I accord her my sincere thanks.

Very special thanks go to Mrs. Sharon Gardner who did a most masterly job of editing the manuscript. I really cannot thank her enough for the infinite care and precision which she put into the operation, thereby giving me a solid lesson in properly preparing the product. I thank her so much.

To my sons Rohan and Paul, I say many, many thanks. Their computer expertise and management ability were most vital, and I daresay, without them there might not have been a book. Thanks to my wife Vinnette, ailing but patient. Thanks for being understanding when I was away for many an hour. Many relatives and friends kept asking if I were still writing the book. Their constant prompting pushed me on and I thank them most gratefully.

Chapter One

My Early Years

I was born on October 30, 1930, in the district of Maidstone, Manchester, the "illegitimate" child of Iva Morris, daughter of grandpa Samuel M. Morris. I was registered, "Gilfred Keith Oliver,"with no surname, as was the custom with "illegitimates" in those days. My grandfather, Samuel M. Morris was the Registrar of Births and Deaths for the region and he did the job of registering his grandson.

In all my years and travels, I have never known of, or heard of, or read of another "Gilfred". Where did my mother dig up that name? But I suspect my grandfather had a strong hand in the selection. In his wide reading, he might have come across the Saxon, Alfred the Great, King of England or Wilfred of Ivanhoe, the gallant Saxon knight who served Richard the Lion Heart, King of England, as told by Sir Walter Scott in his novel "Ivanhoe". It would not be surprising if my grandfather slipped off "Al" or "Wil", and slipped on "Gil", thus inventing a new Saxon name, "Gilfred" - "Gilfred of Maidstone?" Also, I must note that my father's first name was "Gilford". Was there a deliberate connection?

However, I never questioned the origin of my first name during my years up to fifteen, simply because that name was never used, and I was totally unaware that "Keith" was not my first name. Not until I was fifteen years of age when I had to consult my birth certificate, did I discover that the name by which the whole world and myself, knew me, was actually my middle name. Regrettably, I did not pry out of my grandpa and my mother how I came by that name "Gilfred". All through the years after the discovery, people and institutions have insisted on addressing me at various times as "Gilford", or "Gilgred" or "Gilbert" or "Wilfred". The National Water Commission over many, many years maintains "Gilgred" on my water bills and every once in a while a letter arrives with "Gilbert". But I love my initials 'G. K.' and I was always so pleased with one of my Mico tutors who never failed to address me except as "G. K. Chesterton" - I thought it had such an impressive ring to it.

The situation concerning my father has been a common Jamaican one, where the young dandy impregnates the young female and abandons her and his child to their fate. The historian and the sociologist assure us that this attitude is a part of our culture carried down from our forefathers' slave days on the sugar plantation. The young buck, as a slave, was not encouraged to accept any responsibility. In fact, it was a policy of the slave owner to discourage any pattern of what might develop into any sort of family responsibility. The slaves must be kept divided. And so our young buck enjoyed himself and moved on without a glance behind. I am sure my father knew he had a little boy at a home in the hills but it never bothered him. Somebody was caring for that boy, and that was that. My mother said that she was nineteen years old when she became pregnant with me but she miscalculated - actually she was twenty three years. She told the story that her father was most angry and disappointed when he discovered her pregnancy and he gave her a severe beating. His only surviving daughter had let him down. Her mother had died some years before, her father had not remarried and possibly the absence of a mother's strong guiding hand made its contribution to her "fall".

However, it would seem that having delivered that beating, her father decided to make the best of the situation and fully accept the coming child. And so the child was born - I believe that my grandfather was quietly pleased that a boy had arrived and not a girl. Apparently, there was no communication with my father, neither during the pregnancy nor in the years after. My grandmother, that is, my father's mother, who lived about three miles away, told me that when I was born, she went to my mother's home to look at the newly arrived baby. After having a good look she was convinced that baby was her "blood". Here began a beautiful relationship with my grandmother which lasted till her death at one hundred and three years.

My father never accepted me as his child but his mother accepted me fully as her grandchild. Once, as a little child of about four years, my mother took me to spend a week with Grandma. There I met my sister Alma for the first time. She was born a month before me. Ha! You get an idea of how busy my father was at that time. He fathered seven of us "illegitimates" - seven that we know of. Three of us were born in one year: July, September, October. I firmly believe that any one of those highly developed Western European countries, now very worried about their too low birthrate, would today welcome with open arms, a man of such prowess and proven productivity. Seven beautiful "illegitimates"- with how many women? I will not tell you. I must note here that this rather handsome young man had been given a car by his dear mother and one can just picture, in those times, what a desirable prince he was, in that whole region of the island. And so he made merry with heart and soul and body and mind and every other thing, in this his extensive princedom.

Grandma had several other grandchildren, besides us "seven", and she always had at least one at home with her. My sister Joyce, cousins Mavis,

Basil and Gerald, as well as Basil's son, Vern, were all nurtured in Grandma's home. She was so very kind to me. On Sundays, for example, at the end of the worship service at church, you would see this little boy picking his way among the rows of pews, down to the back section where his grandmother sat. There she would have pudding, biscuits or sweets, for him. The little boy loved it and he knew that his grandma loved him. As I grew up over the years, we kept close; many were my visits with her and she had so many stories to tell me. She always encouraged me with my school work, and later on when I began sitting exams, she rejoiced with me when I was successful. Grandma was very intelligent, was well-spoken and had received a solid basic education. She had been married to a schoolmaster who was principal for a short time at our local school, Nazareth. He was a very good organist and on the last Sunday that he accompanied church service many people wondered at his especially brilliant performance that day. A few days later he was dead., leaving Grandma with six young children, no money and no home of her own. But she set to work and singlehandedly built her home and reared her children. She was a farmer all her life and a widow for over fifty years. She never flinched from hard work and as her district people always said of her, she worked like a man.

Strangely, in all my years growing up at home, my father's name was never mentioned to me. Neither my mother, my uncle nor my grandfather ever mentioned his name. But I was kept quite well informed by people in the district about him. They never ceased remarking to me about my resemblance to my father, about the truck he drove, and a lot of other bits of information on him. But inside my home, nothing. I can't remember ever asking my mother about my father. Maybe, even at this tender age I somehow understood that the subject was taboo at home and I kept quiet about it. I forgot to mention that I was given my mother's surname, not my father's. My six "illegitimate" siblings all had his surname. When I was about eleven years old I accompanied an older schoolgirl, Marjorie, who was living at my home, to the railway station at Greenvale, about six miles from home. My father resided and worked at next-door Mile Gully and several times on my visits there, I had seen him from a distance. This time I told my friend, Marjorie, that if I saw him I would go to him and say howdies.

That day, as it turned out, he was sitting nearby reading the newspaper. I walked up to him and said good day. He looked up from the newspaper and smiled and returned the greeting. I cannot remember what I said next but I recall he was smiling and polite and when I left him to continue on my way I was sure he knew who I was. But I never had any thought of striking up any relationship with him. My action was simply the result of a whim. When, sometime later, my friend Marjorie met my mother, she promptly informed her of my approach to my father. My mother was not in the least amused and upbraided me for doing that. She warned me never again to do that and remarked that he had never given me anything, and who knows, if a relationship was struck up, he might want to take me away. I thought her fears were ridiculous but I heard her quietly and silently assured her that I was not in the least interested in any son- father relationship. I was about seventeen years old when my father died. I received the news without any real feeling of loss. He was just a distant figure, of no great significance; it was just another death in the passage of time. I never attended his funeral.

My home district, Maidstone, was, in the slave period, a coffee plantation of three hundred and forty one acres. In 1840, just after Emancipation, it was purchased by the Moravian Church and subdivided into ninety eight lots which were sold to the ex-slave Church members. My great, great grandfather, James Morris, was one of the first settlers in the new village. He purchased a five acre lot valued at twenty five pounds and by October 1841 had completed his payment. Sometime later he added a neighbouring one and one-half acre lot, for which he paid seven pounds cash. Great, great grandpa James, an ex-slave, must have been a solid, upstanding man, and a credit to this new Moravian community. Thus was established one of the earliest Free Villages, which the Church nurtured into a vibrant small settler community.

District Scene

Maidstone lies in North-West Manchester, on the peak of the Don Figueroa Mountains, with a cool climate and picturesque hills and valleys. Its irregular and sometimes difficult terrain precluded its development into the typical Moravian village that the missionaries envisaged, models of which would be found in other parts of the world where the Moravians laboured. But the village grew and prospered, with its large church, school and later its post and telegraph office, active community organisations and able and devoted pastoral and lay leader-ship. This was the community which nurtured me from childhood to young manhood - a region of hills, gullies, sinkholes, bad roads, plenty of hilly land, bits of level land, stones and stony school playground, pimento, coffee, tobacco, citrus, yam, sweet potato, Otaheite and rose-apples, banana patches, corn and peas, cows, goats and many a hardworking donkey - sturdy small farmers at their labours, conservative and devoted to their Church. Such was my community, those dear hills that watched me grow. I came up from those hills and they never cease to lie tenderly in my memory.

I shall regard the period from my birth to age six as the first phase of my life. I take age six as the dividing line because my mother married about that time and left the home to reside in a nearby district. The earliest I can remember is that my mother and I occupied the north bedroom of my grandfather's home. The room was high above the ground and I recall gazing often through the window panes at the barbecue below. The bed was spacious and at that time would have been built of wood, with wooden lathes, and a mattress stuffed amply with "bed grass", a special type of spindly grass which was used in most homes, and was readily obtained in the districts around. "Spring beds" would have been rare in the district at that time. One incident which has been etched in my mind is that of my mother dealing with a scorpion which was crawling quickly on the bed, towards me. I may not have been more than five years old, but it was early morning. We had just awakened and were about to go outside to start the morning's chores. I was still on the bed, with my mother puttering around to leave the room. Then 'wham, wham'. I saw my mother frantically hitting at a scorpion heading in my direction. The third 'Wham' crushed the fellow, and her son was saved. Did I cry or jump off the bed or was I terrified? I cannot remember, but what I do remember clearly is the mother seeing her child in great danger and jumping to effectively protect him.

My mother later got married to a gentleman from nearby Medina district. I can't remember this "gentleman from Medina" coming a-courting and making himself 'nicey-nicey' around the house or making much of his prospective step-son. But I do recall just a little of that wedding day. I believe it was on a Wednesday, because Wednesday, in those days, was the favourite day of the week for weddings. There was always a flower garden immediately in front of the house, and a short rail fence separating the garden from the house. I was sitting on the topmost rail when I saw my mother all dressed up and walking down the path from the parochial road, leading to the house, on the arm of the "gentleman from Medina". I remember clearly that she was crying and dabbing her eyes with a handkerchief, and my new stepfather kept saying, "Don't cry, don't cry". Another little bit I recall was my looking through a window and seeing my grandfather standing in the reception hall, but he was not dollied up in wedding finery. It did strike my little mind but I gave no further thought to it. I don't recall getting cake or drink or any fussing about me. I must have realised that something special was taking place, but that it would mean losing my mother from the home and that she would be living somewhere else, did not filter through my little brain. I have to add that I did not know when my mother slipped away, she never said goodbye to me, no one tried to explain anything to me and I was left to cope as best as I could with the change. Marriage and weddings were adult business and I guess there was no need to explain to children. I seemed to have coped very well, settling down nicely in the new household of my grandfather, my uncle and myself.

Sometime later, whether it was weeks or months I cannot tell, the household was joined by 'Nana', an elderly lady who had lived elsewhere in the district. 'Nana', as everybody called her, took care of the home, cooked and laundered and became a member of the family. She was quiet but could wax eloquent when the situation warranted. She was very neat and took good care of the home. She was kind to me and treated me as a child should be well treated, according to the child- rearing manual of the time. She had three words which she used so often. They were strange and we couldn't figure out where she found them. One was "Condesly" - whenever she wanted to speak to you privately she would say, "I want to speak to you, `condesly'." If I were absent from her presence for a long time, when I reappeared she would ask me, "Where you coming from, Panaucis?" Another time she would say, "Is Nassa you coming from?" Later we found out that 'Nassa' meant Nassau in the Bahamas, but we never could figure out 'Condesly' and 'Panaucis'. She was a disciplinarian and would not hesitate to vigorously express her displeasure whenever I crossed the line. She never used the rod on me but I recall two occasions when she took an active part in having me disciplined.

On the first occasion I had transgressed seriously and my grandfather was determined to give me the switch. However, I dodged him and hung about the garden near the kitchen and hoped that the hours would soften Grandpa. Dinner time arrived and by that time, about five thirty, I was very hungry. Hunger propelled me warily into the kitchen where Nana was busy dishing out the food. I was still wary and anxiously kept my eye on a slit in the wooden window facing the short path leading from the house to the kitchen entrance. I did not want to be 'backed up' in the kitchen by Grandpa. I eagerly stretched out my hand to receive the plate of dinner that Nana handed to me. In that swift moment I must have dropped all caution. I was taught that when taking anything which was being given to me, I should take it with the right hand. So my right hand went out to receive my dinner. Instantly, Nana's hand clamped on my left hand. "Put down the plate, don't drop the food", she calmly said. I put down the plate on the table and Nana led me up to the house and delivered me to Grandpa. I received my whipping, cried for the appropriate length of time, then dried my eyes, wended my way back to the kitchen and duly attacked my dinner which Nana had safely put away for me. I was much displeased with Nana but by next morning we were again good friends.

On a second occasion Nana again had to deliver me to Grandpa. In those days (1930s), many people in the district did not have concrete water tanks. We had our water tank and sometimes neighbours would ask us for a bucket or two of water. On this occasion our young neighbour, Bauz, came up to us to get a bucket of water. This was the time when I did something that was really terrible - so bad that even in my adult years whenever I remember it, I squirm. However, I stood beside Bauz as he filled his bucket. He placed the bucket away from the tankside and then started walking up towards the kitchen to deliver something to Nana. When he reached a short distance from me, I called to him, "Bauz, a gwine spit inna di water". [1] Bauz literally jumped around, "Don't dweet Keet (Keith). If yu dweet a tell Cou Sammy." [2] (Cousin Sammy, my grandfather). And then he turned and continued walking.

When I saw that he was not looking I promptly spat into the water. Then I dipped my right index finger into the spittle and spun it around a few times in the water. In my little child's mind, I was sure the spittle would naturally and quickly blend and dissolve into the water and one would not see any trace of it. But to my horror, Bauz was on his way back and the blob of spittle had settled down and was 'showing off itself' most glaringly in the water. Bauz was now almost by the bucket of water and the blob of spittle was now compact and quietly floating, waiting to greet Bauz. Bauz arrived at the bucket and gave a gasp. He bent over the bucket as if to see even clearer. "Yu spit in deh!" [3] He whirled and quickly went back up to the

---

[1] "Bauz, I am going to spit into the water."

[2] "Don't do it, Keith. If you do it I will tell Cousin Sammy."

[3] "You have spat in the water."

house and Grandpa, and told him of my worthless act. On the way from the house he called to Nana in the kitchen and informed her.

Both Grandpa and Nana were livid.. Grandpa summoned me but I ran into a clump of banana trees nearby. He did not pursue me. That wise old head knew that there were more ways than one to skin a cat. Why did I spit into the water? All through the years I have never forgotten the incident and I keep asking myself the question, why, why? I had never seen any of my friends or playmates do any thing like that - my home was one of discipline, respect and high principles. So it was not a result of any example set. Furthermore, Bauz's family were good neighbours of ours and there was no suggestion of any rancour or ill-feeling between the families. I was not a disobedient or headstrong child. All our neighbours and friends around would have been appalled that "little Keith" did that. So, why did I do it?

I don't know and I have never been able to offer an explanation. I committed the act at about six years of age but I have regretted it all my life. Millions of us parents have had "good children", but can we swear what they will do or what they will not do? Well, what did happen to me in that clump of banana trees, waiting for the inescapable judgement? I sat there, almost crying - I was so sorry for what I had done. I had let down Grandpa, my uncle and Nana. I had let down Bauz, for he was my friend. Dinnertime came. I did not feel hungry but I decided to head for the kitchen. I felt so dejected and guilty that I did not care. I went and sat down on my little bench. Nana calmly walked over to me, took my hand and led me up to the house and Grandpa. There was no resistance I knew I deserved what I was about to get. Grandpa gave me a sound whipping. I cried and I cried but I never thought that Grandpa was unkind for giving it to me. I deserved it and I went to bed greatly humbled and determined never again to be so obnoxious.

Home, for me, was strict. Obedience and good manners were non-negotiable. For us children in those days, there was little display of close affection from our parents. So many of us would never think of jumping on our parents' backs or huddling up close for a hug or a kiss. If we tried it, possibly we would receive a firm slap and be told to know our place. In parents' presence, the child should be quiet and respectful and keep his place. "A child must be seen and not heard". I am convinced that most parents genuinely loved their children but showing it openly was not the way of the times. The world was not yet open to American television and the love revolution which it spread far and near. Disciplining then, very, very often involved corporal punishment. The majority of parents knew of no other method. After all, did not the Good Book warn about sparing the rod and spoiling the child? At school some teachers were known as 'beaters', never being without the cane or leather strap. Many parents, in trying to ensure that their children learnt well and behaved well in school, encouraged Teacher to "just save the eye". Some teachers welcomed the encouragement and were glad to 'lay it on'. I did receive my quota of lashings from home and school. My grandpa was always moderate in his punishment but I was a bit afraid of my uncle who could be very severe at times. He just had to 'look' at me and I would straighten up forthwith.

My home was a good home in the sense that it was one of discipline and order and clean living. There was no looseness of behaviour, foul talk or use of expletives. I was taught to be respectful to all adults. Whenever my playmates took to teasing an adult who had an amusing nickname, I knew I should wisely dissociate myself and move quickly from the scene. In my district there was 'Mass Manny' who, whenever you addressed him as such, declared you were classing him as "Manny Mongoose". He would get most annoyed and raved and promise solemnly to tell your parents. He never understood that the more he raved and ranted, the more enjoyment he provided for his tormentors. Sometimes he would go up to the schoolhouse and inform Teacher of his tormentors. Teacher would deal appropriately with the miscreants, one by one, as they crept into class. Then there was "Willie Cake". He worked regularly on the parochial road and was said to be a great lover of 'cake' (what we now know as 'bullas'). On this particular day, certain of the school children on their way to lunch, taunted him, "Willie Cake, Willie Cake". Willie Cake knew the names of some of his tormentors so he ran up to the school and gave those names to Teacher Romney, the Principal.

As the time for reassembly after lunch approached, the Principal placed himself at a strategic position and, as the tormentors came in, he called, "John Anderson, come and take your cake." Poor John, who did not think his sin would catch up with him, was well 'caked' by Teacher Romney's cane. Next, Isaiah Bentley's head appeared over the hill. Teacher waited. As Isaiah stepped in, he said, "Isaiah Bentley, come and take your cake". Isaiah, who was slightly 'chigga foot'[4], ambled up and was well 'caked', and received a 'running lick' as 'brawta'. And so all the 'cakemen' were dealt with by Teacher and Willie Cake now enjoyed some peace on the road. But this episode reminds that the whole community took a strong interest in their children and their behaviour on the street. You knew that you were being observed and that your parents would be kept abreast of

---

[4] "Feet infested with chigger or jigger or chigoe. This type of flea burrows into the skin of humans and animals and if not extracted, can eventually deform the toes and gait of the infected person."

your carryings-on. There was a greater sense of community then. It was not unheard of that an erring child could be chastised by a non-family member if found to have been flagrantly insolent or engaged in activities which the community members knew would not be tolerated by the parents. Such was the rural community in the first half of the twentieth century.

The Church on the Hill - Nazareth Moravian church

Church was a vital part of the life of my family. We were rock solid Moravians and would never entertain even a very, very remote thought of changing when the Seven Day Adventists, Pentecostals and the various shades of Church of God invaded the district. Neither rain nor sickness kept us from attending church on Sundays. It had to be flood rains or severe illness which would stop church attendance. On a Sunday morning there was Children's Meeting, beginning at eight o'clock, directed by Mrs. Annie Black, wife of the pastor, Rev. James Black. At Children's Meeting, each child attending had to recite the Golden Text from the Bible, along with a verse from a particular hymn. This hymn was chosen by Mrs. Black and each week we learnt one verse until the verses were complete. When we had memorised all the verses, Mrs. Black would teach all the children and the adults the hymn tune after Sunday School. Children's Meeting included young adults below seven years of age up to fifteen years. Here we learnt and committed to memory Bible verses, many hymn tunes from our Moravian hymnal and Bible stories and intensive religious and moral instruction from a most devoted Mrs. Black. She was an overawing personality to us children. You did not play the fool in her presence - in fact it would never cross your mind to misbehave. She was stern but she never used force with us. A look from her would certainly pull us back into line. We felt we did not dare to displease her.

Whenever you started out to Children's Meeting on a Sunday morning and you did not memorise your Golden Text and hymn verse properly, then you would be a very troubled child, dreading that coming contact with Mrs. Black. I can well remember an embarrassing experience I suffered at Children's Meeting. I might have been about eleven years old at the time. On this particular Sunday morning, I was a bit late because I was trying with the last minutes to cram the Golden Text in my memory. Unfortunately, my brain then was always a bit lazy whenever it came to memorising Bible passages and I arrived at Children's Meeting badly prepared. The Golden Text was from St. Luke 18, verse 14, "I tell you, this man went down to his house justified rather than the other ...." When I stepped in, Mrs. Black had just finished hearing the Golden Text from all the children. Mrs. Black turned to me. There was silence and all eyes were on me. I began haltingly but resolved to start afresh and I blurted out, "I tell you this morning ....". Can you imagine the laughter? Mrs. Black gave me the sternest of looks and then ordered, "Sit down." I was so embarrassed and had to live with the teasing for the next few days at school. As for Mrs. Black, maybe we did not love her but we had the greatest respect for her and we knew she had our best interest at heart. In later years, looking back, I have always regarded her as the ideal minister's wife. The Church was her life. She was the sole teacher and leader of Children's Meeting, she was a main cornerstone of the Sunday School, she was Choir Mistress and sometimes Organist. She ran the weekly Sewing Class for young women of the church and taught Country Dancing, now known as Square Dancing, to the girls. Other village organisations did not escape her and she was very active in the Maidstone Improvement Association of the 1930s. As the minister's wife, working with the young people of the community, she could not be surpassed.

Now for Sunday School. This started at about nine o'clock and included all the participants in Children's Meeting, older young people in the senior classes and adults of any age. Teaching lasted for about forty-five minutes and then all the classes came together for a review by the

Superintendent. The Golden Text for that Sunday was again run through and only the very adult classes were not pressured to memorise. As mentioned before, whenever all the verses of the chosen hymn were memorised, then Mrs. Black would teach the tune. These were always interesting mornings. Mrs. Black would teach, line by line, usually without accompaniment. Sometimes she would even teach the bass parts to the older men. Remember, she was Choir Mistress and could also roll a satisfying bass when necessary. I cannot forget the many Cantatas she prepared with us, the beautiful singing, recitations and the appreciative congregational audiences. I remember once she put on a special 'Children's Day', with 'The Home' as the theme. There were the many rehearsals and we dared not miss any of them. My recitation was entitled, "A Boy Needs A Dad". I have always wondered if Mrs. Black specially chose that piece for me. But I did it beautifully and received enthusiastic applause at the end. I remember the big young fellow, Rudolph, singing a solo beginning, "Home, home, dearest to me", and eventually ending with the line "There's no place like home." Oh! Those were great days. Mrs. Black was stern, but she gave her best to us and we are the better people as a result of her selfless devotion to us young ones.

By 10:45 the church bell would be summoning worshippers to 'Big Service,' starting about eleven o'clock. Moravian congregations in those days separated males from females. The women and the girls had their sections and the men and boys had theirs. Wife and husband did not sit together - only much later did this segregation begin to break down. In the boys' and girls' sections the smallest and youngest ones, sat on the first benches, in front, then, as they grew older, they graduated further and further to the senior benches at the back. The singing was accompanied by organ music from a beautiful German-built pipe organ, usually played by a staff member of the nearby school. In these early days we had no choruses, no testaments were given, nobody called out Hallelujahs or Amens, nobody commented aloud as the minister preached. There was a staid decorum to our worship. We sang our hymns lustily, quietly listened to and imbibed the sometimes rather lengthy sermon.

There was very little variation in the format of the services. "Big Service" ended at about one o'clock, after which there was a break. Many members came from far outlying districts and they would usually bring refreshment, which they would consume during this break. At this time too, those who were heading for home would leave the premises. After this break, there would be "Second Meeting", when the various church organisations e.g. Moravian Missionary Society Jamaica (MMSJ), would meet and discuss their business. "Second Meeting" was also the time when, if the

Minister had any special business with the congregation, he could get close to them. During the years of the Second World War, Rev. Black often used "Second Meeting" to bring the congregation up to date on the progress of the War. With "Second Meeting" over, the worshippers could now all go home, after a rather long day. But nobody complained. Sunday, for the folks, was the day of rest, to worship in the house of God and remain quiet. For these rural people, hard working all week, a measure of socializing was welcome too, as many members took the opportunity to renew acquaintances and catch up on the happenings and tid-bits of the district.

My grandfather, in time, I regarded as a very special man. To this child, he knew so much about so many things, so much about old times, with a repertoire of wonderful stories. He could write so easily and beautifully, he registered births and deaths, he gave endless 'legal advice' to all and sundry, he made their wills and stored many at his home. He communicated with big merchant firms in Kingston and abroad, he imported shoes and clothing from Lennards in Bristol, England. In the cellar of his home there were countless old envelops from Thomson Hankey and Company, Fred L. Myers and Son, Lascelles deMercado and Co., John Haddon and Co., and many more. He took the 'Daily Gleaner' regularly, sometimes daily, and kept himself abreast of much of what was happening in his island and overseas. He never borrowed from neighbours. He always possessed the required tools and equipment for his home - on this he was fiercely independent. Yet he was considerate to neighbours who did not have, but he insisted that if you borrowed, you had to return what you borrowed. Many were the times when I was sent to some neighbour to retrieve what had been borrowed. He lent his donkey and its hampers, his cross-cut saw, his fro for splitting roof shingles, his adze, his crow bar, and the use of his coffee pulper and honey extractor. He borrowed money only from the local People's Cooperative Bank, never from any neighbour or local businessman. There was no alcohol consumption nor tobacco smoking in my home, no gambling nor hanging out at the local shops. The end of the workday would see Grandpa with his newspaper, reading by lamplight or telling some interesting story, sometimes posing riddles, telling an Anancy story or challenging with strange or difficult spelling words. He would talk about old landmarks in the districts around, well respected folks who had passed on, past Governors of Jamaica, eminent legislators, well known and eminent planters and pen-keepers, Mrs. Morris Knibb, Barrister Smith from Clarendon, Queen Victoria and her Golden and Diamond Jubilees, and on and on. Regrettably, the tape recorder was not yet in wide circulation.

Every year Grandpa planted his field of yams and sweet potatoes. He reaped some yellow yams but his specialty was the Mozella yam. For sweet potatoes, his favourite was the Blue Bud variety but he reaped also a little of the Breeze Blow variety. This was a sweet potato with a fine, floury white flesh and was delightful when baked under hot ash. There were a number of other varieties which had done their time and were gradually fading from the scene e.g. Costa Rico, Lyon Joseph, Sierra. Sweet potato varieties last only for a time, to be replaced by new varieties. Farmers always declare the latest variety to be the best yet, but when the new variety takes hold, the previous 'best' variety is quickly relegated to a very rear position. In his provision field Grandpa never failed to add his 'Bellyful' beans, okras, cucumbers, bush cabbage, cooking tomatoes, sometimes 'jukutu' (`a rough calalu). He would also have his coco plot, which was a favourite hunting ground for me. You see, I dearly loved roasted cocos - I was always proud of my white, strong teeth and I delighted in cracking them into a roasted, well-scraped tough shelled 'Leftman' coco. Many a time my grandfather went into his coco plot intending to reap, but when he pushed his 'coco stick' into the soft earth around the coco root, it broke nothing. The cocos had already been removed, by guess who?

Some of my happiest moments were spent in the world of the sugar cane. My grandpa and my uncle never failed to plant sugar cane in their fields. Manchester has never had any sugar estates; its mountain climate and often rugged terrain marked it off as unsuitable for that estate culture. But her small farmers planted the sugar cane widely, not the estate varieties, but those which were sweet and soft enough for easy human consumption. I repeat that I had strong teeth and these were always engaged with my sugar friend. Grandpa and my uncle kept me amply supplied. My uncle still had reasonably good teeth and he too loved his cane. He would have his cane after dinner in the evening. He would peel with his knife and when he came to the hard bumps between each joint, he would cut that off and hand to me. Every time, as soon as he sat down to have his cane, I would pull my little bench up close and he would feed me with all the bumps. Grandpa liked his cane juice too but he had to get it from the old 'squeezer' near the kitchen. I have never lost this great love for the sugar cane and even in these my diabetic years I eat my occasional joint.

Chapter Two

I Begin My Primary Education

I started school at seven years of age. In fact, to be exact, I started on January 17, 1938, which would make me seven years and two months old, but since I would not have been accepted in my October birth month, I had to wait until the new school year which began in January 1938. In my district, and the districts around, there was no Nursery School or Infant School to give us little ones a start and our parents had to put up with us for a much longer pre-school period than present day parents. In those times, in our country's history, there must have been very, very few champions of Early Childhood education. Some of us little ones may have suffered dearly from this early 'empty period' of our lives but we must be reminded that very many of us who 'suffered', went on to forge ahead gloriously, despite our late start. But there was one occasion I can remember, when I greatly regretted not starting school a bit earlier. It was the 12th of May, 1937, the day of the coronation of King George the Sixth and Queen Elizabeth, of England. That day was a day of celebration throughout the British Empire, and Jamaica enjoyed its share. School children received a special treat. In my district the school children that morning gathered in the schoolroom and they were joined by the children from the neighbouring school of Medina. I don't remember any singing of patriotic songs but I am certain there must have been. Those were the days of *"Rule Britannia, Britannia rules the waves - Britons never, never, never shall be slaves."* Also *"O Britannia, the pride of the ocean ---- - – –."* then the chorus, *"When borne by the red, white and blue; Thy banners make tyranny tremble, When borne by the red, white and blue."* Such an occasion would not have been complete without lusty expression of the gathering's loyalty and devotion to the British Crown.

Then came the best part of the children's hour - they marched up, one by one, up to the front of the room, where each student was given a rectangular metal pan beautifully decorated with the portraits of the new King and Queen and filled with sweets. Each child bowed as he or she took it with the right hand; a few who did not bow in the first instance, were made to do it properly before the pan was released. I was about a year short of school age and was so disappointed that I was not old enough to receive a pan. As I stood on the sidelines with Grandpa (he would not have missed such a patriotic spectacle), how I yearned for a pan. They were so pretty, the King and Queen looked so heavenly, and most important, each pan was filled with gorgeous sweets. However, I licked my lips in vain as I did not have a friend or relative with a pan, from whom I could get a taste. Later, when I started school, there were many of these 'royal' pans around, used by students to store their pens, pencils and erasers.

But I did reach the ripe old age of seven. I recall sometime before I turned out to school, my grandfather calling out to Teacher Romney as he rode his horse past my home. Grandpa went up to the roadside and I saw both of them turn their heads to look at me as they talked. I could not hear what they were saying but I instantly knew they were discussing my turning out to school. So when that certain Monday morning came, I was registered and placed in A class. That was the class for the beginners. The next class above was B class, then First Class and then a student would normally, in time, go on next to Second Class and up through the school to Sixth Class, which was the highest in the school. On reaching Sixth Class, the student would remain there until age fifteen when he or she would be quietly informed by the headmaster that "your time is up". By law the student's primary education started at age seven and ended at age fifteen. However, all was not 'cut and dried', as gifted students skipped grades and could progress through the stages rapidly. Many students reached the top grade, Sixth Class, by age eleven or twelve and could embark on extra studies long before age fifteen.

On my first day at school I sat beside my next-door neighbour and friend, Joe. We did very little work but sat and looked and looked, as if taking in everything and everybody in our new and strange world. Our A Class was in the south-east corner of this old, large rectangular building which in earlier years had housed the Moravian congregation. A new church building had been erected nearby and this old building was now the school. It was one very huge room with chalkboard partitions between some classes. A Class and B Class occupied the gallery in this corner. In the south-western corner of the building was a second gallery which accommodated Second Class and Third Class, both classes comprising Middle Division, the name given, in those times, to that section of the school. A Class, B Class and First Class, comprised Lower Division and Fourth Class, Fifth Class and Sixth Class comprised Upper Division. Our Lower Division teacher-in-charge was Miss Brenda, wife of the principal, assisted by two monitors, Icy and Mavis.

My A Class days seemed to have been uneventful except for one episode which demonstrated that I, a quiet, cooperative, 'mannersable' student could also be quietly destructive. It so happened that on this particular day, while still a student in A Class, we were returning from lunch. I was about three minutes behind the others and when I entered our galleried area, A and B Classes were already gathered, standing close together, receiving and answering Mental Arithmetic questions. As I ascended my gallery area I saw a 'little slate', placed leaning smack in the walkway, right in front of me. I remember clearly that I asked myself, "If I step on this slate, I wonder if it will break?" I walked straight ahead and stepped on the slate. I heard the cracking sound of the slate and I jumped off nimbly, held my head up and walked to join my classmates at Mental Arithmetic. So far I was sure no one had seen the action; everybody was busy snapping fingers and solving their Mental Arithmetic problems. I entered merrily into the proceedings, snapped my fingers too and answered one or two questions and I was happy.

Then the bell rang for the end of Mental Arithmetic and the beginning of the after-lunch roll call. Everyone was now hastening to his seat. Before I reached my seat, the cry went, "Slate bruk!"[5] I looked agitated like all the others. Then, to my consternation the statement came, "Is Keet Marris bruk it" (Keith Morris). My classmate Yu Yu, had seen what had happened, had kept quiet, but promptly identified the perpetrator when the crime was discovered. The broken slate belonged to classmate, Kenbert, who was quietly shedding copious tears. For Kenbert, this was a sad disaster. In those times, A and B Class students used the 'little slate' which cost threepence, and First Class up to Third Class used the 'big slate' which cost sixpence. Kenbert had inherited his 'little slate' from his older brother, was proud of it and guarded it carefully from being broken. Among us little squabs, where slate breakage was such a frequent occurrence, keeping a slate intact for a substantial length of time was a great achievement. So one can see why his broken slate was such misery for Kenbert. Of course I was hauled up before Miss Brenda, our teacher. I declared that I did not see the slate and had accidentally stepped on it. I was given some stern words but the accused got the benefit of the doubt and the matter was laid to rest in the class. However, when school dismissed at four o'clock I thought it prudent to leave the scene quickly and get home fast. When I reached home I pulled off my school clothes, donned my yard clothes and came out of the house to begin my evening chores.

Then I heard noise and loud chattering coming down the road. When I looked out there was Kenbert, with his broken slate and leading a crowd of school children. Then he stepped down to my front door, the crowd standing by the roadside and waiting expectantly. They must have expected

---

[5] "Slate broken."

that I would be given a rotten time by my folks, maybe even given a sound beating and they would joyfully witness the spectacle. But they were disappointed, for my grandfather was absent from home that day, and Nana, our home caretaker, was in no position to give any redress. She told Kenbert he would have to return the next day. No doubt the crowd felt cheated. It melted away and the matter of the broken slate was no further pursued. Needless to say, I maintained before Grandpa and Nana that I accidentally stepped on the slate. Kenbert never entertained any rancour towards me. He soon had a new slate and we became lasting good friends.

I learnt my letters well and in a very short time I was reading "Mr. Mike rides a bike" and "Twirly and Twisty are two screws". At home there was reading all around me so I had the incentive. In all the learning areas I more than held my own, though I had to wrestle overtime with numbers. The first memory passage from the Bible that I can remember in A Class was from Leviticus 19, verse 32: "Thou shalt rise up before the hoary head, and honour the face of the old man, and fear thy God." We had our full course of memory gems, Bible verses, recitations and much more.

I had very little of B Class as I was skipped early to First Class, where I now had to get my 'big slate'. Here now I had to handle Units, Tens, Hundreds and get into full Addition and Subtraction. Dictation, where the teacher read a paragraph slowly and the student had to write it, taking great care to get every word spelt correctly, and getting in your commas and full stops, was a great test for us at this stage. It was an enormous achievement when your slate was checked by teacher and it came back with a big capital "R" sprawled in chalk across your dictation passage, signifying that all was correct. We always tried to reach home with the big "R" intact on our slates, to show off on our parents. Spelling became very easy for me and my reading level rose rapidly as I had reading material all around me at home. From our "Mr Mike" books we moved on to the Royal Crown Readers in Second Class. We had enjoyed the earlier "Twirly and "Twisty" stories and were a bit disappointed when they later told us that those two delightful characters were "two screws". As we graduated on to Middle Division we handled the new Royal Crown Readers quite well and we enjoyed the numerous interesting stories. In later years there emerged much criticism of these 'foreign' reading material, that these reading material were outside the experience of the Jamaican child and there was need for material to which the local student could relate.

But we, as students and main users of these reading books, were not in the least perturbed. Snow and ice were not here for us to see, but when we read the poem beginning: "Around the fire one wintry night, the farmer's rosy children sat." at least some of us transported ourselves to this cosy, happy and warm scene - outside was cold and uncomfortable and we knew how welcome a warm fire was in such a situation. I developed early, an active imagination which enabled me to transport myself into all kinds of situations. In "The Brook", when I read or recited, "I come from haunts of coot and hern, I make a sudden sally", it did not matter that for a long time I did not know that 'coot' and 'hern' were birds. I saw clearly in my mind the young waters tearing down from the mountain fastnesses and I stood in awe. Or the story of Derrick, a little American boy who was lost in the forest near his home. His parents were in a panic, then an Indian appeared with his dog, and offered to search for the boy. After the dog had scented an article of Derrick's clothing, he bounded away towards the forest, with the Indian closely following. By sundown the dog had located Derrick, who was soon reunited with his grateful parents. I was there in spirit when the Indian arrived and I bounded through the forest along with them. I saw young Derrick's joyful face as he watched his rescuers approach. All these scenes were imprinted in my mind - they were real and I reveled in them. Long years after, my older son was sent off to sleep on many a night with the story of Derrick's rescue. He would ask for this story night after night.

I dearly loved reading - I dearly loved stories, whether they were set in England, America, Palestine, in the desert or here in Jamaica. I became so interested in other peoples, other countries, chivalry and the knights of old, the exploits of warriors and princes, Greek and Roman gods and heroes. The Lower Division song which had the lines: "Little folks in China, where they grow the tea, Little folks in other lands so far away;" always fired me. Later in life I was always puzzled why the subject Geography did not appeal to many people. I have encountered Teachers' College students who had difficulty in locating north, south, east and west on the map of the world. Such was so easy for me as a primary school child. From very early in my life I began to dig up and search and explore down in my grandfather's cellar. It was to pay huge dividends later. Now to return to my tenure in First Class. Overall, I had a pleasant stay in that class and handled the programme very well. Miss Brenda was the opposite of her husband where class discipline was concerned. Teacher Romney was a 'beater', but Miss Brenda was more relaxed with her students and she did not have disciplinary problems with us. Miss Brenda did use her little cane when it was necessary, but to her it was not a way of life.

Chapter Three

Middle Division - My Exploits Therein

At the end of the school year I graduated into Second Class. I had made my entry into Middle Division where Miss Tamson was in charge. Miss Tamson was about middle age, played the pipe organ on Sundays and was involved in other community activities. Teacher Romney did not have a singing voice, so every now and again Miss Tamson would go over to Upper Division (Fourth, Fifth and Sixth Classes) and brush up a song or two with the students there. Miss Tamson was assisted in her Middle Division classes by a Monitor who went back and forth between Second and Third Classes, as she was directed.. Miss Tamson was a quiet, unpretentious teacher and a hard worker. We respected her and I can't recall her having any disciplinary problems with us. Second and Third classes, as related earlier, occupied the gallery in the south-western corner of the school,. thus, when we were seated, we looked down at Miss Tamson at her table. Teacher Romney's platform and table were in the mid-west of the schoolroom so he could monitor us almost as effectively as Miss Tamson could. Many a time do I remember him bounding across the room, up our gallery and executing dire 'justice' on some poor, offending boy.

Teacher Romney was a great teaser and on occasion would humiliate students before the entire student body. One such occasion was that involving my classmate, Harold. Harold was a most "unacademic" fellow and couldn't "hold" his lessons at all. He sat at the very top row of the gallery, so Teacher Romney could see him very well, and he, Teacher Romney. Apparently, Teacher Romney, knowing Harold to be most 'unacademic', decided to use him as a teasing stick. Morning roll-call and after-lunch roll call were quiet times in the entire schoolroom. Those were the times when Teacher Romney would jump on Harold. Out of the blue he would turn in Harold's direction and call loudly: "Arral! Arral!" (dialect for ' Harold'). At the same time Teacher Romney would laugh and laugh uproariously, with his gold tooth gleaming from the right side of his mouth. "Arral". Poor Harold would be quietly furious but he dared not utter a word. We, his classmates would be so amused, but we had to be very careful

how we snickered, as we could get ourselves severely mauled by suffering
Harold later on the playfield. He couldn't get at Romney but he could get at
most of us in his class. But there was one boy in our class whom Harold
could not discipline. His name was Freckleton and he was middle height and
well muscled. He could call out "Arral," at any time and Harold would have
to swallow it and keep quiet.

I recall this particular day when Harold had a terrible teasing from
Teacher Romney. After recess that morning, as we stood in our lines waiting
to lead into the schoolroom, back to our seats, Freckleton decided to harass
Harold.. "Arral!" he called out. "Arral!", and he laughed and he laughed.
Harold was furious but he could not make a move. Harold in his helpless
anger, could only look Freckleton up and down, from head to toe and up
again. Then he blurted out to Freckleton, "Look pon yu footside, how it
pop up"[6]. Replied Freckleton, "Meck it tan de, it no hab chigga"[7]. And what
did this exchange between the two boys mean? In those days all of us boys
went barefoot. In the nights before we entered our beds, we would wash
our feet in a wash pan but here and there would be a boy who was not very
careful with this ablution and the feet would be left with a lot of the days
dirt on - there might be a boy who did not even wash the feet at all. In a
case like this if he had careless parents he, maybe, could get away with it.
After a time, without proper washing, the side of the feet above the sole
would develop lines and grooves because of the dirt accumulation and could
be quite unsightly. Some boys allowed jiggers to get into the deep grooves
and remain there. We regarded such boys who carried the jiggers thus as
nasty and worthless and they were looked down on. So when Harold hurled
at Freckleton how his 'footside' was grooved (pop up), Freckleton could say
to the effect, "That is so, yes, but it has no jiggers". Poor Harold could not
win. No wonder Harold's attendance was so poor. Sometimes he was absent
from classes for weeks.

But I did have my bit of humiliation from old Romney. My first love
letter was written while I was in Third Class. Three of us Third Class boys
were in love with this girl, Bessie. Bessie was in Fourth Class, the class
immediately above mine, and all three of us thought she was the nicest girl
in the whole wide world. In the evenings, after school dismissal, Herbert,
Edward and I would run after her and she would run ahead. She lived in a
neighbouring district and the path leading to her district began some
distance below the schoolyard. In the evenings we three boys would wait
just outside her door and as she came out and spied us she would run off.

---

[6] "Look at your footside, how grooved it is."

[7] "Leave my footside alone. It does not have jiggers."

We boys would take up the chase, then she would stop, and we also would stop, just behind her. The three boys stood there, looking very foolish and not saying a word to her. Then she would run off again and we again gave chase. Again, she would stop, and the boys also stopped, not saying a word to her. Again she would run off and the process repeated, until she reached the turn-off path down to her district and headed for her home. The three boys never went further than this turn-off path. Edward, Herbert and I had much to learn yet about the subtle art of courtship.

But to return to my love letter. One evening after chasing Bessie, I sat down and composed a beautiful letter to her. I then carefully hid it, intending to deliver it to her the next day at school. That morning my grandfather gave me a note to deliver to Teacher Romney and somehow, very carelessly, the two notes were placed in the same side pocket. When I reached school, the teachers were just about ready to mark their attendance registers. I headed directly to Teacher Romney's table and told him that Grandpa had sent a note for him. I dipped into my pocket and the first note came up which I placed on the table. Immediately I saw that it was my precious love letter and I hastily said, "That is not your own Sir". Possibly, he did not hear me, but he pounced on the love note and started reading. When I came up with Grandpa's note he showed no interest in it but went on reading my note and smiling broadly. Almost grinning, he jumped up and headed for Miss Brenda. They read my love note together and had a good laugh. Then with my note, and greatly amused, he returned to his table and took up Grandpa's note.

I stood there, silent and lost, and wanting the floor to open up and swallow me. What a terrible disaster! How would I live down such a misfortune? Teacher Romney only motioned me to my seat, smiling broadly but not saying a word to me. I walked to my seat in a daze, grateful that my classmates had not been informed. For the rest of the day I was quiet and subdued and I did not take part in the Bessie chase that afternoon. But as the days passed I gradually returned to normal and neither Teacher Romney nor Miss Brenda made mention of it. Then, after about three weeks, came the bombshell. It was during the afternoon roll call on this day and we were supposed to be very quiet. Somehow, Teacher Romney, from the distance, caught me talking to my friend, Edward, and I had my mouth very close to his ear. Old Romney shouted out, "You, Keith Morris, what are you telling Walters? You telling him about that big love letter you had in your pocket the other day? You don't want anybody to hear so you whispering it in his ear." Oh! How could Teacher be so cruel? I was sure he hated me. To my great relief, however, Teacher did not pursue the matter any further. Herbert and Edward smiled at me but thankfully they did not tease. Later, that same day, Edward confided in me that about two weeks earlier he had been caught writing his letter to Bessie. His father promptly confiscated the letter and ordered him right away, to go and cut enough grass for the three pigs in the nearby pen. As he hurried away to cut the grass he heard his father give out, "Bwoy can't even wash 'im foot properly but 'im a look ooman[8]."

All these misfortunes put a damper on our romantic beginnings, and we three 'musketeers', Herbert, Edward and Keith, wisely put our experimentations on hold. Too many pitfalls seemed to line the path. But Teacher Romney was really a hard man and seemed to have been devoid of pity sometimes. I remember one occasion when my classmate, Lebert, returned from lunch with a bellyache. At roll call when all of us stood to listen for our names, Teacher noticed that Lebert was sitting and pressing his folded arms on his belly as if to squeeze out the pain. Teacher, on hearing from Lebert that he was having a bellyache, ordered him to go outside to an old wall, pick some 'quakoo bush' and eat it, to cure his belly ache. In his school, if you were 'dunce', you were just 'dunce'. There was no thought about a slower learner, or the need to re-teach a lesson, or maybe the need for a bit of extra help. If 'you could not learn,' then the remedy was licks and more licks.

We schoolboys of ten, eleven or twelve years of age had much to eat. In the fields around were plenty of guavas, roseapples, Otaheiti apples, oranges, tangerines, grapefruit, sugar cane, and we never had to go hungry. Mangoes have not been mentioned as the hills of this part of Manchester were too cool for this luscious fruit. In my years growing up in this region, I can remember only once did we get a whopping mango crop there. I don't know what were the very special conditions that year which made the mango trees so productive, but for the first time, and only time, I was able to climb mango trees, vigorously shake the branches and dozens of ripe mangoes would come crashing to the ground. After this special year, the mango trees resumed their usual unproductive existence. But during these local unproductive seasons, mangoes could be easily had from nearby districts like Mayfield, Greenland, Medina and Amby. These districts were within four miles from Maidstone and were nearer to the warmer St. Elizabeth border areas. In these times, the sophisticated mango that we knew of was the Robin, plentiful on the St. Elizabeth plains and brought by the donkey loads to Mandeville market, specially on Saturdays. How we used to gape at those young light-skinned St. Elizabeth girls, beautiful and barefooted, leading their donkey-loads of mangoes.

---

[8] "The boy can't even wash his feet properly, but he is looking for a woman."

When we visited Kingston, we got acquainted with the Bombay mango. It was later on that the East Indian and St. Julian varieties came on the scene but these were mainly in the urban areas. Other delicious fruits like the sweetsop, custard apple, naseberry were not generally found in my hills- soursop was present but not plentiful and was made into a cool and soothing drink. The old variety of papaya was quite common, along with the jackfruit. But in this era we did not realise the golden bounty of our wonderful rural fruit basket. We devoured these fruits, filled our stomachs, and that was that. We never appreciated the blessing of having such a variety nor did we realise that this was a part of our great national heritage. Later on, in teenage years when we began our acquaintance with the urban areas and sampled American apples, we thought that when we ate that fruit from North America, we were eating a real big- time fruit, and our star-apple, Otaheite, naseberries and the others were second rate 'country products'. We were to wake up, however, and discover how badly mistaken we were. My generation was intrigued with things American but we gradually learnt that not everything 'American' was the best.

For us children, the first meal of the day was "Tea". This was really breakfast, in the very early morning. It included, as a must, not 'Green Tea', but a hot drink made from any of the four varieties of mint, various bushes or even orange or lime leaves. Now and again hot chocolate might be available. Our parents insisted that we had to have 'something warm' in our stomachs to begin the day. The region was a coffee growing area but most parents kept their children away from coffee, maintaining it as an adult drink. 'Green Tea' was a rare treat, then. With our tea or hot drink, we sometimes had a piece of bread, or much more likely, a roasted sweet potato, often roasted on live coals overnight and then warmed up in the morning, or a piece of 'toas nyaam' (toasted yam), which was boiled yam left over from the previous night's dinner, and now thoroughly toasted on coals until it had an attractive, light brown crust. During the later corn season, a favourite with us was the corn dumplings, which in the great majority of cases, were served with dinner, the last meal of the day. Sometimes, when we could summon up the strength of will, we refrained from eating it then, and put it up safely overnight. Next morning it would be lovingly toasted on the live coals and given a nice crust. Getting your teeth into that well-toasted dumpling and washing it down with a can of hot tea was a delightful start to your day.

We boys were convinced that corn dumplings was a sure source of great physical strength, and the 'weaky weaky' boy was weak because he was not eating enough corn dumplings. In the district the school day started at nine o'clock and before the student left for school in the morning, he or she was given "Chacklatta" or a 'catch up' to keep him until lunch time at twelve. This"Chacklatta" could be anything lighter than a meal, maybe a large piece of boiled or roasted yam or a sweet potato roasted, a dumpling or a hefty bulla - something to bolster the stomach until lunchtime arrived. We have to remember that some children, each morning, traveled miles, over very bad roads, over hills and valleys, to get to school. Those children's stomachs needed a solid boosting to face such a journey to school.

The second full meal of the day was "Breakfast", what we now know as Lunch. This was a heavy meal and heavily starch - yams, cocos, sweet potato, banana, flour dumplings- and possibly some vegetables. And the 'salting' part could consist of salt fish (cod) and cooking tomato stewed down, fried fat pork, cabbage or mackerel. A poorer fare included various sauces, shad and herring. Some of our people would not fail to wash down this meal with liberal quantities of 'pot soup', the name given to the water left in the pot when the food was cooked. This 'pot soup' could be tasty if handled by a skillful cook. I have to add here that if any of us had boiled bananas in our lunch we would never breathe a word about it to our classmates. Among us, in those days, boiled bananas was a 'low' food and we did not want our friends to know that we partook of it.

The last full meal of the day was 'Dinner". If by chance you missed "Breakfast," you would make every effort to get to your "Dinner". For so many rural families, "Dinner" was the supreme meal of the day. It was served in the late evening which was the time of day when most families could be together at one time. It was also the time when so many mothers were able to demonstrate their culinary skills and do little extras for their families. During the red or brown peas season, this was the meal where the famous and favourite peas soup was served. In many a cosy and warm kitchen, dinner time was a time of mirth and healthy family bonding. With dinner over, the time could go over into story telling, with Anancy stories, 'duppy 'stories which so frightened us youngsters. Woe unto the youngster who had neglected to bring in the wash pan and water for the foot washing before getting into bed. After a good dose of the 'Duppy" and "Rolling Calf", can you imagine his terror at going into the darkness to fetch the wash pan and water? Often during the corn season, the after dinner session could be devoted to the preparation and eating of 'roast corn'. This was a favourite of the children and many of us will remember the games we played with our 'corn grain'. I remember 'Sip Sale". Two of us children, well armed with plenty roasted 'corn grain', would approach each other. I say, 'Sip Sale'. You reply, 'Sale fast'. I next say, 'How much man inna mi han?' If you guess that I have five corn grain concealed in the palm of my hand and it turns out that I have seven, then you will have to give me seven of your 'corn grain'. After you pay me my seven 'corn grain', then you get your turn to 'Sip Sale'. And so the game would go on until one or both corn would be empty 'cornsticks' without any 'corn grain'.

Now we have to say a word on Sunday dinner. Sunday dinner was always served at mid or late afternoon. Many people observed Sunday as the day of rest - they attended Church and returned home by two or three o'clock. They had their dinner soon after and relaxed for the rest of the evening. Some amount of visiting of family and friends sometimes took place. But Sunday Dinner was a bit more special than those dinners during the work week. There might be cowfoot prepared, or a piece of beef picked up from the shop of the district butcher, goat head cooked down or a solid tripe- and- beans dish or simple cod fish mixed with cabbage or even cho-cho crushed and well seasoned. There could be a big pot of well seasoned red peas soup, and a touch of rice once in a while. Beef and cow-foot would be treats and would come not too often. Some fathers on some Sundays would wend their way into the 'buttry', the storeroom by the kitchen, and approach that beautiful hunk of White Yam which was duly well cured and carefully put away for special occasions. He would delicately cut off an appropriate sized piece and take it to Mother to include it in the dinner fare. The White Yam was a special yam, never plentiful, refined, and on a little higher plane than the rougher Mozella and Afoo (Yellow Yam)

Today, education authorities all over the world are fully aware of the great importance of a proper diet for the young student. Many studies have shown that diet and nutrition are critical to the physical and intellectual development of children, but in "those early years past", parents were not too influenced by the findings of such scientific studies. They fed us and we were full but they were not very concerned about the fine points of a proper diet. We began learning in school about proteins, carbohydrates, vitamins and fats but this very, very often did not catch on at home. My early school years was the period when students did not yet get to enjoy a hot meal at school. Most students who lived a far distance from school and would not be able to travel home for lunch and be back on time, carried their 'shut pan'. In that shut pan was a cooked meal, to be eaten at lunch time. School started at nine o'clock in the morning and by lunch time at twelve, that 'shut pan' and its contents would be cold. But the student by this time was hungry. He had no alternative but to settle down and dig into the cold food. Those of us who lived nearer to school could run home and receive a hot cooked meal.

There was also a mild hazard for the 'shut pan' people. Every once in a while a 'shutpan' or two would be raided and emptied by some hungry student who could not be provided with lunch from home. There was always that student from a very poor home who had to sometimes stoop to raiding. We did not sympathize with such students or try to help them - we simply despised them. A hot lunch finally became available to our students a few years later. Teacher Romney had left the school and district, a new and young principal had taken over the headship and new ideas and a new approach were now on stream. One result was the erection of a small kitchen in the schoolyard for the preparation of a hot lunch for students who came from far away homes. This marked the end of the "shut pan' period and was a welcome improvement in the diet of many students.

Whenever I return on a visit to my home district and look up to the hillside where my old school stood, I am amazed at how we negotiated the rocks all round. Many Moravian churches are sited on hilltops. This part of Manchester is very hilly, and our school, which was once the church building, was located on this rocky hill. There were stones all around; nearly all of us were barefooted but there were very few 'buck toes (toes crushed and cut against stones), or bodies falling on the rocks. At that time it was the normal thing for the great majority of us students to attend school barefooted Teacher Romney's daughters were well shod but his sons sometimes went barefooted like us. My classmate, Herbert, wore shoes. He was a Kingstonian; his father operated a truck to Kingston and his family was only temporarily in the district. His sister and two younger brothers also wore shoes. My next door neighbour's daughter, Millie, also wore shoes from the time that she started school at seven. In the top class of the school, Sixth Class, maybe about two or three of the big girls would be wearing canvas shoes or 'puss boots. Bright students who later became Monitors or began to take 'private lessons' from teacher, preparing for the Jamaica Local Examinations, wore shoes. Notwithstanding, a goodly number of us students each had a pair of shoes, only one pair, at home, but that was for special occasions, for example Sunday service at church, a concert or other village function. School was not one of those special occasions and we who had our one pair at home, knew we did not run around in them.

But in all this, we were happy; we never knew we were poor; we had more than enough food. Clothing was not plenty but we had our Sunday clothes and our school clothes. Pocket money was unknown; if we came into possession of a sixpenny piece we would regard ourselves as rich. A penny piece could buy a huge bulla, and a half penny piece, a smaller one. A child's favourite, head sugar, was two and one half pence per head, so a school child with one half penny, could buy a decent piece of head sugar for that price. Cod fish sold for three pence per pound; mackerel was even cheaper; ordinary brown sugar was two pence half penny per pound. Clothing fabrics in the stores were cheap. Hearing now about these prices, the later post-war generation might tend to be amused but they should understand that prices all round were low. The prices of the commodities that we had to buy were low, but also, the prices of the commodities which we had for sale were also low. Even the price of labour given was at rock bottom. There was the story of a St. Ann farmer of the 1930's who decided to leave home for a week and seek some work to boost his meagre resources at home. At the end of the week he returned to his home and family and presented the princely sum of five shillings to his wife. His wife stared hard at the proffered five shillings, then looked up to him, and snarled, "Go to hell". She could not be convinced at the moment that after working for one whole week, only five shillings were earned.

But the story tells you a hard fact of the times. So the net result was that low-riced labour and low- priced commodities which the small farmer had for sale could barely purchase the low- priced commodities and other necessities which he needed to procure from the merchant. In those far- off years when the prime lands of the Brumalia property, just outside of Mandeville, were being subdivided and sold, it is said, for six hundred or seven hundred pounds sterling per very large lot, how many of our people could find six hundred pounds? You might hear the bright young man of the 1990's pompously trumpet: "If I were around at that time, I would buy at least three lots". But, would he have been able to hang on to even one? Most small farmers and labourers in my area depended on tree crops like coffee or pimento and the sale of ground provisions. They also had to depend on the few animals they could afford to rear and on occasion even hired out their labour. They had to work hard and manage their meagre resources astutely. When I think back and recall certain small farmer families in the district, I have to lift my hat to them. Their children were well fed and well clothed. They attended school most regularly and were actively encouraged by their parents to excel. There was not much money to go round, but what there was, was well utilised. Those parents of ours must have been great practical economists.

My years in Middle Division (Second and Third Classes), moved on rather uneventfully. Miss Tamson, our teacher, was quietly efficient and I liked her very much. It was in Third Class that I was spurred to improve my attitude to memorising. I had earlier been humiliated in Mrs. Black's Children's Meeting, because I did not properly memorise the Golden Text for that Sunday. Now I was down for another piece of humiliation. Miss Tamson had given the 'Magnificat' to be memorised by both her classes, and so, on Monday and Wednesday mornings before roll call, we had to recite to her or to Monitor Gladstone. As for me, I made a bad job of it - I just could not,or would not, settle down to memorise it, but since I was in the 'bright section' of the class, I got away with it. Everyone took it as a given that Keith Morris would know the passage thoroughly. But then came this particular morning when Miss Tamson brought every one down from the gallery to recite individually. She took Second Class and Monitor Gladstone took my Third Class. As we recited, those who knew it well were allowed to step back on to the gallery and resume their seats. Those who did not know the passage well had to continue standing down on the floor. As the action progressed, I became very perturbed. Monitor Gladstone was getting nearer and nearer to me and I saw no avenue of escape this morning. Then Gladstone was on me and I could not deliver the passage. Monitor Gladstone was visibly taken aback, as if he was saying to himself, "Am I hearing or seeing right?"

I now had to remain standing down on the floor while so many of my classmates had passed the test and were back on the gallery. I was so ashamed to be down there standing with the academic 'ne'er do wells'. And to make matters even more bitter, my classmate, "Mongoose" Williams, who was almost always at the foot of the class, called out to Monitor to say that he knew the "Magnificat" right through. The Monitor had a look of disbelief, but he said to "Mongoose", "Say it". "Mongoose" then recited every word, right to the end, correctly. Monitor Gladstone gave out a hearty laugh and sent "Mongoose" to take his seat in triumph. When Miss Tamson came across to check and saw me among the 'ne'er do wells', she looked me straight in the eye and exclaimed, "You? You?" This experience convinced me that I had to mend my ways with regards to memorising parts of the Bible; my academic reputation was important and it had to be repaired.

A Geography lesson on "Rivers", given by Miss Tamson, stood in my mind for many, many a year. In that lesson on "Rivers", Miss Tamson made the point that some rivers were like 'Big seas'. The 'big seas' idea specially stuck and being a young Manchesterian who had never seen a river, I longed for the day when I would get the opportunity to see one of these great rivers. At age fifteen I made my first visit to Kingston. I travelled by train and I knew that the railway bridged the Rio Minho at May Pen. At May Pen I would at last get my first sight of a river. When the train reached the bridge and I looked down to see the big river, I was virtually dumbstruck. Where was the water? I could not believe my eyes. How could it be a river without a mass of water flowing? It was during the dry season and I was not prepared for a dry river bed. Only here and there a small spot of water could be seen. I was sadly disappointed and never did see any 'big seas' river until I visited North America many years later. Miss Tamson might have done a bit of exaggeration but her lesson certainly fell on fertile ground.

In Third Class we began to get our first taste of handling pen and ink with an exercise book. Our regular class-work was done on our 'big slate'. Remember, our two Middle Division classes were accommodated on the gallery, so there were no desks or tables for us to work with pens and books. However, there was a special exercise book which we had to buy. It was kept in the press and was called the 'press book'. It was special and you would be allowed to use it, maybe, once a fortnight. On 'press book' day, place would be made for us Third Class students in the Fourth Class desk area. The Fourth Class students might be taken outside under the tree so that we could occupy their desks for the writing period. Here we would be seated at long desks so we could work in our exercise books. The 'press books' would be distributed; we would be very closely supervised as we took our early and unsteady steps into the world of pen and ink. Now we had to copy an exercise into the 'press book'. That exercise would have been done on your slate, marked by the teacher, corrected by the student, marked again by the teacher, and when the teacher was satisfied, then it could be copied into the 'press book'. That 'press book' period was a real hectic and stressful time for the student. He was seated at a strange desk, a long one and usually a bit crowded. His fingers were not yet familiar with the pen - he had to learn to use the inkwell, not sinking his pen nib too deep into the ink so that too much came up on the nib and so blot the page. Woe be unto you if you overturned the inkwell on the desk, and triple woe if you overturned that ink across your or your colleague's page. Teacher's cane always had much work to do on 'press book' day. Everybody was so tense and there were always some 'accidents' and teacher seemed not in the least understanding and sympathetic. When the exercise was completed, those 'press books' would be carefully collected and stowed safely away in the press until again required in another two weeks.

Mention was made earlier of long desks accommodating us for our 'press book' exercise. There were no 'short' desks in the school. I imagine 'long desks' allowed our teachers to pack in as many as possible. You can imagine how hot we were, so closely packed, especially on a hot summer's afternoon when we returned from lunch - all that sweat under the heavy khaki oozing from boys who had a most active lunchtime. It brings back to mind some very humourous incidents directly connected to our celebrated long desks. Imagine one of these long desks with about eight students closely packed together. Teacher is working in the area and is constrained to give a 'lick' to the boy at her end of the desk. The other boys see her upraised arm with strap and are poised, and as she comes down on that poor first boy, the one next to him lurches violently away lest he be 'accidentally' hit. But his violent sideway lurch unbalances the rest of the fellows and they all nearly fall. Even more hilarious was when teacher directs them all to move out of the desk and they move out too slowly. Teacher jumps up and makes a swing at them with the strap and every fellow tries to get out of the desk at the same instant. If you were in that desk you would be scampering for your life. If you were away at a distance and could view the scene, you would laugh until 'you die'. There was mirth even among the 'licks'.

Students reacted to their corporal punishment in various ways. Some cried long and hard, some boys would not cry and liked to be regarded as tough - some girls sulked and pouted and said angry things about the teacher. One girl, Hazel, was a special case. Hazel was quite able at her work but inevitably she and Teacher Romney would clash at some point. She was terribly afraid of the cane and when the licks connected she cried out and called the Lord's name 'in vain'. After crying for a time she would quiet down, put on her most vicious- looking countenance and 'cut her eye' at Teacher for a long time. Gradually she would simmer down and eventually rejoin the class but she would be mum for the rest of the day. Among us boys there were always stories about 'big boys' who had challenged their teachers, 'scored' the cane so that when the teacher hit with it, it broke into pieces, or hid the cane where teacher could not find it. We enjoyed those stories but we were never bold enough to try out any of those tricks. Despite the occasional 'misery', we enjoyed ourselves and had a lot of fun among the stones and the hillsides.

Chapter Four

Upper Division, Here I Come

When I moved over to Fourth Class I was about eleven years of age. I now had to discard my 'big slate' and take on fully my exercise book and pen and ink. Fourth Class was the first class of Upper Division and when you arrive there you know you are nearing the 'big league'. Fourth, Fifth and Sixth Classes were the direct responsibility of Teacher Romney, assisted by his daughter, Daffy. We disliked Daffy very much. She was about nineteen years old and we thought of her as being rough and 'feisty'. She handled some of our Arithmetic and Reading classes. She never smiled with us and never saw anything humourous in our classes. Teacher lumped all three classes together for his Science, Geography and Scripture sessions. He took all the boys for Gardening and Drill (Physical Education). He taught Fifth and Sixth Classes English and Arithmetic, with Daffy assisting wherever needed. As I remember, Science involved facts on Gases - Oxygen, Nitrogen, Carbon Dioxide, Argon, and their properties. Then there was some information on Foods - Proteins, Carbohydrates, Fats, Vitamins. A lot of facts we learnt by heart e.g. 'Nature abhors a vacuum'. We stuffed so many bits of information, some we really never understood. Sometimes there were not the connecting links. There were no experiments or any form of science equipment. Geography took in countries of the world and their capitals, Land and Sea Breezes etc etc. Scripture was simply stories from the Bible.

In these days we speak of Physical Education, in those days we spoke of Drill. For Drill, Teacher Romney took all the boys of Upper Division to the playfield, to a spot just outside the cemetery wall. Here we lined up in straight lines. Teacher Romney's cane sometimes had to do quite a bit of work to get those lines really straight. But once they were straight to his satisfaction, the 'drill-master' got to work. 'Hips firm!', 'Feet, astride, leap', 'Feet, forward, lunge', 'Feet, forward lunging by numbers, begin! One two, three!' The 'Drill-master' never left his cane behind. This class was supposed to be good fun but 'bitter medicine' was occasionally dispensed. My classmate, Basil Grayson could attest to this. There was one exercise that poor Basil could not master. At a particular Drill class, the order was given, "Hips firm! Feet astride leaping by numbers, begin. One, two, three –". The student, obeying, will have his two hands firmly on his hips as he does the 'astride' leap. Now, whenever Basil leaped and got his legs astride, his right hand flew from his right hip - he just could not keep both hands rightly placed as he leaped. Teacher Romney observed him and went down to see that the exercise was correctly done. Teacher whacked and whacked but Basil could not get it right. Eventually frustrated and angry, Teacher Romney left Basil. Basil soon dried his tears and quickly returned to the spirit of the occasion. This was one occasion when Teacher Romney and his cane did not win.

We always enjoyed Gardening, which was on Thursday afternoons each week. All of us boys gaily trooped down to the school garden, not because we were anxious to learn something new but because we were simply glad to get out of the classroom and enjoy the freedom and chatter in the garden. We grew yams, potatoes, bananas, sugar cane and a few other things, but we really did not learn any thing that we did not already know. What we did in the garden were things we already knew from our parents. Nevertheless, we boys would never have given up our Garden period. It was the time when we swapped spicy stories from the district: the recently buried resident whose 'duppy'[9] was seen several times, the man who was seen in the church cemetery with his shut pan catching 'duppy', the middle-aged gentleman who was caught in a serious indiscretion and was soundly whipped by the aggrieved party. This last incident was the talk of the district for about two weeks, and my friend, James, who lived in that part of the district where the deed took place, came to school, hot with the glowing facts. He regaled us with the juicy bits and we had a whale of a garden session. One night two weeks later I overheard my grandfather telling his wife, Miss Ann, the story in low tones (so that the boy, Keith, would not hear). I was so amused. I chuckled to myself, "'A now you jus' a hear the story? A how yu late so?"[10]

So many stories were passed among us: 'duppy stories', Rolling Calf[11] and Whooping Boy,[12] Mermaid and G[13], Old Table,[14] 'big man' stories, and many others. James' grandmother was a great storyteller and he in turn

---

[9] Ghost.

[10] "Are you just hearing that story? Why so late!?"

[11] An aggressive ghost in the form of a large cow calf, with a jangling chain around its neck.

[12] A ghost in the form of a boy in the old days, who drove and whooped cattle on the way to the market, in the dead of night.

[13] Certain ponds and lakes were said to be inhabited by a mermaid who would sometimes be seen combing her hair on shore but would dive into the water immediately if startled sometimes leaving her comb.

[14] A Golden Table was sometimes reported to be seen afloat on the water but would immediately disappear beneath the water if humans tried to capture it.

would bring her stories to us. On one of these garden sessions he said that his grandmother told him that when you go to Heaven, you will see a bell continuously ringing, and it is saying: "Today fi me, tomorrow fi you, today fi me, tomorrow fi you." Teacher Romney was not much of a farmer and he left us very much to ourselves in the garden. Every once in a while he would let a pair of bigger boys cut some sugar cane into small pieces so that each of us could get a juicy piece for our consumption later.

Teacher kept a horse to transport himself around the district. The animal had the run of the church and school lands, many acres, but there were times when the grass on the commons was sparse and had to be supplemented with grass from outside. This was done by schoolboys who were dispatched to the lands of a neighbouring farmer who always had plenty of grass. We were pleased when we were detailed for that job as it gave us even more freedom from the school environment. In addition, that farmer's lands always had various fruits and other edibles and we boys could enjoy ourselves to the full. As said earlier, we learnt very little from the school garden but we would never have entertained the thought of our school being without one.

Chapter Five

Grandpa Remarries - Marjorie's Interlude

Grandpa's first wife, Frances, or 'Fanny' as he fondly called her, had died some years before I was born. The little I knew of her came from Grandpa who every now and again would make some reference to her. Quite strange, neither my mother nor my uncle talked about her. It was as if they saw it as a closed chapter and had no desire to talk about her. My mother would sometimes refer to 'my father, my father' but never a reference to 'my mother'. Grandma Fanny came from the Santa Cruz Mountains in St. Elizabeth, from the Malvern area, and bore five Morris children, two boys and three girls. The older boy as well as two of the girls died early and so Grandpa Morris was left with my mother, Iva, and her brother, Florizel. This was the household that I was born in. Then when my mother married and left to set up her household in a neighbouring district, Nana came to take care of us but Grandpa seemed to have become increasingly lonely. He was a very unemotional individual and one could hardly detect the toll that was being taken on him.

However, Grandpa fell in love with Miss Ann Foster of nearby Mayfield district and the knot was duly tied. Miss Ann was a Presbyterian and so the wedding ceremony was performed at her Medina Presbyterian Church. I might have been somewhere between eight and nine years old but I remember at the end of the ceremony when parsons instructed the groom to kiss the bride, Grandpa gave his new wife a resounding kiss, much to my disgust. I was not used to this kissing between man and woman and I did not approve of my grandfather, of all persons, kissing before all these people. But I could see that he enjoyed it as when he had done the deed, he laughed heartily and looked unabashed at the gathering.

Miss Ann was a tall, full bodied light skinned lady. She had spent many years in the United States, was not well educated but had worked with upper strata folks in New York and so was quite polished and well spoken. The district folks respected her very much and to many of them she was "Aunt Ann". She dressed well, was quite jovial and could turn on a bit of 'Americanese' whenever she thought it appropriate. She loved dancing and among her 'American things' were a large, standing victrola, a smaller portable gramaphone and a quantity of records which included Fox Trots, Waltzes, popular songs, music from the movies, religious selections and a few classics. One classic piece I remember was the 'Hallelujah' piece from Mozart, and my first acquaintance with the great Afro-American contralto, Marion Anderson, dated from those years.

Miss Ann was very light on the dance floor and so very often pulled Grandpa up and worked him on the floor. Even my uncle often got into the act and enjoyed himself. I never forgot that day when her brothers, Manny and Jackie, came up from Mayfield to visit her and she pulled Manny on to the dance floor. Manny, who possibly had not been on a dance floor in decades, was pulled and twirled and twisted in all directions, but he stood up manfully to his sister and seemed to have enjoyed himself immensely. But I suspect that on his return to his home that night his old bones demanded an extra rigorous dose of several ointments. Miss Ann brought much laughter back into the Morris household and the house was often abuzz with visitors and her relatives. The house was located very near to the passing parochial road and so the music and laughter and dancing could be easily heard and seen by passers-by on the road.

Miss Ann's period at home was an enjoyable one in another way. About ninety yards away from our house stood a tailor shop, occupied by a master tailor, fondly referred to as 'Mas Eitel'. 'Mas Eitel' was a great personality, intelligent and highly respected by all. He had three very decent young men as apprentices and his shop was a gathering point for several of the steady and ambitious young men of the district, especially those who were 'studying'. He was a real role model for us young ones. In addition, 'Mas Eitel' was an organist at our local church. Miss Ann and 'Mas Eitel' became great friends and she treated him as a son. Many an evening after work he would walk over to our house and there would be a joyful and enriching session. Grandpa, Miss Ann, 'Mas Eitel', and sometimes my uncle would tell stories, discuss current events and talk about local and overseas personalities, put forward and solve word puzzles, spell difficult words, etc. Miss Ann had a storehouse of Anancy stories and terrible Duppy and Rolling Calf episodes. As a small boy I could only listen, but I learnt so much from these sessions and my storehouse grew in preparation for later years of academic activity.

The Morris household also enjoyed a short and merry interlude when we had a young Miss from "Town," living with us and attending our school. Marjorie was the town girl. Her full name was Marjorie McDonnough and she was a few years older than I was. She was rather short in stature, of medium build, was light-skinned and had a head full of long, flowing hair.

She was good humoured, with a ready, infectious laugh and attracted the attention of all wherever she went. Of course, Marjorie wore nice shoes to school. She had a full set-out of school uniforms: immaculate white blouses and navy blue, pleated skirts. When she arrived in Maidstone, she had a pair of dark glasses which added an extra touch of elegance to her presence. Marjorie spoke very good English and was very articulate and self-confident. Her vocabulary was quite wide and she sometimes used words which made the eyes of us 'country bumpkins' pop out widely.

Marjorie arrived at our school in the early 1940s, when I was in Middle Division, and she was placed in Sixth Class. She was one of those students who had moved very quickly through the grades, so she arrived in the highest grade, Sixth Class, at a young age. She would spend, possibly another two years there before reaching the school leaving age of fifteen. She was Kingston-born and bred and received the great bulk of her elementary education in that city. Her mother was a very good friend of Miss Ann, my grandfather's second wife, and her sister, Miss Mary, who resided in nearby Greenland district. Possibly, Marjorie's mother felt that her daughter would greatly benefit from some time in the countryside and since our school, Nazareth, was known as a good school, and Grandpa and Miss Ann had a good home, she was willing to send her Marjorie for a taste of country life. And so she arranged with Miss Ann that Marjorie would stay with her and attend school at Nazareth. This was how Marjorie came to live at my house. Suddenly, there were now two children at home. I had never had to share. I had never had a playmate to push around, to tell tales on, or to make into a victim of some annoying tricks. From now on, on each school morning it would be two heads passing under the huge Otaheite apple tree, out to the road and on up to our school. Life could become quite interesting.

I don't remember if there was anything very special about Marjorie's first morning at my school, but I well recall her first lunch period there. Our home was about half a mile from school so we could easily walk home for lunch. On this particular Monday, by lunchtime the word had spread widely that there was a 'new' girl in our midst. We were dismissed for lunch at twelve o'clock and as Marjorie stepped out to walk down to our home, a few students tagged along behind her, not beside her. Then the numbers increased and by the time that she had gone half the distance, there was a small crowd behind her. Now, picture the scene: nice brown girl, immaculately attired in blouse and skirt, long and beautiful hair and dark glasses delicately perched on a nicely chiseled face. Marjorie must have quietly enjoyed it all - her moment of supremacy. She walked with a firm gait, talking to no one and looking neither to the right nor to the left. I walked to the back of the crowd, not that I was amused at the scene, but I think I was just as awed.

When we reached the step-down to my home, under the big Otaheiti apple tree, I stepped behind Marjorie, not looking at my friends but thinking how they 'mus grudge me'. An early embarrassing situation for me was on that Saturday night after she arrived from Kingston. Miss Ann, Grandpa, Uncle Zel and I were sitting in the drawing room. Then 'Mas Eitel', our neighbouring tailor friend, came over to share in the welcoming of Marjorie. As time went on, Mas Eitel requested that Marjorie dance for us. Marjorie obliged and pulled me on to the floor. This was possibly the most embarrassing moment of my life. While she happily 'la, la, la-ed' and tripped around merrily, I hung on for dear life. After what felt like an eternity, the demonstration came to an end and I sheepishly slunk back to my seat. Needless to say, Marjorie made a powerful impression - she did Kingston proud.

Marjorie settled down to life in the countryside and she adapted well, both to rural school life and life in general in the district. As children we had our little quarrels and 'bex-up'[15] days but I respected and liked her and felt good that she was living at my house. I can well recall how my classmate, 'Mongoose' Williams, responded when he found out that she lived at my house. I earlier related that Teacher Romney did not sing, so at intervals, Miss Tamson, our Middle Division teacher, would go over to his Fourth, Fifth and Sixth Classes and 'brush up' a song or two. In the meantime, Miss Tamson's Middle Division students sometimes had to stand or sit quietly on their gallery and listen and attend to what was being done in the Upper Division singing class. On a particular day, Miss Tamson was having that singing class and we, her Middle Division students, were attending from our gallery. By this time Marjorie was well integrated into our school society and stood in the front row of the singing class. Merrily the singing students belted out the lines,

"Let the hills resound with song, as we proudly march along,
For as of old our sires were bold, proud hearts have we
While Cambrian Mountains stand, Like the ramparts of the land..."

The song had a bouncy tempo and Marjorie was certainly enjoying it. As she sang, she vigorously marked time with her feet, 'left, right, left, right', and she laughed and laughed. Miss Tamson had no idea what was taking place below the platform, as Marjorie gleefully distracted her classmates but

---

[15] Vexed.

was careful to behave perfectly when Miss Tamson's head turned in her direction. My classmate, 'Mongoose', sat beside me on the gallery and noted with tremendous amusement, Marjorie's antics. This was 'Mongoose's' first good look at this new brown girl and he was almost jumping out of his pants. "Massy, look pon her nuh. Jeesam, a whe she name?"[16] He was transported with delight. Then someone nearby said that she lived at "Keet yard".[17] 'Mongoose' spun around to me and excitedly questioned, "Keet, a true say a fi yu yard she lib? How yu nebba tell mi?"[18] 'Mongoose' was just beside himself with wonder. He looked at me with a wide grin, a look which clearly meant, "A how yu lucky so?"[19]

Marjorie brought a few books and other reading material with her from Kingston and I enjoyed reading them. My favourite was a book on English Literature with Shakespeare, Milton, Dryden, Pope, Swift, Lord Tennyson, and many others. I remember Shakespeare and Milton were pictured as, possibly, nineteen- year- olds. I held that young Shakespeare was the more handsome, but Marjorie was adamant that the more serious-looking Milton was far more handsome. I can't remember the title of that book but I learnt so much from its pages. One of the names I threw at her when we quarreled was "Audrey, the country wench", a title which she did not like, and which I had got from one of Shakespeare's plays. Also, Marjorie had a few lovely school songs which she brought from her Kingston school. She sang them often and I learnt one or two of them. One of the sweetest was "Strawberry Fair" - the first line, "As I was going to Strawberry Fair...", then she would sol-fa the rest of the line. Marjorie was bright and one could always learn something from her. I remember when Neville Chamberlain died, early after World War 2 started, and she brought home the news. Well I remember her comment on the death, "I am certain he died of a broken heart." In dance, she brought some of the Kingston moves to us. The Glen Miller hit tune, with our words of the first line, "Mister What You Call It What You Doing Tonight?" was very popular then and she delighted the girls with the 'townie' steps to the tune.

Marjorie's sojourn in the countryside was all too short. She spent one full school year with us at Nazareth and then her mother decided it was time for her to get back to the city. She had brought good laughter and a brightness to all who had to do with her. Her intelligence and self-confidence gave a boost to so many of us. Her navy-blue pleated skirts were

---

[16] "Mercy! Look on her. Jeesam, what is her name?"

[17] Keith's home.

[18] Keith, is it true that she lives at your home? How is it you did not tell me?

[19] How is it that you are so lucky?

pressed every evening and her white blouses were as white and smart as could be. We had no house maid at our house so Marjorie had to get the job done all by herself. Added to all this, her shoes were clean and shone. Even at this young age she took pride in being so neat and well groomed. She certainly was an example who was pointing out to us, in that quiet way, some of the qualities we should aim at. Her not-aggressive sophistication, self-confidence, good use of language, sunny, positive disposition were good for us and Nazareth's gain was indisputable. In the years following, we never lost contact and in the mid 1940s I had my turn living at her house for a short period. She attended Excelsior High School after returning to the city, then Bethlehem Teachers' College where she qualified as a teacher. She is now retired, still short of stature, but the strong, infectious laugh and bright personality are still there.

But this period of enjoyable and productive experiences was not to last. With the progress of World War 2 and the American need for extra manpower in her agriculture and the war effort, 'Mas Eitel' was recruited for farm work in the United States. Grandpa and Miss Ann quietly bid him goodbye and you could see that they were sad when he had to go but they wished him well and godspeed. Miss Ann did not last very long after 'Mas Eitel's' departure. Her health began to deteriorate and she now had bouts of depression. She eventually moved to her sister's residence in nearby Greenland district, for rest and nursing. There she died, thus ending that short, bright chapter in the Morris household. This was my second taste of loss by death as Nana, our faithful housekeeper, had died sometime after Grandpa's marriage to Miss Ann. Grandpa was now a widower again and resumed his loneliness. As was his way, he was unemotional in all this and we were surprised when sometime later he admitted that throughout his adult life he had cried only twice, the second time when he sat beside the dying Miss Ann. And so life returned to the Morris household as it was when Nana arrived: Grandpa, my uncle and I. But this time I was more equipped. Miss Ann had taught me to sew on my buttons and polish the floor and do other chores in the house. I now had to begin my early apprenticeship in the kitchen. I never liked this as I was always fearful that my classmates would refer to me as 'kitchen jack'. I had to learn to prepare a tolerable meal but I never developed a love for the culinary department.

Chapter Six

The War Years, 1939 - 1945

World War 2 began in September 1939. Britain and France declared war on Nazi Germany on September 3 and the second war to end all wars, now raged in earnest. Britain's colonial family, from self-governing Canada, Australia, New Zealand, South Africa, down to even tiny Barbados, "Little England", now set to work to aid Mother Country, England, to crush the Nazi monster. I was two months short of my ninth birthday and my reading level was climbing very rapidly. The 'Daily Gleaner' had become more and more my friend and I had started to delve into varied reading material around the home. In addition, by this time I had soaked in much of my grandfather's stories - I knew about serge suiting from England, pocket knives from Germany, much about America and the 'badness of republic' (Cuba and Panama); I was told of the Ashanti Wars, Botha and Lord Roberts in South Africa, Kaiser William fleeing to Holland after "the first war", Scots and their bagpipes and kilts, etc, etc. There was a picture in our drawing room of a column of Scots bagpipers marching, and below it was the comment, "Dinna ye hear the pipes?" Later I was to learn that the marching Scotsmen were marching to the relief of a beleaguered town during the Indian Mutiny. "Dinna ye hear the pipes?" was the joyful exclamation of a keen eared woman, anxiously waiting to be rescued.

Grandpa had a story on Winston Churchill as a young war correspondent in South Africa during the Boer War. Grandpa said that when he read the newspaper to the old folks in his district about the Boers inflicting defeats on the British, the old folks were amazed and could not understand how "dem de hog so terrible an a give de English soldier dem so much trouble" ('Boers' 'Boar hogs'). Grandpa also told me that during the Spanish American War between Spain and the United States, they could hear the roar of the American naval guns when the Spanish Admiral Cervera and his squadron tried to break out of Santiago Harbour to escape the waiting American fleet. He told so many of these stories, about local and international events and people. He was a mighty amateur historian and he readily passed on his knowledge.

And so, when the War came, I was already fertile ground and my general knowledge was quite extensive for a rural nine-year-old. Grandpa received his 'Gleaner' every day and he allowed me to read over his shoulder. I quickly learnt the names of the outstanding British, German, American and Russian military, naval and political leaders - Germany's Rommell, Von Bock, Paulus, Von Manstein, Von Rundstedt, Keitel, Raeder, Doenitz; Britain's Montgomery, Wavell, Auchinleck, Alexander, Lord Mountbatten; America's Eisenhower, Patton, Bradley, Mark Clark, Nimitz, Halsey, McArthur; Japan's Yamamota, Nagumo, Ozawa; the USSR's Marshal Timoshenko, Zhukov, Koneiv, Malinovsky, Rokossovsky. When the brilliant young Russian, General Vatutin, took ill and died, I was so sad. I wanted to continue reading about his hammering of the Germans. There were the lesser names, in my opinion, of the Italian Marshal Graziani and the Duke of Aosta; the French Petain, Weygand, DeGaulle and Admiral Darlan. There was a young fellow in my district who was very loudly talkative at this time, and we thought he had a huge mouth too; so we labeled him "Mussolini", the bumptious Italian ally of Germany's Adolf Hitler. Winston Churchill was Grandpa's darling, while I thought President Roosevelt was the greatest. The reader can imagine how disappointed I was when I learnt later in the War that he was a polio victim. To me, it was so wrong that such a great man should be so struck down. As for the Italians, I developed a disdain for them. The newspaper reports of their military non-performance convinced me that Italians were near useless as fighting allies. Not until the late 1980's, when I visited Italy and toured some of her sites and viewed her great engineering feats in the Italian Alps, was much of my respect returned.

The War indoctrination was very effective. To us the Germans were cruel monsters who should be totally destroyed. Teacher Romney told us that the only good German was a dead German. The young adults of our district sang, "War, war, cruel war, oh what a dreadful war; We'll bomb the German soldiers and..." We were also told that if Germany and her allies won the War, we blacks would again be enslaved. The term 'Huns' was sometimes used for the Germans and it created a picture of the Germans as arrogant, bloodthirsty villains who had to be vanquished. Oh, how I rejoiced when the tide turned against the Germans; Stalingrad was a great victory for the Russians as well as for this boy, Morris. I lapped up greedily the progress of the Allied drive across Germany and was very disappointed when the Russians did not grab Hitler alive. I would have so liked the spectacle of the captured maniac exhibited across Europe in an iron cage and then his neck severed by a French guillotine.

But my feelings towards Germans were to change drastically later in the early 1970s when I sojourned for a short period in Manitoba, in Western Canada. There I met and talked with several Germans; one gentleman, a plumber, had fought in the German army on the Russian front. Another, a shoemaker, had fought elsewhere in Europe; another was principal of a small high school where I worked. These Germans had migrated to Canada at the end of the War and I found them to be normal, nice people. To top it all, two of our very best friends in Winnipeg were a German couple who came from Bingen-on-the-Rhine. One of my old school books had a poem relating to Bingen-on-the-Rhine. In the poem, a mortally wounded German soldier during the Napoleonic Wars, spends his last minutes recounting the joys of his home town of Bingen-on-the-Rhine. I thought it was such a wonderful coincidence that I should now meet real live Germans from good old Bingen. This German family were really beautiful people - father, mother, two boys and a girl. My family and I spent many great hours in their home.

How did the War affect our lives in my rural location? From the very beginning our Minister, Rev. Black, was appointed Air Raid Precaution (ARP) warden. I guessed that a big part of his job was to ensure that, should there be an air raid at any time, the villagers would be properly warned and they would know what to do in such an emergency. I remember two occasions when the church bell rang in the night and we all knew that that was the signal to put out all lights. Other than the bell in the night, I cannot recall any other preparation. In our schoolroom there were now displayed big attractive pictures of the war effort in places like India, Malaya, Uganda and other parts of Africa. We were stirred by all this activity, this show of intense loyalty to the embattled Mother Country. Certainly, our struggle against Nazi Germany was a righteous cause and God was on the side of Mother England and her Allies.

Teacher Romney had regular short sessions with the whole school on the progress of the War. I recall one of those sessions, when Monitor Gladstone was informing Teacher on the latest news. He informed Teacher that "Albanya" had fallen to the Germans. His pronunciation was immediately corrected by Teacher Romney, to "Albania". This was the time when my schoolmate, Shirley, acquired his nickname. At one of these sessions, Shirley stood up to give a fact on the Americans. Instead of saying 'the Americans', he said, 'the America'. Teacher Romney made fun of his answer and thoroughly embarrassed the fellow before the entire school population. We clapped on the nickname immediately and he had to carry it through the rest of his school life. We addressed him as 'America' or 'Merican' or 'Americs.' Shirley had to endure a lot of teasing from us but he took it in good spirit and never allowed anger to get the better of him.

Rev. Black had his War information sessions with his congregation at "Second Meeting" after Sunday service. Grandpa was another source of

War information for our district people. He received his 'Gleaner' daily, read it thoroughly and so was always full of news. A passerby would call out to him, "Cou Sammy, a whe de German dem a do now?"[20] Then Grandpa would pass on his latest news and his grandson would be near to back him up if he forgot the name of the German city recently heavily bombed or the name of some German general. I remember three young fellows from my district who joined the Royal Air Force. One of them returned at the end of the War, severely shell-shocked, while another remained in England and never communicated with his family for sixty years. Then in the early 1940s the United States needed manpower for her farms and factories and large numbers of Jamaicans were recruited to work on contract in the United States. Many of the men stayed for extended periods and earned good money. Most had only short periods and did not return with much. Some married American women and were able to take up permanent residence there. My family's good tailor friend, Mas Eitel, had a long stay, married an American girl and settled down to a productive life there.

There were shortages of various goods which we used in our daily life. Gasoline was short. It greatly affected the taxis and trucks which plied between our district and market centres like Mandeville, Christiana and Balaclava. Kerosene was often in short supply and this led to the discovery of alternative materials which could be 'burnt' to produce light. At this time there was a gifted tradesman living in our district whose name was Leonard Carpenter. He was a skilled carpenter, cabinet maker, and was skilled in other useful areas as well. He originated from South Manchester but adopted our district and made it his home. He built simple tin lamps which were able to use Castor Oil or Coconut Oil as fuel. The lamps worked tolerably well and came in handy when there was no kerosene to be had. Years later I read where the Kingston barrister, Ethelred Erasmus Campbell, member of the Legislative Council for Kingston, in 1942 designed a special tin lamp, which used pure Castor Oil as fuel. His demonstration of it produced a bright flame and he had high hopes of his new lamp ushering in a bright future for his lamp and the local castor oil industry. Interestingly, I must add here that this man, Ethelred Erasmus Adolphus Campbell, B.A., LL.B (Hons), M.Sc., was a great Jamaican lawyer, outstanding research chemist, politician and pioneer trade union leader. An intensely loyal Jamaican, he gave outstanding service to his country. His biography, available at our National Library, is an inspiration to any thinking man with drive and ambition.

---

[20] "Cousin Sammy, what are the Germans doing now?"

The drastic shortages forced many people to be innovative and inventive in order to cope. Leonard Carpenter and Ethelred Erasmus Campbell were two such people. Even the ackee pod was utilised to produce some soap 'power', when the traditional soap was scarce. So often the lone two taxis which plied from my district had to be 'off the road' because of gasolene shortage. In such a situation folks had to retain their love for walking long distances. Fortunately, the now all-conquering automobile had not yet mastered the traveling public and we survived handily. Our deep rural community, in normal times, had modest consumer demands and so when the hard time came, they braced themselves and weathered the storm. We must note here that in the town areas the buggy took on a new lease on life and many are the stories which older folks will tell of these gaudy four-wheeled vehicles pulled by clip-clopping horses and mules transporting well-off kids to and from school and being so useful in so many ways.

For us children at school in our community, the War brought a brief experience which we thought was special. There was the shortage of ships to transport our Jamaican bananas to Europe, so a lot of bananas were piled up with no market. Rather than allowing the bananas to rot and go to waste, the Government arranged for the distribution of ripe bananas to the schools. Some came to my school. That distribution period was short and there were only about three distributions at my school. At the appointed time the student body gathered in the schoolyard as the male Monitors and a few senior boys brought the bunches of ripe bananas from a storeroom in the Manse, over to the schoolyard. The big boys bearing the bunches, in response to entreaties from students standing along their path, would sometimes give a quiet shake of the bunch and a few bananas would fall off on the ground, to be readily gobbled up by the lucky students nearest. Well, we all received our banana and enjoyed it immensely. When the banana supply stopped, no one explained why - whether it was that more cargo ships were available or that the supply of bananas could no longer meet the demand.

The school distribution had a short life, we enjoyed it but bear in mind that the rural child in this part of Manchester was no stranger to the ripened fruit. At some time in his life he might have been the one to discover a bunch of ripening bananas in the kitchen patch, and had feasted before reporting his find to his parents. So, why did we think this one-banana distribution was so very special? My classmate, John Lindsay, must have had a not- so- sweet memory of the banana distribution. John was absent from school on the day of the first distribution. The next day when he arrived at school, a friend was excitedly telling him of the bananas of the day before.

Apparently, John was not impressed, and made the comment, "Me no want none a dem flaw"[21]. John's words, by some means, reached Teacher Romney's ears. John was called up and was given a sound lashing. To Teacher Romney, John must have been simply 'mannish and feisty' and had to be dealt with promptly - the chap was downright ungrateful for the government's kindness and should not be allowed to get away with it. I cannot recall if John partook of any of the succeeding banana distributions.

A highlight for us schoolchildren in the very early War period was a 'Bazaar' held in Mandeville. 'Bazaar' was the name given to it but I cannot recall any exhibits on display and for sale, but I imagine there was. What I remember was the wide assortment of candies, cake, gizzadas, patties etc etc. The Bazaar was all part of the War effort and I suspect that an unspoken aim was to waken us all, young and old, to the fact that there was a great emergency in our midst and loyalty and devotion to the British Crown was most vital. It was held on the grounds of the Mandeville Government Elementary School, and oh! It was a huge crowd of teachers, students, parents, well wishers and many others. Trucks collected students from the various schools in Manchester. There was a big platform area, beautifully decorated, and it had the royal standards of England, Scotland and Wales. There were several speeches from the platform which was occupied by impressive- looking men and women. The crowd was so huge and there was so much milling about that I could not get close to the platform, and I, a nine year-old, could not make much of the goings on up there. The Jamaica Military Band was present in full regalia. They played beautiful music and I gazed mesmerised at the range of shining instruments which they had. When they completed their presentations, they broke up and I had the good fortune of going up close to a few bandsmen. I was intrigued by their shoes and their 'funny hats' with their tassels hanging.

But there was another side to the day's proceedings which I do not lovingly cherish. Grandpa allowed me to travel on the school truck and attend the Bazaar, and I bless him for that. I take it that he was very concerned about the amount of money that he should allow his nine year old grandson to handle that day. Thus he decided that three pence was the amount that I should spend at the Bazaar. He did not give the three pence to me, in my hands, but he gave it to Teacher Romney, for its safekeeping, until we reached Mandeville. I soon got very hungry but I could not locate Teacher Romney and my three pence. There was so much food on the grounds, beckoning at every turn and not a half penny to spend. Teacher Romney himself, I believe, did not have a thought of that little boy, now so

[21]"I don't want any of their trashy food."

hungry, or his pretty three penny piece. A brief respite came when my classmate, Ken Watson, turned up with a nice cake in his hand and gave me a piece. That was the best piece of cake I had ever eaten, considering how hungry I was. After a while, Ken sauntered off to continue his explorations and I continued my seemingly fruitless hunt for Teacher Romney. Eventually, the hunger god took pity on me and led me up to a corner near the platform. There was Teacher Romney sitting and observing the world passing to and fro. I went up to him boldly, no doubt driven by hunger, and I asked him for my money. He jumped up, "Oh, oh! Where were you?" I took my three pence and headed for food. How much food could three pence buy? It was a small sum, but bear in mind the time was late 1939, and three pennies could buy a lot of cake then. Overall, I had a good day - I saw much that was educational, my loyalty to King George was assured and I finally arrived home safely after a pleasant truck journey.

The War raged on but we in our rural district never felt any insecurity from enemy activity. The news releases were so carefully handled that we in our rural retreat and possibly ninety five per cent of Jamaicans were unaware of German submarines prowling in waters quite near to us. We knew of the American base at Fort Simmonds in South Clarendon, popularly known as "Sandy Gully." A few of the men from my district secured employment there, and there were quite a few jokes about these men and others from other areas who worked with the Americans - their hastily acquired Yankee accents and the airs which some of them put on. Little was known of Gibraltar Camp and its foreign detainees. I recall acting in a school play, where I played the part of a young farm worker, returned from America, who wanted to locate the 'Nearest pub' for some fun. The man from whom I asked the direction looked me up and down and when he saw my new slacks out of my pants, he said to his companion, "You si whe him shut de?"[22] Anytime you si a man wid him shut outa him trousers, him a tun wutless". This demonstrates how the War was changing us - our speech, our dress, our manners, etc, etc. My new slacks out of my pants had shocked this poor man. How would he cope with the quarter dressed bodies of the early twenty- first century?

By the end of 1944, the German 'Hun' and "those little Japanese men with buff teeth" were solidly on the run and we knew the War would soon be over. Grandpa Morris was distraught at the death of President Roosevelt just before victory. After all Roosevelt's yeoman labours he was not permitted to taste the final victory. VE Day came in May 1945 and it was

[22] "Do you see where his shirt is? Whenever you see a man with his shirt out of his pants, he is becoming worthless."

greeted with quiet joy in my home district. The Japs held on for a little while longer but the horrors of Hiroshima and Nagasaki immediately put their resistance to an end. Japan surrendered on Sept. 3, 1945. And so the World, after six years of death and destruction, could breathe free again.

The shortages and the inconveniences gradually passed and life seemed to return to 'normal', but how many of our adults had even a slight inkling of the vast changes which this postwar world would bring? On the subject of the use of the Atomic bomb on those two Japanese cities, there is much controversy over the 'rightness' or the 'wrongness' of the deed As a fourteen year old at the time, I saw nothing wrong with exterminating so many Japanese. They had unleashed terrible suffering on a large part of the world and they received what they deserved. To me, 'Enola Gay' and her crewmen should be enshrined. But War brings out the worst in men and it is fortunate that, as the years pass and we get further away from the harsh memories, our judgement matures and we can see things in a more reasonable light.

Yet I hold on to the view that there is the danger that the next generation who did not experience the conflict, will tend to minimise the memories and maybe even deny some of the truths. We may note, as an example, those who deny that there was a Jewish Holocaust. I am much, much older now, but still cannot fault the Americans for dropping the atomic bomb on the two Japanese cities. President Truman must have agonised long and hard before he gave the order to use the bomb. Surely it ushered in a great danger to the world's security but when we look at all the factors in the situation of mid-1945 in the Pacific, there is no doubt that the Americans had very good reasons to unleash the bomb.

Chapter Seven

Party Politics Comes To Jamaica

In mid 1938 I was barely eight years of age but I remember there was trouble at a place called Frome and I heard my grandfather mention the name several times. I never understood what the trouble was about – I cannot recall if Grandpa was in favour of or against the Frome workers. But I sensed that the trouble was serious as extra security men had to be recruited and sent to the estate. About three of our district men were recruited and sent there and I remember them, dressed in khaki uniform and being referred to as 'ex–police'. I believe that my district folks understood 'ex' to mean 'extra' or 'special', and not 'former'. The name 'Bustamante' became well known but I don't recall the waterfront troubles. By the time I was twelve or thirteen years of age I knew many of Jamaica's political names. Grandpa talked a lot about Barrister Smith, the Hon. J.A.G. Smith, member of the Legislative Council for the parish of Clarendon. He said that Norman Manley was second to Barrister Smith, as a lawyer. I used to read the 'Gleaner's lists of the elected members of the Legislative Council and the early 1940's lists had Erasmus Ethelred Campbell from Kingston, Charles Archibald Reid from Manchester, E.V. Allen from St. Elizabeth, Harold Allan from Portland, Rev. F.G.Veitch from Hanover, Maurice Hugh Seagre from Westmoreland, Arthur Benjamin Lowe from St. James, Roy Lindo from St. Mary, E.A. McNeil from St. Catherine and Rudolf Ehrenstein from St. Thomas, also the members for Trelawny, St. Ann and St. Andrew. These were elected members of the island's Legislative Council.

The Official membership of the Legislature came from the very top civil servants or heads of Government departments, for example Simon Bloomberg (Collector General), B.H. Easter, (Director of Education), Major T. J. Hallinan (Director of Medical Services), and the Director of Agriculture. The Officer Commanding the British Forces in the island, with the rank of Brigadier, always had a seat on the Council. The Colonial Secretary, Attorney General and Collector General were ex-Officio members. Other members were Robert Barker, Lawyer Douglas J. Judah, industrialist O. K. Henriques, planter Theodore Rowland Williams and Robert L. M. Kirkwood, manager of the English Tate and Lyle sugar interests. There were fourteen elected members and fifteen nominated members, which ensured that the Governor and the Administration would not be outvoted on any important issue. The Colonial Secretary was the head of the Civil Service and was the automatic acting Governor when the Governor was absent, had died in office, or in the interim between the departure of a Governor and the arrival of a successor.

I remember that when Governor Denham died in office in June 1938, the Colonial Secretary, Mr. C. C. Woolley, acted as the Governor, until the arrival of Sir Arthur Richards. I remember so many of those names as I took great pleasure in reading the reports from the 'Gleaner', whenever the Council met. Names of Mayors, Custodes and other movers and shakers in the society were of great interest to me and I easily memorised them. At the present time, Custodes of parishes come from the ranks of teachers, medical doctors, the clergy, businessmen, lawyers. In my childhood days who would ever think of a Custos coming from the teaching profession or even from the clergy. In that period, the class of great landowners supplied most of them, men like Clarke, Thursfield and Anderson from Manchester, Sir Thomas Roxburgh and Lt. Colonel Moulton Barrett from St. Ann and Capt. Henry McGrath from St. Catherine. The Corporate Area had Sir George Seymour Seymour for St Andrew and Sir Noel Livingston for Kingston.

I remember the old Parochial Boards, forerunners of the present Parish Councils, the Road Headmen who distributed and supervised work on the various 'parochial roads', the District Nurse or midwife, who delivered many of the local babies, the Sanitary Inspector or Health Officer or 'latrine man' and the Inspector of the Poor. All these were employees of the Parochial Board. As we saw it, the Sanitary Inspector's main job was to inspect the pit latrines in the district. In my early years there was only one butcher in the district and he handled only goats and there was no meat inspection. In later years this butcher stepped up to butchering cows and now the Inspector had to do meat inspection. Also a lot of cow's milk was collected for delivery to the Bog Walk Condensery and the Health Officer now had to have sessions with the milk suppliers, sensitizing them to the need for care and cleanliness in the handling of the milk being supplied. Two outstanding Sanitary Inspectors who worked in my area were Lesley Maxwell and Vesta White. Both men were avid cricketers and worked hard and successfully with our local cricket club. Old-timers, whenever discussing their local cricket, would always refer to "Maxwell time" as the glory period of the Maidstone Cricket Club. They would always relate with glee, how the Maidstone Club, under Maxwell's captaincy, challenged and beat the mighty, conquering Siloah Cricket team of St. Elizabeth. The later Vesta White was a great people's man and he also did great things with our Cricket Club.

These Local Government employees lived in our community, interacted well and were popular and well liked.

Now, a last word on one of the services provided by the old Parochial Boards, that of road repairs and upkeep. The Road Headmen who oversaw the provision of this service rode mules or horses in those days and were naturally popular in the district. I well remember the occasional blasting of troublesome rocks on the roadway. Workmen using long crow bars would first drill holes in the troublesome rocks. Then, when the holes were of the required depth the holes would be plugged with paper, old cloth or clumps of dried leaves, to await blasting day. On blasting day the workmen would place the sticks of dynamite into the holes, light the fuse and then scamper for safety. After a short interval the roar would be heard, with broken stone fragments flying in every direction. Sometimes a horn or shell was blown to warn people of the dangerous operation. We children always kept clear of these plugged holes as we held it firmly that these were real danger areas. This was well reinforced by a story told by Evelyn, one of our older schoolmates. She told the story of a man walking on a road that was prepared for blasting. This man was attracted to one of these plugged holes. He approached the hole and used his walking stick to scratch away the plug. Suddenly there was a roar and the rock was blown apart, taking the unfortunate man's head completely off his body. As the head flew up into the air it uttered, "Lawd God". We were too terrified to question the veracity of such a tragedy and we all kept clear. I, for one, specially kept clear of these drilled holes as my uncle, some years before, had lost his thumb and the next two fingers, of his left hand, after an accident with a dynamite cap which had been carelessly left on the road after a blasting operation.

But, to politics. I don't recall much of the events after the 1938 troubles, but the name "Lord Moyne" stuck in my mind. I knew from Grandpa's stories, that he came out from England, and came to find out 'what the troubles were about'. The reports on the Moyne Commission's investigations and sittings, and finally, its findings and recommendations would have been far above my head then. Grandpa also spoke of a man named Sir Stafford Cripps, that he was a friend of Mr. Norman Manley. I can't remember when 'Party' first came into the consciousness of our district but I do remember when the People's National Party group was formed at Johns Hall, a neighbouring district of Maidstone. It is interesting to note that this political group was not formed by teachers or the parson, who were usually the natural leaders in the community. It was formed by very ordinary district people; a few of them, over the years, had experience of city life and they brought some of that new political awareness to their district people. They were very enthusiastic and spread the PNP fever. However, there were some people who were suspicious of the move by these 'uneducated' local lads.

These political enthusiasts had no more than basic elementary schooling but they were so committed t o Mr. Manley and his Movement. They had their lively meetings and discussions, spiced up with the new party songs. I, myself, as young as I was, was always specially impressed with the party song, "Rally to the PNP" and the clenched fists didn't bother me then. They sent delegates to party Conferences and the first time that I had ever seen the group leader, Carpenter, in a suit was the morning after he returned from Conference in Kingston, and all dolled up, he came to report to my grandfather.

I failed to mention that my grandfather was drafted in as chairman of the group and I remember him preparing for meetings, thumbing through various books and other literary material, hunting for inspirational quotes, etc. to fire up his audience. Of course my grandpa was a great admirer of Mr. Manley. He was not a rabid political enthusiast, but clearly he had strong political views and was prepared to follow the leadership of the great lawyer and he must have been convinced that Mr. Manley was amply qualified to lead the Jamaican people. Interestingly, little was said about Bustamante in my home. Manchester never had sugar estates; it was a parish with a strong 'small settler' element, hardworking and independent. Maybe this was a reason why the 'Bustamante and Labour' phenomenon did not take on strongly in Northern Manchester. The PNP group in my district was vibrant and the leaders enthusiastically prepared the ground for the first General Election under Universal Adult Suffrage in 1944.

I earlier mentioned that there were a few people who were sceptical about this new 'party politics' craze. A lot of 'small, simple' people were actively involved and a level of political consciousness was gradually rising. The sceptics did not understand this new consciousness and felt that these gullible small people were being fed 'unhealthy' ideas and getting them all mixed up. Some people felt that these small people were just 'uppish' and were going into areas where they just could not fit in. I recall that the girl friend of one of the top party group leaders was a woman from a family that was at the lowest rung of the district 'totem pole', but this woman was very active in the party group. There were all sorts of adverse comments about this very low- grade woman. One of the 'high grade' women of the district was most incensed at this 'low grade' woman and made the acid comment that "any thing that Pikey Thomas head an head inna, can't be good something." How could this new 'party' movement be good, with people like Pikey Thomas so active in it?

Later, there were murmurings when gleanings about the PNP and its Socialism began to filter in. At this time there was no understanding of this new philosophy in our community, and I doubt if the Party did much to begin that education on the Party's stand, that was so necessary to people's understanding. As a result, one of the 'great truths' about Socialism that spread in our community was that sharing in Socialism meant that if you had two pigs then you would have to give one to your neighbour who had none. To so many of our community people, this type of sharing seemed like 'foolishness'.. This, however, did not deter people in this area from giving their support to the new movement. They trusted Norman Manley - he would never put anything that was unworthy on their heads. By the sterling work of these PNP pioneers, a solid foundation was laid. Note that this part of Manchester, since 1944, has voted JLP only once in a General Election, in the Seaga landslide of 1980.

And so on to the New Constitution which was granted to Jamaica, following on the Moyne Report. From my vantage point in time, I wonder if some of those very people who had agitated so strongly for self-government, were not a bit pleasantly surprised at that New Constitution with its grant of Universal Adult Suffrage. There must have been some doubts about the wisdom of granting Adult Suffrage to a population with such a high proportion of illiterates. Imagine a man who has nowhere to lay his head tonight, he has no job, no skill, does not know where his next meal will come from; he is over twenty one years of age but has not made anything of his life. How can you take the dangerous risk of giving him the vote? How can such a man or woman properly use that sacred trust, the vote? This must have been discussed, argued over on verandahs, in clubs, boardrooms, bedrooms, offices, at high tea, etc, etc. Prophecies of doom and destruction must have been heard here and there. But the General Elections of 1944, under Universal Adult Suffrage, came and there was not doom and there was not the destruction that some might have feared. I was almost fourteen years of age at this crucial time in our country's history and Teacher Romney did a reasonable job in giving us students some information about the New Constitution.

I can well remember the beginning of that election campaign, with the Jamaica Labour Party, the People's National Party, the Jamaica Democratic Party and one or two other little groups fielding their candidates. Informed observers saw the Jamaica Labour Party, led by Alexander Bustamante, as the party of the working class on the sugar and banana estates, the waterfront, the factories, lowly artisans, domestic servants etc. The People's National Party, led by Norman Manley was the party of the upper working class and much of the middle class and the professions; the Jamaica

Democratic Party, led by Abe Issa and Gerald Mair, represented the upper monied classes.

My parish, Manchester, had two constituencies, North Manchester and South Manchester. There was a spirited campaign for my North Manchester seat. There was Norman Sinclair, the PNP candidate with the booming voice. Sinclair had lived in the Maidstone area for some years, had operated a grocery shop and farmed on nearby lands. The family of his wife, small daughter and himself were well liked. Lawyer T. H. Sharpe from Christiana was the Jamaica Democratic Party's candidate and a less than warm campaigner. Also, he was hardly known before. The Jamaica Labour Party fielded no candidate in this area. A. John Anderson, pharmacist from Porus, campaigned as an Independent candidate. He was quite a strong speaker and many people spoke well of him. Nomination Day came on Nov. 29, 1944. The 'Gleaner' later carried the names and pictures of the candidates and constituencies for which they stood.

I well remember that night after I collected the 'Gleaner' at the post office, Grandpa and I going through the pages with the candidates who were nominated. Names which come back to mind are F. A. Foster and Gerald Mair for the Jamaica Democratic Party, pipe-smoking Gaston G. Girvan in one of the Clarendon constituencies, Rev. R. E. Phillips, John Regeorge Henry, W.D. Linton, Dr. Ivan Lloyd, Mrs. Dalton James, Manny Chin, Stennet Kerr Coombs, F.A. Pixley, Linden Newland, Florizel Glasspole, Dr. E. H. Fagan, Leslie Washington Rose, B.B. Coke, Norman Sinclair, Lawton Bromfield, W. W. Benjamin, Isaac W. Barrant, T. H. Sharpe, A. John Anderson, among many others. When we came to the name and picture of Isaac Barrant, from St. Thomas, my grandpa looked hard at him and was most unimpressed. As he commented on Barrant's 'sheepy, sheepy' appearance, he gave out, "All you, you nah get in." But Grandpa Morris had to later eat his words, as Barrant won his seat comfortably, and in many years to come, no one could defeat him in that constituency. He later became Minister of Agriculture and actually died in office. If you now ask old and retired Agricultural Officers who worked under him as to who they think has been our best Minister of Agriculture to date, the majority will unhesitatingly say, "Isaac Barrant". This simple and unsophisticated man had enormous common sense and drive and made a success of his portfolio. Many of my generation will recall the amusing, but often fictitious stories about Barrant's lack of drawing room manners and the embarrassing situations he fell in as a result of his ignorance of the social graces.

By the 1944 General Election, this fourteen year-old was rooting for the PNP and Norman Manley. I naturally followed my folks' sympathies, also I was influenced by the 'propaganda' of that lively PNP group at John's

Hall and my 'pickney' admiration for Norman Manley. I took great pleasure in Norman Sinclair's victory in my area of North Manchester. South Manchester's race was extremely close and the final count gave the seat to Lawton Bloomfield. I had prayed for Wendel Benjamin's victory as I felt it would have been so nice for my beloved Manchester to have both its seats occupied by PNP members. But that was not to be. I was so bitterly disappointed when sometime later, Lindsay, one of the leaders of the local PNP group, called out to my grandpa to tell him that Bloomfield had finally won. I suppose that this was an early demonstration to the young fourteen-year-old 'politician' that politics come with victories and defeats and he would have to learn to take his 'medicine' gracefully.

The results of the 1944 General Election is now a part of Jamaica's political history. We know that the Jamaica Labour Party, under Alexander Bustamante, won handsomely with 23 seats; the PNP could only muster 4 seats. Only Florizel Glasspole and Dr. Ivan Lloyd of the top leadership of the PNP were successful. Norman Manley, the PNP leader, was clobbered in his constituency by lightweight, Dr. E. H. Fagan. Alexander Bustamante became Chief Minister and our Jamaica had embarked on the road to self-government.

Chapter Eight

My Last Two Years With
Teacher Romney

Those years were 1943 and 1944 and I would be two years in Sixth Class, the very top class in the school. Teacher Romney was his usual self, always armed with his 'psychology' and ready to dispense a 'tarring' wherever and whenever he thought it necessary. 'Tarring' was one of the terms used by Teacher when he was referring to a solid thrashing given or one which was threatened to come. This reminds me of my friend, Rayton, a year or two before. Rayton was a senior student in Upper Division, when, on this particular day, one of his relatives was getting married. Of course Rayton attended the wedding and did not attend school that day. Weddings in those days were held mostly on Wednesdays, so there would have been the wedding taking place in the Church and the school would be in full session nearby. We bigger boys usually welcomed a wedding on a school day as there would be a good chance of two of us being asked to go over to the Church and pump the organ - electricity had not yet come to Maidstone. But back to Rayton. After the wedding ceremony, Rayton followed some of his male relatives up to the village shop, which also had a rum bar. He must have been taken in by the merry occasion and he hung around, possibly hoping to have his share of Ginger Ale or Cream Soda or Kola Wine or Herring and Bread. He was certainly bent on enjoying this merry day away from school.

But fate would scheme to spoil his future with Teacher Romney. For some unknown reason, one of his school colleagues, Selvin Ashton, informed Teacher Romney that Rayton was at this shop and bar, busy drinking rum. Teacher was outraged; he never tried to investigate the truth of the information, but promised solemnly to give Rayton the 'tarring' of his life when he returned to school. But Rayton quickly got wind of Teacher Romney's 'evil intention' towards him, and he seemed to have made up his mind there and then. As Rayton must have seen it, continuing his education wasn't worth that coming 'tarring' from old Romney, and he never, never returned to school. That was the end of Rayton's formal education. Didn't his parents care? Maybe they themselves were quietly glad that they could now have him for full time assistance in their provision fields. For Rayton, he could do a little reading and writing, and that was good enough for him.

We young ones of Maidstone, despite our little fears and uncomfortable moments at school, had much respect for our learning institution. Teacher Romney told us that we attended a First Class A Grade school and though we had no means then, to verify his word, we believed him and felt good about the distinction. Teacher took pride in his Jamaica Local Examination 'private class', and each year he had successes in that examination. I can well remember the excitement when the Jamaica Gazette came off the press in October, carrying the names of the successful candidates who sat the Local Examinations in the previous July. Teacher Romney had contacts in Kingston who would get the Gazette as it came out, extract the successful Nazareth names and then telegraph them to him. Then a day or two later, the Gazette itself would arrive at the local post office and great would be the joy of the successes and much sadness and tears for the failures. I can still hear the joyful shrieks and foot stomping as the successful names were read out and more shrieks if that successful candidate 'capped' a subject, meaning obtaining a distinction in the subject. We regarded it as a distinction to be drafted into Teacher's 'Private Class', to be prepared for the Jamaica Local Examinations. Most of these fortunate students, as a natural result of their new status, began to wear shoes to school; some of the boys, now fifteen or over, received their first pair of 'long trousers'. Teacher Romney alone conducted the classes, for about an hour down to nine o'clock in the mornings, and then after school dismissal at four in the afternoons. These students were to pay a certain amount per month for the tuition but I am sure Teacher was never able to collect much of these fees.

Teachers at that time in the Jamaica countryside would sometimes experience situations where a parent strongly desires his or her child to 'study', but the teacher knows that the student is not yet ready or is academically unfit or 'her head too tick'.[23] The parent is unconvinced and insists, but the teacher does not bend. This sometimes led to 'bad blood' between teacher and parent, the parent declaring that the teacher does not like her child and is 'prejudiced'. Another disappointed parent might sneer, "If Maggie Smith daughter in yu private class, mek fimmi pickney caan in de to?"[24] There were parents who did not like other children to succeed ; there were more than one story whispered about a certain mother who 'consulted somewhere' to ensure that certain students did not 'pass'. In the district

[23] She has little academic ability.

[24] "If Maggie Smith's daughter is in your private class, why can't my child be there too?"

there was a certain family who were very successful, academically, but their mother was very openly caustic about other children. But these were not uncommon situations which some rural teachers had to contend with as they laboured in these communities. But I must add that, although I was two years in Sixth Class, with Teacher Romney, I did not reach his 'private class'. At the Annual School Inspection in 1943 by the Department of Education, I acquitted myself masterly. All the Inspector's questions were answered correctly, and I repeatedly 'saved the class' that day. Teacher Romney was beside himself with joy and the next day he told me, in the presence of my peers, that he would place me in his 'private class'. But he did not and I did not summon up the courage to remind him. On another occasion he was again very pleased with my performance and he again made the promise, but he did not follow up. I am certain that I would have been in his 'Private class' the following year, my third year in Sixth Class, but he left the school at the end of 1944.

Teacher Romney never organised big school concerts but at the end of each Summer term we had what we termed, 'Breaking Up'. This was an informal afternoon session to mark the end of the Summer term, and the whole student body would remain in their seats and individual students or groups would perform in the cleared area in front of Teacher Romney's table. He might give out a few pieces to be performed but the bulk of the pieces were put together by students and their parents. There were a few parents who could always find nice pieces to give their children - gems and extracts, poems for reciting, jokes, riddles and a skit here and there. Poor Jamey from Fourth Class, on one of these sessions, was roundly embarrassed by Teacher Romney and driven back to his seat in disgrace when he went out before the audience and posed the riddle, "Hell a top, hell a bottom, hallelujah inna middle; what is that?" Now the answer to that riddle is "Pone", as we then termed a special baked pudding. 'Pone' was made from corn or sweet potato or cassava flour, baked in a covered iron pot or "Dutchie", placed on a controlled fire and topped with hot coals. Hence, hell (fire) on top and hell (fire) at the bottom. Of course, the delicious baked pudding was the 'hallelujah' in the middle. For some unknown reason, Teacher immediately rejected this riddle and verbally tore into Jamey as if he had uttered something foul and despicable. Was it too 'rootsy' or disgraceful to talk about the lowly 'pone' before such an audience? And so Jamey had to 'lap his tail' and cower back to his seat. I remember in preparing for one of these 'Breaking Up' sessions I came upon Longfellow's poem, "A Psalm of Life", and I got together three of my classmates and we four recited the poem. It was well executed and very well received by the young audience, though we all had little or no understanding of the depth of thought expressed in the poem.

Looking back, I like to think that I contributed to a bit of pioneering on one of these 'Breaking Up' sessions. On one of my regular search and 'digging up' under my grandfather's cellar, I came upon a copy of a book of Jamaican pieces written in dialect, entitled "Constab Ballads". I believe it might have been one of the very first works written in Jamaican dialect. I showed it to my friend, Ken Frith, and he selected a piece to perform at the 'Breaking Up'. The piece selected was "Cotch Donkey' which involved him riding a lazy donkey, and he got classmate, Ivor, to be the donkey. And so Ken came into the schoolroom riding Ivor, but as soon as donkey Ivor came into the middle of the audience area he suddenly slumped down and would go no further. Ken had to quickly jump off Ivor's back and he now tore into his lazy donkey in full, raw Jamaican dialect. This was the first time we all were hearing a full piece rendered in dialect before an audience. Remember, these were the days when Jamaican dialect was not respectable and you could be well punished by your teachers for using dialect in class. I recall myself, while in Third Class, being flogged by Teacher Romney after he heard me, in raw dialect, taunting Clarence about his "chigga foot". The taunting was done, not in the classroom, but out in the schoolyard, during the recess period. So, that skit by Ken and Ivor, done in full dialect, before an audience, was an important departure. Within a few years 'Miss Lou' would be revolutionising our whole attitude to our dialect, but our local pioneers were certainly Ken Frith and Ivor. Ken seemed to have had a special appreciation for our dialect. He always brought home from Mandeville, tracts of songs composed and sung by the noted duo, Slim and Sam. One of those early tracts that he brought to school was "Jamaican Woman". As he sang, instead of singing "Manchester gal dem", or, "Hanover gal dem", he would localise: "Maidstone gal dem" or "Shirehampton gal dem" ------ or "New Hope gal dem" – – –referring to various districts in our immediate school area.

Miss Tamson continued to come over to Upper Division for the occasional singing class and fed us with a diet of patriotic songs. She taught the French "Marseillaise" and the "Pomp and Circumstance" favourite "Land of Hope and Glory". But she did mix these with a few others like "Jamaica, the Beautiful Island of Springs" and "The Huntsman", and "Merry Christmas" at Christmas time. We boys were like spectators, we were never encouraged to actively participate; it was unheard of for any boy to do any solo singing. But this would change mightily before long.

Entertainment in our community was not easy to obtain and for us children the big event for the year was the annual Sunday School picnic on

Queen Victoria's birthday, May 24, or Empire Day. This picnic was held on the Church and school grounds. Bear in mind that Maidstone was a strict Moravian community and the picnic was closely planned and supervised by the Church leadership. No unsavoury elements or activities were allowed - dancing to the music of drum, fife, triangle and horse skull had to be circumspect and 'harmless', and not many people indulged. There might be a maypole, there were swings, but little else to entertain. In the morning before the picnic got underway in earnest, all the Sunday School children would be gathered at the school building where each received a can of 'sugar and water', flavoured with sour orange juice. That was accompanied by a smallish round bun, which was supplied by Parnell's Bakery at Balaclava in St. Elizabeth. Jim Parnell, the owner of the bakery, was the brother of Mrs. Black, minister's wife. There was little else for the day.

Many parents came out for the day's outing, and laughed and joked, swapped stories and caught up with the latest tidbits and gossip. We children frolicked and enjoyed ourselves and did not complain. After all, we were not used to more. It was sometime before radio invaded our community and television was not yet on the scene to show us a taste of what was outside. On August 1, our neighbouring Presbyterian Church at Medina had its annual picnic on its grounds. That was a much more relaxed community and their picnic was always much more lively and had more attractions. There would always be the very popular Maypole with all the merry parents and young people, and sometimes even a dance booth, a great attraction, and was always well patronized. A few of us boys from Maidstone never missed the Medina picnic. I was always there because I had the perfect excuse: my mother's house was a few chains from the picnic grounds and I was certain to visit with her every August 1. A further incentive was that Medina was a mango area and picnic time was smack in the mango season.

Our annual Missionary Service at our Nazareth Church was another special day for us young ones. The Moravian Church had been a great missionary Church and they were the ones who brought the gospel to the Jamaican slave population, beginning with their landing in Jamaica in 1754. Hence the Missionary Service was a very special occasion in each Moravian congregation. Our Missionary Service at Nazareth was always in early December and was held on a Wednesday. Sometime after the War, the day was changed to Sunday. For us children the great delight of that Wednesday was the presence of cake sellers, bun sellers, patty sellers, candy sellers, and many others, all trying to cash in on the big crowd, many of whom would be very hungry after the long Missionary Service. They were all gathered on the grounds just below the church building, and came from areas as far away as Greenvale, just outside of Mandeville.

Some of us young ones would have up to a shilling to spend and how we yearned for the Service to end so we could rush out to sample the tasty wares. Many of us had saved our three-pences, sixpences or maybe up to a shilling or more, from collecting 'rat cut' coffee or gathering the 'Leavings' of the pimento crop, after our parents had gathered. Our little collection of 'rat cut' coffee or pimento would be sold at the village shop and for a very short time we would feel rich. Another very important feature for us children was the array of visiting speakers at the service. In the early years there were always a goodly number of ministers from other Moravian congregations; the Presbyterian minister from nearby Medina was always present, and at least once the Anglican rector at St George's, Mile Gully, was one of the speakers. But we were so impressed by that long pew in front, holding the several visiting speakers. In those days the Moravian Church in Jamaica always had a number of English missionaries working in the countryside. Some had experience in other foreign mission fields and how we sat up as they told us about their work in Labrador, Africa and other areas. We enjoyed just staring admiringly at these white men and their wives. The lusty singing of "From Greenland's Icy Mountains", still rings in my ears.

1944 saw me as a big boy in the school. I was now in Senior Sixth Class, a veteran of the 'Romney System", and enjoying a few 'perks' from my seniority. The ink we used was mixed from powder supplied by the Department of Education. Every Monday morning, Teacher would issue an appropriate amount of ink powder to be mixed. About three or four Senior boys would be detailed for the mixing. The powder would be properly watered and the resulting ink would be poured into jars with spouts. Then these Senior boys would go around to the various desks and replenish the ink wells. It was a job with responsibility and I liked it. Also, the little ones from Lower Division, and even part of Middle Division, showed you some respect. Sometimes, Teacher Romney made a senior boy supervise a number of small boys in the school garden. In addition, there were times when the boys assembled for Drill and Teacher Romney could not be there right away. In such a situation, he would direct a senior boy to line up the boys and direct some of the exercises until he arrived. One might even get the chance to write up the homework for the next day. This would entail a battle with the chalk to keep the writing straight on the chalkboard. There were several other little ways in which our seniority was felt but one was never too senior to be out of the reach of Teacher Romney's 'rod of correction'.

Interestingly, I can remember very, very few squabbles among us. I never knew of Teacher Romney having to step in and part two fighters. We had our little squabbles occasionally, but usually after a short period of 'bexing up and cut-eye and throwing wud'[25] we would be back to normal. Our fisticuffs were really with the fists and there was the serious wrestling or 'throw-dung', which demonstrated strength and dexterity. We did not even think of using weapons - where a boy had a pocket knife, it was for the purpose of peeling his orange or sugar cane. There was none of that viciousness that we see demonstrated so much by our young people today. I remember a lone weapon incident when, some years before, a senior boy had attempted to cut another boy in a dispute. That boy was doing his last few months in school and I must have been about eight years of age when it took place. But I remember that the horrible news flew around the districts and people were astounded. The boy never returned to school and in later years when we saw him, our minds always echoed, "There goes the cutter", and he was always avoided. In a way, he paid dearly for his act and the area never did forget. It is interesting to note that this young fellow came from a neighbouring district which we always distrusted. Not many children attended school from that district and we never gladly played with them.

Sometimes, during our district wanderings, we had to pass through that district and we always made haste to get out of the area. So when this young man made this serious mistake, there were many people who were not surprised. But this man settled down, reared his family, lived a peaceful and productive life and has been so respected. Be at peace with all men and do not judge! One case of a severe beating remains in my memory. It took place in a certain mango season and the victim was a strong, muscular man who repeatedly and defiantly gathered mangoes from a certain 'mango walk'. He was warned again and again but he scoffed at the 'walk' overseers. Eventually, the three overseers grabbed hold of him and gave him a severe beating. He took his beating, then ambled home quietly and a few days later he was back in circulation. Nobody teased him and he never tried to take revenge. These were 'good days' and 'Man to Man was so very less unjust'.

Of the games now being played, we knew nothing of Football or Soccer. In those times if we at Maidstone wanted to witness a game of football, we would have had to descend to the St. Elizabeth plains, to Munro College, to satisfy our curiosity. The 'Daily Gleaner,' at that time, carried a 'Missing Ball' competition, where players would be shown in various playing scenes, and the reader, if he wanted to enter the competition, would make a cross where he thinks the ball is. If he were

---

[25] Vexation and ignorance.

correct, then he would win a prize. Cricket was played by all. We used the occasional tennis ball, a green orange, or a 'kende', which was roughly rounded out of wood and could inflict a very painful blow to one's body. A golf ball was used on at least one occasion. In other words, we used whatever was available. For a bat, we used all sorts of pieces of wood or board, coconut bough, barrel stave etc. etc. The standard cricket ball, or 'red lion' was used by the adults.

Other games like Tennis or Golf were for the upper classes and the scions of the prestige high schools. Volley ball was unknown and Baseball was 'something' up in America. Later, when television came and showed the first pictures of American Football, we saw it as that strange 'buck up' game - big men running up and down with a funny- shaped ball hugged tightly to their bodies. Pshaw! Among us, there were other 'soft' boys' games like Marbles, Flags Game, Belt War, and a little wrestling or 'throw dung' as we called it. The girls played Catch Ball with any type of ball available. A little Basket ball or more correctly, Netball, was played, but overall, little was done to organize ball games for the girls. In fact both boys and girls were sadly neglected where organised games were concerned. We had to make do for ourselves and provide for our play activities as best as we could.. These were the great days of girls' Ring Games - 'The Grand Old Duke of York', 'One and Twenty, Two and Twenty' – ---- – and a few others. There were girls' baseball, hopscotch, bull-in-the-pen, dog and bone. Really, we enjoyed ourselves on our rocky terrain and we were adept at inventing ways of getting amusement.

Recess period among the rocks of the schoolyard was also the time for relaxation and 'education in various tings'. It was during one of these recess periods that I first learnt that a woman was subject to 'monthly periods'. My classmate, Sarjie, was the guy who delivered that 'education'. Now, Sarjie had six grown sisters who at this time were all away from home, employed in Kingston and one or two other areas. How I saw it, Sarjie's parents had these six girls, and then there was a long, long break before Sarjie and his older brother were born. Hence these two young boys had six adult sisters. As we thirteen or fourteen- year- olds relaxed that day among the rocks, Sarjie related to us that one of these grown-up sisters was at home on a short leave from her Kingston job. She talked a lot with him and told him that if she were still residing at home she would tell him a lot of 'tings' that would help him to 'tun man'[26]. Among the 'tings' that she told him was the fact that a woman had to 'bleed ebry month'. At that news I very nearly jumped out of my trousers. I had never heard such 'utter foolishness' in my

---

[26] Become a man.

whole life. I fired back at him, "Go whey, you too lie; nutten coulda go so; yu sista no know whey she a talk bout."[27]

To me it was so ridiculous, there was no sense to the whole thing. If one received a knife or machete cut, or some other accident, naturally you bleed and lose blood. What would be the sense of bleeding without some sort of cut. Preposterous, utterly stupid! The whole story seemed so senseless to me that I never repeated this 'fool, fool' information. It was so foolish that I wouldn't 'waste mi time' to pass on the information to my peers who were not present when Sarjie dropped the bombshell. But looking back, we see that Sarjie's sister was ahead of her time. Those were the days when most parents would take flight in panic if sex education for their youngsters were mentioned. That was not for children, and 'dem mus wait till dem grow up'. So many of us got our 'facts' from older boys who were so often misinformed and had their facts twisted and exaggerated. The magazine "Sexology", which came on the scene in our later teen years, supplied us with much basic information. How times have changed! Compare us naive thirteen/fourteen year-olds with ten year olds of the late twentieth or early twenty first centuries - the gap is ultra enormous.

Youth organisations were notably absent in our community at this time. Scouting or Girl Guiding did not reach us and 4-H Clubs came after Teacher Romney left. Youth Clubs, which by this time were making headway in the urban areas, never invaded our district. Our youth training came solely from Church, school and home. The adults had the local branch of the Jamaica Agricultural Society and a Maidstone Improvement Association did well for a number of years. They had debates and lively discussions on various local and national issues. There was elocution, singing and poetry reading. They had visits to their meetings from their Member of the Legislative Council, Member of the Parochial Board and several other notable people from outside the community, including an eminent retired teacher who had laboured in the Calabar region of Nigeria. Facilities and opportunities were limited, but our people lived their lives and made the most of what was available to them. Life was very less complicated and more easy paced and we were not yet exposed to the pull of the 'joys' of the outside.

School life for me, under the Romney regime, was rapidly drawing to a close. But two situations stand out in my mind. The first concerns an 'analyse and parse' homework, given by Teacher Romney to his Fifth and Sixth classes. On this particular evening, just before dismissal at four

---

[27] "Go away, you are too lying; nothing could go like that. Your sister does not know what she is talking about."

o'clock, Teacher wrote up the first two lines of William Wordsworth's poem, "The Brook:" "I come from haunts of coot and hern, I make a sudden sally."

This was the homework for the following morning: to analyse the two sentences and then parse all the words contained. This homework should be submitted immediately when we gathered for devotion and would be marked by Teacher's daughter, Daffy, who assisted him with the two classes. As soon as she completed the marking, which would be sometime after roll call, Teacher would bring the two classes together for him to go through the homework exercise with us. He dealt with each book and the student owner individually, and he dispensed 'justice' accordingly. On this morning over ninety per cent of the class failed to do the 'analysis' correctly. Three of us boys were exempted from the 'operation', as for sometime on the evening before, we three were working on a clean-up project at the Teacher's Cottage. Thus on that evening we did not get the homework, so we were safe next morning and could observe fully the 'misfortunes' of the rest of the class. Teacher Romney was irate that nearly everybody did not know that in analysing the sentences in question, they should slip in 'and' between the two simple sentences to make them into a 'Compound Sentence'. Teacher and cane worked vigorously - student after student was 'worked over' and many, many were the tears shed.

Teacher repeated and repeated and repeated: "I come from haunts of coot and hern, and, I make a sudden sally". He had in fact taught that in such a case, the conjunction 'and' was not written between the sentences but it is understood to be there. So when you get to work to analyse, you should know to put in 'and'. The angry Headmaster was very disappointed that his 'teaching' was not followed and he waded into the erring students with his ever ready cane. Oh! There were tears, tears. I couldn't remember so many licks being dispensed in one session. 'Analyse and Parse' was very difficult for many students who could not make sense of especially the 'parsing ' section. Every word had to be given its special place and relationship in the sentence and some students just could not do it. Teacher Romney perspired profusely that morning. I suspect that Miss Brenda at lunch time had to 'noint' that right arm of his. Those arm muscles had every right to be sore.

In these years there was a pair of twin boys in my class and we were very close friends. Leslie was a rough and tough character but good homoured and kind. I was sure that Teacher Romney secretly admired his toughness and he would always refer to Leslie as 'Hard Morris' and to twin brother Clevon as 'Knock Softly'. Clevon was a more placid personality, but still a good friend. Leslie and I were especially close friends and we took great pleasure in pulling off tricks right under Teacher Romney's nose. As the corn crop ended, we young ones had to turn to corn that was dry and hard. Those with poor teeth had to call it a day as far as their roasted-corn eating was concerned. Boys like Leslie and myself, with sound, strong teeth, could deal with the hard, dry corn, roasted. Every day, after lunch, we returned to class with our pockets loaded with this roasted 'dry corn', as we called it. Fifth and Sixth Classes were very often gathered, standing together around Teacher's platform, and while Teacher held forth, Leslie and myself had our fill of 'roast corn'. We developed great expertise in cracking the tough grain without the noise reaching Teacher and we were never betrayed by any movement of the mouth. On the converse, during the earlier 'soft-roast corn' period, despite all the expertise, one could be betrayed by the strong 'roast-corn' smell. With the roasted 'dry corn', you did not need to worry about the smell. How we were amused that Teacher Romney, despite 'his great wisdom and know-how', never detected us, feeding away under his very eyes.

Then Leslie was a great listener to 'talk' among the farm animals. Morning after morning he would bring the news of what he heard the donkey say to the cow, or the old hen to the new hen who had just arrived in the farmyard. He had a choice one about the bull which was tethered adjoining to the pen of the young heifer who 'did tink she nice'. Then he gave us this one about the ram goat who was upbraided by the quiet but efficient ram sheep, about the rumpus he created when 'going about his business'. He also related what the cat said to the dog, as she was perched up in the avocado pear tree, and looking down at the angry and hungry dog. Sometimes in our Reading class, when Teacher made us read collectively, as a full class, Leslie would make the most hilarious comments and jokes as we read. Teacher would be convinced that our wide smiling faces mirrored the enjoyment of the subject we were reading about. Little did he know how Leslie's humour carried us. But despite Leslie's expertise in dealing with Teacher Romney, every now and again he would run afoul of Teacher, and Leslie would be 'tarred' solidly. On one of these occasions, Leslie, who never cried when he received a caning, cried and cried. He was so upset with Romney that he cried, "I hate him, I hate him." We were so sympathetic to Leslie as we realised how hurt he felt. But two hours later and Leslie was his old self again.

Leslie's twin brother, Clevon, was quiet and more reserved. And I remember one occasion when he was extensively whipped by Teacher Romney. The occasion was a Reading class and the lesson was entitled, "How Pat won the Victoria Cross." Pat was a dog which was closely attached to the colour sergeant of a British regiment. During a battle with the Afghans somewhere in the East, the British soldiers came under great pressure from the Afghans. The colour-sergeant went down and was at the point of being killed by a giant Afghan and the colours being captured. Pat, seeing his master in mortal danger, rushed at the Afghan and gripped his knife hand in his jaws. He held on, receiving very severe wounds, but his brave intervention enabled another British soldier to shoot the Afghan dead, and so save his master's life and the regimental colours. Pat slowly recovered from his wounds and for his bravery and devotion was awarded the Victoria Cross. But back to dear old Clevon. In this reading class, we were reading individually to teacher. When Clevon's turn came, he had to deal with 'the Afghan' at several places in his paragraphs, but he could not say, "the Afghan"; instead, he kept saying 'the Affigan'. Teacher Romney jumped up from his seat, bent on having Clevon say the right word, 'the Afghan', not 'the Affigan'. Teacher brought the cane down on Clevon, 'the Afghan'. Clevon replied, 'the Affigan'. Whack! Whack! went Teacher's cane, but 'Affigan' came from Clevon again, again and again. - Affigan, Affigan, Affigan. Teacher's cane could not extract 'the Afghan' from Clevon's mouth, and Clevon just had to be left with his 'Affigan'.

Leslie and Clevon and their sister, Yvonne, later went off to the United States to join their parents, and so we lost their company. I especially missed Leslie as he was such a great humorist and made our young lives lighter. It was after Leslie left that I discovered that I had come under serious suspicion because of my close association with him. The story came out that Leslie had taken hold of a registered letter belonging to a resident of his district. It was believed that he had got the slip signed by his great friend, Keith Morris. We never did hear how Leslie got out of this one, but I recall a visit that was paid by Leslie's grandmother, to Miss Ann, my grandfather's wife, at my home. The two ladies were not such great friends to be visiting each other and it was not until later that I realised the purpose of the visit. At one point, during the visit, I walked past the open front door and I noticed Miss Ann walking from the direction of my room with an exercise book partially hidden from view in the folds of her ample blouse. I wondered at that, but put it out of my head almost instantly; maybe she was only showing off my nice handwriting.

That afternoon when Leslie's grandmother was about to go home, Miss Ann called me to say goodbye to her. I clearly remember, as I stood before her, that long look she gave me, and her eyes seemed to bore through me. I noted her eyes and I was convinced she was a bit 'cock-eyed'. And so later on, I was able to piece the bits together and see the story. Leslie had taken the registered slip and it was suspected that he got me to sign it. We then appropriated the letter and its contents and shared it. That explains his grandmother's visit, in order to check my handwriting and her taking a probing look at the co-

conspirator. But it seems the evidence was just not there and they could not make an 'arrest'. Poor me! I was never aware of Leslie's wrong doing; he never told me, his good friend, of any such shenanigans. But justice was served and my good name remained unsullied. Leslie, even if he transgressed, remained my good friend. I spent so many happy hours with him and I cherish our merry times in that old schoolhouse on the hill.

Chapter Nine

The Revolution

Teacher Romney and family left the district at the end of 1944 and he and Miss Brenda took up teaching duties at a school in St. Elizabeth. He was succeeded as Principal by Mr. L.B. Reice, a young man who came up from a small school in St. Elizabeth. I refer to this period as 'The Revolution', because there was a whole new vision at work in our community. The school's place in our district was re-energised, parent-teacher relations took on a new meaning, and school, for more and more students, became the place to be. Corporal punishment was not banned - a strap was present; it was kept in the drawer and not flaunted at every turn. When it was used, we felt it was deserved. There was moderation and we were sure there was no joy in using it. Learning became not a chore, but an experience which you wanted to have.

On that school morning in January 1945, when Teacher Reice took up duties, we all turned out early, anxious to have a good look at our new man. We in Senior Sixth Class felt proud of ourselves and held our heads high. Teacher Reice started out quietly, with no great fanfare and any lofty introductory speech. Right away he began settling in and we noted that he was sure of himself and knew what he was about. If you had asked us then, what we thought of him in the first few hours, we would not have been able to express it in so many words, but we did have the feeling that though he was not trailing a strap alongside him and he was not glaring fiercely at us, he was a character not to be played with. On that first day, about fifteen minutes before four o'clock dismissal time, he told us in Fifth and Sixth Classes to sit quietly. We had completed our assignments and were ready now to go off home. In that little time left, Teacher just wanted us to be quiet while he went into a nearby book press to start checking on the school documents and other equipment stored away there and which would have been new to him. We all sat quietly and in order, except my classmates Joe and Stanley. They began sparring quite actively and were spoken to by the new Principal. Things did not improve and he spoke to them another two times. Joe and Stanley seemed to have been bent on testing him and would not stop their sparring. Then we saw Teacher Reice bound across the space up to his table on the platform, pull out the drawer and extracted a hefty leather strap. Then he delivered his first act of corporal punishment in this school. We watched speechless, but with little sympathy for Joe and Stanley; after all, they had brought it upon themselves. But all of us 'big boys', when we saw the execution of the operation, quietly came to the full conclusion that here was a man that was not to be trifled with..

Teacher Reice was an accomplished musician; he arrived with his own piano, which he played very well. He took over as organist at our Church and naturally became the Choir Director. He sang a gripping baritone and over the years graced our church services with many a baritone solo. Later on he formed and maintained a community choir which brought great distinction to our community in various parish competitions. Within our school our Singing classes were now on the top agenda and everybody was involved fully. Under Teacher Romney, the boys were hardly more than spectators in the singing class ; there was not the encouragement for us to take a real interest. On Teacher Reice's first day with us, he gathered Fourth, Fifth and Sixth classes together for singing. This first Singing class took place immediately after the return from lunch on that Monday afternoon. He placed the boys in front, with the girls lined up behind. We boys understood right away that this was no 'joke class' and this new man meant business. He then gave us a few breathing exercises and the running up and down the scale. Then he launched into a Round, the first we had ever had. The words were: *"Great Tom is cast, and Christ Church bells ring one, two, three, four, five, six; and Tom comes last".* He quickly taught us the tune, and then the different entry points. How we sang, boys and girls, and we enjoyed the whole exercise immensely. Teacher Reice's students were all so impressed and fired up and many were the joyful reports related to parents that evening..

Two other popular Rounds we were taught were 'Whittington', and 'Oh, every sleeper waken, the Sun is in the sky.' Years afterwards, at a function honouring Teacher Reice, a certain grandmother, in her tribute, harked back to the first few months of Teacher's tenure and told of her granddaughter coming home on an evening of his first week there and joyfully exclaiming, "Grandma, we all a sing Round now." We now had Singing classes twice per week and we looked forward to them. Instead of the old patriotic songs, we had "Nelly Bly", the first full length song he taught us, "The Lass With the Delicate Air" and "Early One Morning Just As the Sun Was Rising." Just before Teacher Romney left, Miss Brenda, his wife, had been struggling with Shakespeare's "Where the Bee Sucks". When Teacher Reice came, he took it and polished it up with us. The boys were now singing like mad and a few beautiful voices did emerge. Our place was always in front of the girls and we did our best to please him. He taught us boys the male parts; one example was the bass part of "The Lass With the Delicate Air."

For our Science classes, he had a veritable treat for us. He brought to us a brand new Science kit and we could witness close up, various science experiments. Potassium Chlorate and Manganese Dioxide were being combined and the resultant Oxygen gas was being collected under water. Hydrogen was made from pouring Hydro-Chloric Acid on Zinc and then we tested for the pale blue flame which verified the presence of Hydrogen. It was all a new wonder for us and we basked in the new light that opened around us. Our lessons on Foods, Soils, in fact the whole Science course, gave us ideas of how much interesting things were out there to be learnt. Geography classes were of very great interest for me as we studied Climatic Regions of the World: Tropical Grasslands, Mediterranean Lands, Cool Temperate Oceanic Regions, their position on the map, climatic characteristics, people and products. I was a great lover of Geography, so one can well imagine how I revelled. Another innovation which Teacher Reice brought was the start of an Upper Division Lending Library. It began in a medium-sized bookcase and was stacked with much of the Hardy Boys series and many other titles suitable to our age groups. My favourite was The Hardy Boys; I would borrow a copy in the afternoon, read it through in the night, check it back in next morning, borrow another copy for the following night, and so it would go on and on until the collection was exhausted. Then I turned to others – one of these 'others' that I remember well was 'Glengarry Schooldays'.

I recall that the story, "Glengarry Schooldays" made a great impression on me, as I identified with this schoolboy who was experiencing changes in his school life, even the coming of a new Principal, and that new Principal's initial lack of interest in his favourite field game, Shinny. Often when I drive down Constant Spring Road towards Half Way Tree, there is this old residence with the name "Glengarry' on its gate pillar, which takes me back so many, many years to my old schoolhouse with its new bookcase and its exciting collection. A whole new world of information and possibilities was being opened to so many of us, thanks to this little beginning of a library.

Then in Industrial Arts, we also got an introduction. Teacher Reice brought his collection of basic carpentry tools and started the senior boys in making simple and useful things like photo frames and wooden savings boxes. On Friday mornings we would be busy with our saws, chisels, planes, scrapers, screwdrivers, sandpaper, glue - trying to make something we could show off at home. Sad to say, I did not do very well in that exercise as, trying hard as I did, I could not develop proficiency with those tools. Friday attendance at school, which in earlier times had always been sparse, now picked up very significantly. Teacher Reice's 'Friday School' had interesting things to do and students responded accordingly.

The School Garden now had a new lease of life. Teacher Reice was a more active farmer and could be seen on some weekends plying his fork in his private plot near his cottage. In the School Garden there was a greater variety of crops and there was a greater accent on vegetable production. Work in the garden was much more purposeful and we now had less time to'skylark'. Teacher Reice saw not only to our academic well-being but he also addressed our physical well-being. His first year saw the holding of our first full-blooded Sports Day. The school population, from First Class up to Sixth Class, was divided into four Houses and the spirit of competition was aroused. Sports activities was the area of most intense rivalry and we duly prepared for our Sports Day. Our sports field was bumpy and 'hill and gully' but we had to make the best of it. Day after day our practices went ahead: running, jumping, throwing the cricket ball, relays, girls with the skipping races, and others. The high jump was out of my range as I just could not lift my body over eighteen inches. Hence I was determined to do well in the flat races. My classmate and neighbour, Joe, declared that he could not run, so he concentrated on jumping. He was my friend and I did not have the heart to tell him that he was pathetic in his chosen area. On Sports Day he failed miserably, his long feet 'hurling off' the cross bar every time he jumped.

As for me, I did reasonably well on Sports Day. - I was second in the hundred yards and the two hundred and twenty yards (these distances were not yet expressed in metres). My team won the sprint relay and I received one shilling as my prize for my part in the victory. I had ill- advisedly entered the mile race and ended being badly humiliated. My schoolmate Yu Yu, (who betrayed me when I broke Kenbert's slate in A Class) was the champion athlete. It was a great day for all of us - our parents came out in full force, cheered, and enjoyed themselves, and a few took part in the Parents Race. It was so amusing to watch the Father's Race as Mas Eddie manfully and 'slowly' lumbered around the track, with his younger brother, Cecil, toying with him, and then finishing the race with a flourish. Mas Eddie did not give up and insisted on making it to the tape. The Old Students also had their race, which was won by Mico student, Leander. Parents and teachers were brought closer together in a real partnership and Teacher Reice never lost their esteem and cooperation. Also, in Teacher's first year, he launched the first of his several grand school concerts. He brought his piano up to the school and rehearsed the songs with the girls. He wrote the plays and skits and made full use of the dialect. He went into common topic areas for his material, like returning farm workers, workers at 'American Sandy Gully', the new political meetings, domestic issues and school life. For so many of us, this was our first real exposure to full audiences and we grew the better for it.

In so many ways, school became a place which beckoned you, as if to share in good things. This was the time when school took on such a new meaning and I wanted to be at school. The summer holidays of 1945, to me, seemed so long– I wanted to be back in school. I was happier, I was not learning under stress; there was so much now that was new and exciting. In my home there was no hesitation about schooling; education was a must. Books, magazines, newspapers were all around me. I had heard so many comments and stories on national issues and personalities, plus the world overseas, but it was now that my mind was beginning to open to the realisation of performance and achievement. Now it became important to me how many math problems I worked correctly today, who in the class did better than I did, how much out of ten did I score on my English exercise. Class tests became serious for me and I found myself always checking on other students' grades. In the Summer Term examination, Daisy beat me by one mark but I received a beautiful dictionary as prize for my second place. I was intensely proud of this new dictionary and I felt totally crushed when it was stolen in Kingston sometime in 1946. For me, that year of 1945 was a momentous year. Franklin D. Roosevelt, one of my war heroes, had died on the eve of victory, then came the surrender of my arch-enemies, Germany and Japan, and the world could breathe easier and make a new beginning. It seems I too was making a kind of new beginning at months before I turned fifteen. Looking back, I am amazed that so many experiences in my life took place in one short year, 1945. Much was in store for 1946.

Chapter Ten

High School Ahoy!

One can seriously say that in 1946 high school education was not for the son or daughter of the poor Jamaican parent. The child of the poor teacher or nurse or native minister of religion, lower civil servant or the Sanitary Inspector (Health Officer), and who was academically gifted, might have had a reasonable chance of gaining one of the few parish scholarships, among one or two others, to one of the then prestige high schools. But for the peasant farmer who was ambitious for his child, he had to find other avenues to push his child on. No child from my district had ever moved on to high school and no parent had the resources to pay school fees and boarding away from home. We as children knew that three of Teacher Romney's daughters attended a good rural girls' high school. Then his oldest son attended a top high school in Kingston, and we were used to them arriving home for holidays and coming up to the school to occupy their time. There was not much association with us humbler ones and we really thought them to be in a little different world. Later on, Teacher Romney's younger son won a scholarship to a very prestigious rural high school for boys and I can remember his father showing us pictures of where his son would have classes, where he would have his meals, his playfields, where he would have his Science classes, etc. How we marvelled at this glorious situation in which young Romney would be basking for the next several years. We just had to remind ourselves that we lesser mortals could not measure up to such distinction.

At about the same period I had the unpleasant experience of a sample of the prejudice which some high school people had for us 'elementary ones'. It so happened that a big business man in this large village about six miles from my school, sent his young son to Teacher Romney to have him prepared for the entrance examination to the same prestige high school which Teacher Romney's son would be attending. He was about my age, very light-skinned, with a mixture of three-quarters Arab and one quarter black. He was placed in my class at school. He knew my father very well and we became good friends. He visited my home regularly, and he, privileged and not having any morning chores to perform, often turned up in my kitchen as early as eight o'clock and watched me about my chores: 'scalding' cow's milk, sweeping out the kitchen, 'chumming 'coffee, and others. Oftentimes we sat down and I did his homework (academically, he was merely competent). During all this while, we, his classmates, never knew he was being prepared for the examination and he never breathed a word to any of us. In the same way we never had the slightest inkling that Teacher Romney's son had sat any examination to enter high school. It was at the beginning of the new school year when the young 'three-quarter Arab' did not turn up for classes that we learnt that he was off to this said high school. Well, that was not for us, and we carried on our lives as usual.

But, to return to my 'three-quarter Arab' friend, he never spoke to me again, after he entered his high school. During the school holidays he would be at his father's business place and I would see him occasionally, but he would never speak to me. We crossed on the street on more than one occasion but he held his head straight and pretended I did not exist. But I had the last laugh. He attended the rural prestige high school, then an urban high school of equivalent prestige, then back to his home village, with nothing achieved. There he helped to pull down his father's business, became little more than a drunk and run-around and was almost arrested for stealing gasolene. Eventually, he died, a little higher than a derelict. I am not laughing, as if in triumph but the 'three-quarter Arab' situation reminds me of Teacher Romney's Eleventh Commandment: 'Man, mind thyself, thou knowest not what lies beyond the bend'.

I have heard many people pour out accusations that, in that era, school teachers ensured that the very few scholarships or available places to high schools, went to their children, that relevant information on existing opportunities was kept away from the rank and file and only the teacher's children knew of them. One may say, in Jamaican parlance, that 'parson christen him pickney first"[28]. I do believe that this was true in many, many cases and I saw it in my very own school. But there is the other side to this situation. I hasten to remind that there were so many cases of teachers labouring in our country's elementary classrooms who were utterly devoted to their charges and would go to the limit to push them on. Also, we have to remember that many, many of these teachers' children did not get into high school and had to travel the path of the ambitious within the rank and file. In so many rural areas, even if 'good students' were identified, parents never had the resources to pursue secondary education for them. Also, there were parents, I verily believe, who did not think that high school education was 'in the cards' for their children. In reality, the teachers' children were the ones with the home opportunities, the books and access to much

---

[28] Parson christens his child ahead of all the others.

information, the push to achieve. Their parents were aware of the 'wickedness' of the system and knew of the very few openings, and they pushed their children in. Their children would certainly have a great advantage here, over others of the rank and file.

So let us be fair to our dear teachers. They were very human and naturally would 'look after their pickney first.' The education system then was very severely deficient and made very inferior provision for the poor and unprivileged. Secondary education was a privilege, not a right. My generation can remember personalities like Vivian Blake, Dr. Ivan Lloyd, Esmond Kentish, Ian Ramsay, Professor Mervyn Morris, Professor Errol Morrison, Dr. Olive Lewin and many others. These outstanding Jamaicans are children of teachers' cottages from all over this island and we are proud of them. They have given yeoman service to their country and teacher's cottages from all over can jump and burst their roofs with pride - they have produced mightily.

Well, as you know by now, with Teacher Romney's departure from my school, and the arrival of the new principal, a new refreshing wind was blowing through our community. I was fast approaching my fifteenth birthday and I had so much enjoyed the new regime. Come the 30th October and I would be quietly told, 'your time is up'. But things took a nice different twist. I cannot pinpoint when, in 1945, that the thought of my going to a high school, was born. But, Teacher Reice, at some point began to talk to my grandfather and 'put things in his head'. It would seem that I began to warm to the idea, that there was a chance for me and I could actually step into a high school. I remember I began to consult the 'Gleaner's' high school advertisements nearly every day. Grandpa would look with me at the various school advertisements. There were those schools which sought applications to sit their scholarship entrance examinations. We looked at their addresses but we did not have a clue where in Kingston these addresses were.

We did not spend time on schools like Jamaica College, Calabar or K. C, for right away we knew these were out of our range; we had to look to the private high schools who seemed more anxious to welcome students from 'my rank and file'. We read advertisements from private high schools like Bodmin College, Gaynestead High School, St. Martins High School, Tutorial College, Buxton High School and St. Simon's College. I applied to Bodmin College and St. Simon's College. These were the two schools that caught my fancy and to me, the name "St. Simon's' had a nice ring to it. Then I got down to writing to the two schools, requesting application forms. I remember Grandpa taking the envelops, laying a ruler across their faces, and using the pointed end of his 'pen-stick' to rule a faint line so that

I could write the addresses straight. The replies to me were quite prompt and both schools pointed to their several scholarships and half scholarships. For the first time in my life I was receiving my own letters, and addressed directly to me. I was proud 'caan done'[29]. Grandpa and I went through the letters and application forms and we decided on St. Simon's College.

Arrangements now had to be made to come to Kingston to sit the entrance examination. I cannot remember in what month the examination was held but it would have had to be early enough so there would be enough time for me to get my result and, if successful, get myself ready - (uniforms, other clothing, shoes and socks, a nice 'grip' for my belongings, financing,) in time for January's beginning of the new school year. So I travelled to Kingston, enjoying my first train ride from Greenvale railway station to Kingston. I travelled in the coach nearest to the engine and received, at regular intervals, a good dose of the coal dust. I was a bit intrigued by the Porus rail station and noted the great array of fruits offered for sale by vendors. My grandfather always commented that 'if you don't get fruits at Porus, slim chance you will get anything worthwhile on the rest of the way to Kingston'.

As we sped through the Clarendon plains, I did not like the vegetation scene very much. It was a dry period and when I gazed through the carriage window I wished I could transplant some of the more lush plant life in my dear North-West Manchester hills, to the less fortunate Clarendon plains. Then the thatched houses we passed repelled me; most were indicative of real poverty. In my area of North-West Manchester thatch houses were rare and we always associated them with the very, very poor. I had great expectations of May Pen, as there I would see my first river. But I was so shocked when we rode over the bridge and I could see only small patches of water here and there, below. Where was the placid, extensive sheet of water slowly flowing along? I expected to see water stretching over a wide area, 'a river full a water'. Was this the same famous Rio Minho that I had learnt about in Middle Division? Shame! Shame! And so we sped on.

The rest of the journey to Kingston was uneventful. I was disappointed with some of the stations - sometimes merely a building in need of maintenance; at one or two stations the train did not bother to stop. Also, on this train ride I made the acquaintance of well- known railway characters like biscuits and sweets vendor, Keith, who rode the coaches for the whole trip, and Jeshuran, 'the hard nut', who supervised the coaches and collected the travel tickets towards the end of the journey. We duly arrived at the Kingston Railway Station and I was clearly a bit surprised by the

---

[29] Without limit.

crowd. Everybody seemed to be on the fast move, scurrying from one place to another; people, as if agitated, shouting questions and answers. This fifteen year old country boy did not understand it. But I was rescued in good time by Uncle Roy, our 'town-girl Marjorie's father, who transported me all the way to their residence in Rollington Town.

I would stay for the time with Marjorie's family, who would see to it that I reached my examination centre on time and later, get me back home safely. I was struck by the many 'pretty houses' which I gaped at as we travelled through Franklin Town on to Rollington Town. These two areas in the 1940's were very respectable residential areas, well fruited and with some imposing residences. I quickly got used to the electric lights, both in the home and on the streets in the nights. The night sounds, however, remained so different from the sounds of my native countryside - all sorts of insect sounds, from insects, which, I was sure, did not exist in my native hills. I saw that fireflies also lived in Kingston and that they gave out the same light as in the countryside. But those insect sounds, so different and pulling on my ears, stayed with me and I never fully got used to them until I took up residence in the city a few months later. In my young mind, the night sounds was one of the most striking differences between town and country.

On the morning of my high school entrance examination, Uncle Roy towed me on his bicycle to East Street where the St. Simon's campuses were located. The boys' campus was about four chains above North Street, and the girls' was just a short distance below the Manchester Square end, on the same side. Uncle Roy and I arrived well on time. He deposited me at the boys' campus, wished me well and then he sped off to work. There were about sixty boys gathered for the examination, and placed in three rooms. As the roll was called, one name specially drew my attention. This boy, very light-skinned, had his middle name as 'Eisenhower', and as Mr Foster, the vice-principal, called it, he let out a laugh, and said, "Ah, the General", meaning General Eisenhower of World War 2 fame. I was pleased with my performance on the first paper but the second paper stretched me quite a bit. But overall, I felt optimistic about my chances. Uncle Roy, before he left me in the morning, had carefully and at length, given me the instructions how and where to get the bus, to return home after the examination. I duly got on to the Fernandez Avenue bus and reached home safely. That bus that bore me had a sort of wailing horn and later on I found out that the residents of the area referred to it as the 'Cow Bus'. The examination was now behind me and I now would return to Manchester to await the results.

In time the St. Simon's result arrived, addressed to my grandfather. The letter said that I was awarded a half scholarship to the school and that I would be required to pay four pounds and five shillings per term for tuition.

At the time we never wondered how many full scholarships were awarded and who won them, or, how many of us received half scholarships. Most of us boys and girls were just so glad to get into a high school that such questions did not occur to us. About six months after we had started school I chanced to hear three 'town boys' discussing what they thought of the school's recruiting system. One boy said his father worked at Lands Department and his dad knew all about the 'system', that it was not fair. I was shaken but I put it out of my mind. But the St. Simon's result had me in high spirit and Grandpa appeared very pleased. We now had to get to work and begin preparations for my advent into high school in Kingston.

Looking back over the years now, poor Grandpa did not realise what he was getting himself into. There were now school fees, equipping me with uniforms and other clothing, shoes, boarding fees. He did not have a pension and his present income came from crops, meagre income from his job as Registrar of Births and Deaths and from his medium- sized apiary, and a cow or two. But he manfully stuck to his undertaking. He equipped me with two pairs of uniform - I really should have been given four pairs. I had one pair of shoes. I remember the pair was bigger than my feet, as if he wanted my feet to grow in them and I had to take a bit of teasing from two of my classmates. Fortunately, the other boys were too busy with their tricks and otherwise, to take notice of my 'sail boats'.

Grandpa also fitted me out with a nice new 'grip' which was made to hold all my possessions. I was certainly in for some very frugal living. So I arrived at Marjorie's home in Rollington Town on the Thursday before the Monday's start of term at St. Simon's. Marjorie's mother had kindly consented to board me; Grandpa never did tell me what was the fee per month. On the next day, Friday, I located a gentleman at Potters Row in Rae Town, to finalise a business deal. This gentleman was a stamp collector and had advertised in the 'Gleaner' for used stamps. I dug up in my grandfather's cellar and found hundreds of old letters with stamps in all sorts of condition. I gathered the best of the stamps and had eventually what I thought was a fair collection. This was the collection I took to this gentleman at Potters Row. Many of my stamps were rejected as flawed and I finally received a little more than four shillings for my labour. With four shillings from this little wealth, I bought my first fountain pen. It was a good buy and it served me for a reasonably long time.

So I arrived at St. Simon's College on that early January morning in 1946, was registered and my fee collected. Then we were placed in our classroom and our introduction to life at St. Simon's began. The boys' campus, part of which is now 'Gleaner' territory, had its two- storey building, mostly of brick, with a reasonable playing space. There were about seven classrooms, along with the Principal's office and conveniences. I don't remember any general staff room. The school population was about two hundred, with seven teachers, including the Principal. The Principal was a Mr. E.B. Hazelwood, regularly addressed as 'Professor'. I told myself, at the time, that he might have been in much earlier years, a Professor at some American college, but it was in much later years that we were to learn what an outstanding educator he was and that he had a brilliant student career. He was a British Guianese native and had the accent, was tall and imposing and you tended to feel 'small' in his presence.

I must take time to tell you that in 1913, as a student of the Normal Training College, London, he passed the Associateship Teachers' Diploma Examination, being one of two teachers throughout the world to obtain Quadruple Honours, and winning the Normal Silver Medal.. Back in his native Guiana he pioneered extensive secondary education for the masses and achieved outstanding success and honours there and from abroad. In 1933 this eminent educator, Edward Benson Hazelwood, A.C.P., F.C.I., founded St. Simon's College in Kingston (Boys, Girls and University Departments). He had the distinction of being the first Private Secondary Master to train students successfully for Inter B.A. (London), Cambridge Higher School Certificate Examinations and for Advanced Commercial Diplomas (A.C.I) in Banking and Currency, Company Law, Commercial etc. In January 1946 when we new boys arrived through the gates of St. Simon's College, little did we suspect that our now aging Principal was such a giant educator in our Caribbean and a pioneer in providing extensive Secondary and Post Secondary education for the masses of the region. Certainly, we had to take some time here to get informed on this great and not too well-known West Indian educator. His Vice-Principal was Mr. F. A. Foster, a good Latin master who had worked for some time in West Africa and was one of the candidates fielded by the Jamaica Democratic Party in the 1944 General Elections in Jamaica. There was Mr.George Brown who later went off to study law and became a local attorney. The late Mr. G. Arthur Brown, distinguished civil servant and Governor of the Bank of Jamaica had completed his studies at the school some years before and was an honoured Old Boy. We new ones at first wondered if our teacher 'Mr. George Brown' was this same past student.

Mr. Gordon taught General Subjects but some years later left to establish his own private high school (Waulgrove, I think), There was a Mr. Bonner, who did not stay very long at the school. Then there were three women; the eldest of the three was one Mrs. Robinson, who was sister-in-law to Professor Leslie Robinson of the Mathematics Department of the University of the West Indies. Looking back, the staff was not an outstanding one; nobody on that staff, excepting Principal Hazelwood and possibly Vice-Principal Foster, had a Bachelor's degree, and most were amateurs. But they worked and I would not say we were shortchanged. We found out later that when we began our career at St. Simon's, the school had seen its best years and was actually on the decline. G. Arthur Brown, Archbishop Samuel Carter and former Prime Minister Hugh Shearer, who all were outstanding servants of Jamaica, had already passed through the school, and there were other notable graduates too. But, as with most of the other private high schools, it did not generate sufficient income to be able to afford top teaching talent. Hence these schools lumbered on, and had to take second and third rate teachers. Then when times became even harder, most of them folded. Bodmin, St. Martin's, Tutorial, Windsor, St. Monica's, Buxton, and St. Simon's too, eventually had to close. Professor Hazelwood retired to his native Guyana where he died some years ago.

As mentioned before, the school population was about two hundred. I can remember only one white boy in the whole population. There were quite a few light-skinned ones, a few Chinese, about four East Indians, and the overwhelming majority, blacks. I well remember at lunchtime one particular day when a black boy purchased his delicious fudge and had just stripped off the paper cover and was settling down to lovingly enjoy his fudge. Then, 'Whoosh!' That lone white boy rushed past him, to escape another boy in play, and knocked the fudge to the ground. Well, can you imagine? The 'cup' was right up at the hungry lips, when it was dashed to the ground. The black boy was furious, and I believe, even if that white boy had prayerfully begged for pardon, it would not have been granted. The black boy, a 'country boy', attacked, but the white boy, a 'town boy', ably defended himself with his fists. Things were getting really serious when a 'sambo-coloured' boy rushed to the defence of the white boy. ('Sambo' is an old term referring to dark-brown skin colour, just a little above black). It turned out that the 'sambo-coloured' boy was a great friend of the white boy, and the aggrieved black boy now had to cool his temper. A little later when the bell rang for re-assembly in our classrooms, a big black boy from a higher form attempted to upbraid the 'sambo-coloured' boy for siding with the white boy against his fellow black. The 'sambo-coloured' boy spiritedly tossed back, "Rex (the white boy) is my friend and I not 'lowing any man to beat' im up, and dat is dat."

And that reminds me of a formula for dealing with a 'town boy' if you have to come to blows with him. It was given to me by the son of the lady I boarded with after I left Marjorie's family. Her son was about my age and he attended the then Kingston Senior School. He said to me that I, as a 'country boy' should never 'jump around' and try to box with a 'town boy'.

The 'town boy' is usually faster with his fists and will knock you out. So then, don't try to box. Wait for an opening and then give him one 'helleba lick'[30] that will rock him to the core. Then you move in and work him over and settle him for good. Fortunately, I never had to test the formula at St. Simon's.

Clayton Blythe was always the top student in my form. Others I can remember were Linton Darien from Thornton in St. Elizabeth, 'Lashie' Linton from Westmoreland and Rupert Richardson, a serious and hardworking student who was so very disappointed when he did not get the chance to sit the Junior Cambridge examination. There was one of the Spence twins, of Jamaica athletic fame, in the lot, and the sole East Indian, Ganga, who would fly into a rage, when called by his nickname 'Ganja'. There was 'Chocho', whose mouth was always watery. 'Stringy' was from Constitution Hill in St. Andrew, and he was no more bulky than a stout pencil. On one occasion I greeted Mr Stringy by his nickname. He did not attack me but he promptly ran up the stairs up to the Principal and reported that I had called him by his nickname. The Principal sent for me and would not allow me to give any sort of explanation or excuse. In his sternest voice he told 'Stringy' that if I ever did that again to him, he should come and report it straight away. Then he glared at me, a most wicked look, and ordered me back to my class. I never liked 'Stringy' but he was never again molested by me. We never came into much contact with the older boys who were next to sit the Senior Cambridge examination. However, there were two whom I remember well, maybe because they were so short and still wore short pants. They were Holness and McMillan. McMillan later entered the Anglican ministry and became Bishop of Belize. He died many years ago.

At the beginning of our stint at St. Simon's, we heard a lot about the Junior Cambridge examination and saw this as the goal for the end of our second year. But in January of that second year, we were informed that the Junior Cambridge examination had been abolished. Now that the examination was no more, we would have to do another two years before we arrived at the Senior Cambridge. This was not good news for me as there were a few questions now being asked, at home in the countryside, about this 'Keith Morris high school thing'. But more on this anon. I mentioned earlier that the St. Simon's staff was not top notch, but I learnt. Mr. Foster was a very good Latin teacher and I enjoyed learning my Declensions, Conjugations and Irregular Verbs. I had just begun to tackle easy Unseen passages and was looking forward to moving on to 'Caesar'. Spanish lacked

---

[30] "One hell of a lick, a massive blow."

a good teacher and I never became a good friend of that language. Arithmetic gave me some bother but as I did well at Algebra I was very often able to use it to solve Arithmetic problems. English and History gave me no trouble and I was always in the top five in my form. I should mention at this point that my boarding situation had changed as from the third term of the first year at St. Simon's. Marjorie had a large family and adequate space became a problem, so I knew that after the summer holidays I would have to be in new boarding quarters. My Principal recommended a lady in Allman Town and she agreed to board me as from the beginning of the last term of 1946.

My new boarding home was a good home - I was well fed and protected and became, in time, like a member of that family. Miss Fanny, my new 'mother away from home', was an ardent church lady. Her husband was a clergyman and I went to worship very regularly with the family. Her grown children were successful and I learnt so much of the knowledge of Kingston from her fifteen- year-old son, Cotty, then a student of the respected Kingston Senior School. Cotty was a few months younger than I, but we became great partners and have remained lifelong friends. There were always many visitors to the family - Mico College students on the weekends or during the week after classes, teachers who came in from the countryside for a day or two, young male teachers who were friends of her two teacher daughters and church people who had business with her clergyman husband. Parson, as we called her husband, had two churches in the rural areas, and so did a lot of travelling. Hence, we did not see as much of him as we wanted. He was a quiet and reserved man but a powerful preacher and was chock-full of wisdom and fun. Miss Fanny was never short of boarders; she was so kind and longsuffering even when here and there a boarder was persistently delinquent. She loved people and she gave so much to so many. Her home was a landmark in old Allman Town and it was widely known for its healthy environment and good attractive human relationships. Miss Fanny made the best beef soup in the county of Surrey and her superbly cooked cow tail could not be surpassed. Regrettably, my high school career came to a close in December 1947, after two full years at good old St. Simon's College. I now returned to my old school in Manchester and began my studies for the Jamaica Local Examinations.

My two-year residence in Kingston had given me a fairly good knowledge of the city and its ways. I came to know many of the important sites, business places, government offices, Hope Gardens, Rockfort, Bournmouth Baths, Institute of Jamaica and many other places of note insomuch that, when my grandfather paid a visit to Kingston early in 1947, I proudly shepherded him around. This brings back to memory an amusing little episode. Grandpa and I had been busy for most of this morning and we became very thirsty, so I asked him for a fudge. He promptly bought two and handed one to me. The other he placed in his jacket pocket, to be eaten when he reached home. I had to quickly remind him that he had to dispatch that fudge right away or it would melt away in his pocket. You see, my grandfather never ate on the street - that was one of his firm principles. So he had to make an exception on this day, and he enjoyed his first fudge.

Interestingly, when I returned home for this second summer holidays, I began to get the feeling that things were not quite what they seemed. I knew that Grandpa was having a tough time meeting the various expenses, and twice the Principal had called me in regarding the payment of my Summer term fee. But in his letters Grandpa never breathed a word about his difficulties. Then one day, while on this summer holidays, I had to go to one of the village shops to make a purchase. Just as I was about to step through the door of the shop I heard talking inside, "An dat boy deh, dat him hab a high school, no waste a money dat? Look how long him diddeh, an him no pass nutten"[31]. I backed away from the door and passed on to the other shop to make my purchase. I went home quickly and I felt so humiliated. So, that was what they were saying about me. I had already known of a certain mother in the district who was not enamoured with my being at 'high school' and virtually campaigned to get my grandfather to end my high school career from the middle of the first year, but Grandpa stood firm. I had told myself that I understood this woman and would not allow her to discourage me; that that was her nature. But what I overheard at the shop cut me to the quick and I realised that others must have been saying the same thing. I did not say anything to Grandpa about what I had overheard at the shop; neither did he say anything on these matters to me.

So I returned to St. Simon's for the final term of the year, not knowing that the axe would fall so quickly. Those district people had little understanding of the then high school system and expected to hear of exams passed, one after the other and great news on the student constantly coming. To be in the high school for four years, or even five, before sitting the Senior Cambridge examination was something they did not understand. When you did the Jamaica Locals, you sat an examination every year, and glory to you if you kept on passing. That they did understand. And remember, high school education, at that time, was not for the rank and file. Perhaps many thought my grandpa was a bit 'uppity'[32] when he embarked

31 "And that boy that he has at high school, is it not a waste of money? Look how long he has been at the school and he has passed nothing (not one examination)".

32 "Overambitious, cheeky, uppish."

on his project with me. Oh, my dear, dear Grandpa. My last term at St. Simon's was a good one and I did very well in my end of year examinations. With school ended for the year, I headed back home to spend the Christmas holidays. I still did not know that I had taken my last train ride as a high school student. A few days before Christmas, Grandpa gave me the news that I would not be returning to St. Simon's College in January and would have to go back to Teacher Reice and do my Jamaica Local Examinations.

Looking back over the years, I like to see myself as half of a pioneering pair. In mid 1945, when the high school exploration was embarked on, two of us from Sixth Class journeyed to Kingston and sat the entrance examination to St Simon's. The other member of this pioneering pair was a young Miss by the name of Dorraine. Dorraine was a bit younger than I was and had just come up to Sixth Class and was the daughter of highly respected Mr. Robby. She had very close relatives in Kingston so she had no problems with accommodation in the city. Dorraine and I did not have any discussion on our pending high school plans and I don't know if Grandpa and Mr. Robby talked together about their coming project. But we sat the Entrance Examination and both of us were awarded half scholarships. Dorraine lasted for a very short time at St. Simon's and very early headed back to Manchester to resume at her old school and do her Jamaica Local Examinations. I never did get her story of why her high school stint was so very short. Our sojourn in high school was cut short and the 'experiment' seemed not to have succeeded.

Dorraine and I were pioneers from our region, in that quest for high school education for the rank and file. High school education for the rank and file was not to come firmly, until the 1950's, with the establishment of the Common Entrance Examination for entry to high schools in this country. Dorraine and I were the first from our district to begin this quest, and though we could not complete the course, we like to think we began the lighting of the candle. Now, I had the rest of the Christmas holidays to think on my changed situation; how I would face and live down the acute embarrassment of returning to my old school and rejoining classmates who had seen me 'fly away to town'. Was it that I had gone away 'pim', and had come back 'pam' - with nothing? There were those of my former classmates who had done their First and Second Jamaica Local Examinations and had passed and could boast that they had two successful examinations to their credit, and I had none. It would have been such a good thing for me if my grandpa or my uncle or any other understanding person had taken me aside and given me some encouraging and reassuring words. As it turned out, I had to face the music all by myself.

Maybe, this is a good time to take a few minutes to look back and do a little reflection on the efforts of those stalwarts who were determined to make high school education available to so many of the poor and unprivileged who could not approach the doors of the traditional high schools. And we have to pay homage to those individuals who boldly took the initiative to establish private high schools. In these private high schools, they endeavored to provide quality education for those who could not afford to attend the traditional high schools like Wolmer's Boys, Wolmer's Girls, Jamaica College and St. Andrew High School. Before the advent of these private secondary schools, thousands and thousands of brilliant children of the Jamaican masses could not access education above the primary or elementary level. The traditional high schools were not many and it was most difficult for the children of the poor to gain entry into any one of them. We ask the questions: Did these high schools deliberately discourage the entry of children of the masses? Did they have any real interest in having high school education extended to the masses? Maybe they felt that admitting the masses would only create an overwhelming social problem for the traditional high school system. What subtle strategies did they evolve to effectively bar the son or daughter of the poor?

But there were the heroes who came to the assistance of the poor but gifted sons and daughters of the masses. We have to specially take note of Mr. E. B. Hazlewood at St. Simon's College, Mrs. Ranger-Jones at Windsor High School, F. A. Buxton-Thompson at Buxton High School, Mr St. George Gaynair at Gaynstead High School, C. C. McArthur-Ireland at Tutorial College, Rev. Ivan Francis at Lincoln College and A. S. Clarke at St. John's College. There was also Leandro Stevenson's Bodmin College, St. Martin's High School, Stratford High School and one or two others. Some of these private High Schools were launched from as far back as the mid 1930s. Buxton High began in 1937. I suspect that St. John's college was as old. St. Simon's began in 1933.

These private high schools did not set any age limit for their students, which was especially welcome to students who were later developers. This was also a great boon for the bright student in the elementary school who had completed the elementary course very early but had to languish because he or she could not gain entrance to any of the traditional high schools. There were certainly many of our poor bright children who had successfully completed the First, Second and Third Jamaica Local Examinations but were now effectively blocked. A small relief for this particular group came in the later 1950s when the Jamaica Ministry of Education, under the Honorable E. L. Allen, awarded tuition places to a number of students who had passed the Third Jamaica Local Examination. Mr. Powell's young

Excelsior High School must be commended for readily accommodating some of these students as did about three other traditional high schools. These said students had got their feet through the door and they performed very creditably. In fact, one of these selfsame students later won the Jamaica Rhodes Scholarship. A slow process had started which would gradually gain some momentum.

Some of these private high schools had a good variety of courses. St. Simon's trained students successfully for the Cambridge Junior, Senior and Higher Schools Certificate examinations as well as the London Matriculation and Inter BA. There was the Commercial Dept. which secured Advanced Diplomas in Company Law, Banking and Currency, Auditing, Secretarial Practice, and Economics. At Buxton High School, Buxton Thompson provided training for the Cambridge Junior and Senior examinations. He had classes preparing students for the Jamaica Local Examinations, and for entrance to the Teachers Colleges. His Commercial Dept. prepared for City and Guilds and Pitman's Examinations in Typing, Shorthand and Bookkeeping. He also had Evening Classes as well as Summer Classes, even lessons by Correspondence. Well can my generation remember the Buxton cry, "Buxton does it again" which the "Gleaner" carried when publishing Buxton's latest examination results. A. S. Clarke at St. John's College and Rev. Ivan Francis at Lincoln College also presented a good Course variety. Not all of these private schools could provide this variety of courses and some concentrated on the Cambridge exams up to the Senior Cambridge level. Some of these schools, despite handicaps, did very good work, and here we are reminded that eminent literary figure and Editor of the "Daily Gleaner", Theodore Sealy, was a product of A. S. Clarke at St. Johns College. We have already made note of a few of Hazlewood's products from St. Simon's College.

Most of the heads of these private high schools were well qualified. Buxton Thompson, C. C. McArthur-Ireland of Tutorial and A.S. Clarke of St. John's were Mico men, McArthur Ireland with a BA Honours in Geography. E. B. Hazelwood of St. Simon's was an outstanding intellect. Rev. Ivan Francis of Lincoln College and Mrs. Ranger-Jones of Windsor High were not far behind. The quality of their staffs varied. There were a number of trained teachers in the private high school system, not with University degrees, but with strong commitment to their teaching task. So many of the teachers were people with London Matriculation, Cambridge Higher School Certificate and the Intermediate Bachelor of Arts. Some continued to upgrade themselves via correspondence courses from overseas. Overall, the quality of staffing of these high schools varied. A few maintained strong staffs and produced very good results. Others were less strong but they all were providing opportunities for which the poor Jamaican sons and daughters were eagerly grasping.

But time was moving and the grand era of the private high school began to pass away. There was to come the period when a number of new high schools came on stream, not the old traditional, and were not bound by the strictures and old exclusive attitudes of the Wolmers, the Jamaica Colleges, the St. Andrew High Schools, the Munros. We see now the emergence of Merle Grove High School, nurtured from 1924 by Nathan and Miriam Speid. The very able Ivy Grant nursed Camperdown from 1930, and by the 1950's, these schools were beginning to bloom. Excelsior High had been founded by A. Wesley Powell and his father in 1931 and this Powell enterprise grew mightily. Then Gaynstead High was launched by St. George Gaynair in 1941. Clarendon College came in 1942, launched by the Congregational Union. Glenmuir High School and Meadowbrook High School were launched in 1958 and were poised for the new thrust in Jamaica's education from the late 1950's. Glenmuir was established by the Anglican Church, while Meadowbrook High had a Presbyterian mother. Here we are firmly reminded of that great role that the Church has played in the provision of education in this country. Merle Grove High is now sponsored by the Associated Gospel Assemblies and there is the close association of the United Church with the Ivy Grant-founded Camperdown. And most of us are aware of that wise and early alliance of Mr. Powell's Excelsior with the Methodist Church in Jamaica, an alliance which has prospered so very much.

So, we were moving into a new phase in our educational growth and the earlier privately- owned high schools had to give way. The Hazlewoods, Buxton Thompsons, Ranger Joneses had aged, and their younger successors found the going much too difficult. Financing rental, paying adequate staffing and other requirements proved too much in the new era which was approaching. Teaching standards would now decline as top teachers could not be attracted and maintained and despite the government now beginning to extend subsidies to some private schools, most were now sliding down. New schools, like Wesley Powell's young Excelsior, now partnered with the Methodist Church, greatly expanded and, not hampered by the strictures and prejudices of the traditional high school system, were serving ever increasing numbers of the sons and daughters of the poor. By the later 1940s when I attended St. Simons, Excelsior had so grown in numbers that it had to acquire more commodious premises on North Street.

Then, in 1957, the Govt. of Jamaica introduced the Common Entrance Examination, beginning with its first award of 1400 places to high schools in Jamaica. This opened the doors of secondary education to larger and larger numbers of those who previously could not qualify for entry. It was the opening of a great new era for the poor of this country but it also sounded the death-knell of the individually-owned private secondary school. These private schools had served the country so well, but in the changing times, with increased Govt. participation and input, and the emergence of new high schools which served their students, irrespective of social background and wealth, they could not survive. The privately- owned high schools did not merely fill a gap. They provided a greatly needed service at a crucial period of our education march and occupy a very special place in our country's educational development.

Chapter Eleven

The Young Man Returns
To His Community

That Monday morning in January 1948 when I headed up to the schoolhouse to start 'private lessons' with Teacher Reice, I was filled with dread. In the mornings the students would gather around the tankside, outside the school building, and await Teacher's arrival. Teacher would arrive, open the door, we would troop in and lessons would start at eight o'clock. On this morning I arrived at the tankside, said hello to the students gathered there and tried to make small talk with those who were nearest to me. I could feel some tension in the group - they had greeted me cheerfully but I could also see that they also felt slightly uncomfortable. Then the big 'chibung' came. The school building and the tank stood on the very summit, on a sort of tableland, and the paths leading to our several districts led down the hill in about four directions, so when you are ascending to the tankside, you can't see anybody until you are almost at the summit. So, on this morning, there were about half dozen students ascending on the west path. One of the boys ascending on this path was several feet ahead of the others, and he spied my head first. In a flash he whirled around and sped back down to his fellows to announce the 'joyous' news of the morning: my presence at the tankside. I remember he laughed heartily, as if in enormous triumph - the 'high school man' was back in all humility. They all now arrived at the summit and greeted me politely. It is interesting to note that the young man who whirled around to take 'the good news' to his companions was the son of the said woman who had virtually campaigned to get my grandfather 'to take that boy away from that school'. I never confronted him about his unkind action that morning and I doubt that he realized I had seen him in action. But I stored it away in my mind, one of my early experiences of the unkindness of humankind.

Teacher Reice had advised me beforehand that the sensible thing for me to do was to forget First and Second Jamaica Locals and prepare for the Third Jamaica Local Examination. He said he was confident that with my two years at St. Simon's, I would be able to handle the Third Year programme. So on this morning I went and sat with the Third Year students. Our first assignment was to factorise about six Algebra problems. When Teacher Reice dictated the problems to us, I did not hear the instruction that went with them and I wondered aloud what he wanted us to do with them. One of my near colleagues, who had failed the Examination the previous year, heard me, looked at me pointedly, did not say anything, and laughed heartily. But then I quickly now realized what was required and got down to work. I had already done Factorisation at St. Simon's and had become quite proficient and I had no difficulty with these. As the days rolled by I settled in and the Third Year programme had no terrors for me. Teacher Reice alone handled the three Local Examination classes and I marvel how well he organised the programme and how much work he effectively covered in a day's classes, one hour in the morning and about two and one half hours in the evenings. He had us as a team and there was nothing he could not extract from us. In a short time I became well reintegrated and the embarrassments were in time left behind. Our Third Year group was quite bright and hardworking and we set our sights on our July examination date.

In the meantime I took on full chores at home. Our household still consisted of my grandpa, my uncle and me and I was the chosen one for the bulk of the cooking duties. You can well imagine how annoyed I sometimes was, when, on arriving home after six o'clock in the evenings I found my grandpa and my uncle patiently waiting on me to start the dinner fire. I had to cover all the chores, cooking, my own washing, cleaning, procuring all firewood, etc, etc. I did them all but never developed a love for that sphere of activity. My Fridays were well mapped out: 'private lessons' in the early morning, then a little relaxation at Teacher Reice's 'Industrial arts' work area for a maximum of one hour. I then had to head home and begin to soak my week's soiled clothing. I had to get them all washed, then ironed, and ready again for Monday morning. Clothing was not plentiful and we had to take care of what we had. I resigned myself to the care of the home though there were times when I felt embarrassed.

At that age I was sensitive to being regarded as a 'kitchen man' by my fellows, and the girls too. My house had one exit and one entrance, through the double door at the front of the building and squarely faced the Parish Council road. So you will realise how I looked or peeped right, then left, then right again before I bolted with the plates of dinners. They must not see me bearing the dinners from the kitchen or kneeling and polishing the floor. If I were sighted with the 'chimmy' on a morning, I would not be able to show my face in Maidstone for six months. Along with my washing and ironing schedule, I cleaned the floor at the weekend and got a very good shine after the 'salindine' treatment. Also, I had to ensure that there was an ample supply of firewood to tide us over the weekend. Many a pimento tree felt the sharp edge of my cutlass and yielded high quality wood for my cooking fire. So I kept house and did my lessons and became quite good at them. I could put together a decent meal and give a brilliant shine to my floors. I washed very well and my ironed clothing passed creditably. The housekeeping chores did not excite me but I reconciled myself to the fact that I was the very junior one in the home trio. My grandfather and my uncle were never handy at the fireside and so I naturally had to fall into the slot. Furthermore, they must have seen me as the one who was most trainable.

We Third Examination students continued to work purposefully and the months passed rapidly. We became quite close and a healthy esprit de corps developed. There were Mendes and his sister who traversed miles of rocks and paths to reach school at eight o'clock on each school morning. After the morning session they would stay on the school premises, under the famous 'Anancy tree' and work at their studies. There were Belzie and Daisy, very serious young ladies, and Perry and Alfred, the most naturally gifted of us all. So, July arrived, and the examination date. Our Examination Centre was at Mile Gully, about six miles away, and we all had to walk down on two successive Fridays. On the second Friday we finally wrapped up our examination exercise and headed for home on foot. We now felt so light, as if a heavy burden had been lifted from our shoulders, and we let our hair down. Cigarettes were lighted by some of the older boys and one was duly offered to me. I took it, took one pull and then handed it back. That was my last encounter with smoking and I could never develop an interest here. A number of the boys were already having their tastes of rum and I remember on several Monday mornings there were the excited reports of how a quarter-quart had been consumed over the weekend. But such, whether the 'spirited liquid' or the fumes of the tobacco, did not excite me. I could not, for the life of me, understand why an individual should tolerate that scalding liquid galloping down his throat or his head being clogged with tobacco smoke. To me, they were not nice to the taste, nor smacked of any elegance. I very early looked on these two habits as a waste of time and totally unnecessary. Neither my uncle nor my grandfather smoked or drank and I certainly received no encouragement from that quarter. These were two choices that I made, without any external prodding, and I am thankful.

We now settled down to await our Examination results, due sometime in October. The results were published in the Jamaica Gazette which reached our post office a bit later than the publication in the Corporate Area. So the city students would know their results by Thursday afternoon, but we in the countryside sometimes would not get it until Friday evening or

Saturday. This year about two telegrams had come from Kingston, on the results, but these messages were incomplete. Our Gazette arrived late on Friday evening and so many waiting students remained still in the dark about their results. But by Saturday morning, Teacher Reice had fully perused the results and handed over the Gazette to the waiting students. For some reason, which I cannot recall, I did not head for the schoolyard that morning. Then, possibly about eleven o'clock, I heard a screaming coming down the road, in the direction of my house. The screaming came nearer and nearer, and louder, and I rushed up to the roadside to investigate. There was my neighbour, Candy, running and throwing up her arms in great joy. Candy had passed her First Jamaica Local Examination, after three attempts, and she was in her twelfth heaven. When I asked her if she had seen my name, she said she had not seen any 'Keith Morris', but there was a 'Gilfred Keith' there. I now jumped and exclaimed, "That is me, man". "But a no so you name?" she replied. "Yes, a my name dat".

Then I had to explain to Candy that my full name on my birth certificate is, "Gilfred Keith Oliver". Everybody, including myself, knew me as "Keith Morris". For the first time, when I signed up for the Third Examination, I had to produce my birth certificate and I then discovered that "Keith" was my middle name. But we rejoiced, that is, those who were successful. The unsuccessful cried and began to brace themselves to repeat their programme. And we might just note that in those times one of the criteria for judging a Principal's worth was his level of success in coaching students for the Jamaica Local Examinations. If his success was considerable, then his stock within the community, and reaches far beyond that community, would soar. Numbers of parents in far- off areas might forsake their less performing schools and send their children into the tutelage of the high performing Principal. Teacher Reice enjoyed such a distinction.

Well, I had passed my Third Jamaica Local Examination. What next? I really did not know and I had no concrete plans. I would be eighteen years of age at October end and would be eligible for employment. Then fate threw its weight solidly in my corner. There was a vacancy on the staff of my school for a Probationer, as from November 1, 1948. The job, with a salary of nine pounds ten shillings per month, was given to Daisy and me, at four pounds fifteen shillings per month each. I was so glad for the job that for the first two days on the job I was not sure what to do with myself. Then on this second afternoon of my employment Teacher Reice sidled up to me and quietly said, "Keith, you have a job now and you have to jump around and get down to it". I had not been given any specific instructions hence my uncertainty as to what I was required to do. But now Teacher told me that I was to assist him with Fifth and Sixth Classes. This ' assistance', as I quickly learnt, entailed marking students' written work, mainly Mathematics and easy English exercises, collecting homework and sometimes marking them, sometimes conducting the after-Lunch Mental Arithmetic session with the two classes, supervising the boys in the School Garden, supervising classwork given by Teacher Reice and giving students any assistance they might need with their classwork.

I became a very busy Probationer and rather enjoyed my work. And all this performance was for four pounds and fifteen shillings per month.. But then, what would I have been doing, without this job? I was not a lover of farming and had no intention of planting tobacco or Irish potatoes. Also, I did not yet have any vision of becoming a trained teacher. This little job was very low paying but I liked it and I felt it gave me even more status in my community. I was living at home, was not paying rent, and my food was assured.

I was a Probationer. Who was a Probationer? A Probationer teacher was a young man or woman who had passed the Third Jamaica Local Examination and was employed as an untrained assistant in a primary or elementary school. At the same period where we are now, the late 1940's, there were also Pupil Teachers; they sometimes had not yet passed their Third Jamaica examination,, and were, sort of, junior to Probationers. These Pupil Teachers, salaried one pound and some shillings per month, gave general assistance to teachers. In some small, poorly staffed rural schools, the Pupil Teacher might have to take on quite responsible duties in the school. Very often you would encounter Probationers who were towers of strength in small or large schools in town or country. They learnt much about the teaching craft from good Principals and other trained, experienced teachers.s The Probationer was usually more academically advanced and so had more status and more responsibility. When you had passed the Third Jamaica Local Examination, your feet now closely approached the first rung of life's ladder. You were now at the stage when you had to think seriously on what career you would pursue.

The Third Jamaica Local Examination certificate, was like a passport for us elementary graduates. Some of us Third Year graduates chose Teaching and went on to the Teachers' Colleges, some chose to pursue Agriculture and went on to the Jamaica School of Agriculture or 'Farm School'.Others chose to become Health Officers or 'Sanitary Inspectors', a few headed for the Theological Colleges and served with distinction in the religious life of our country. Others went into other areas of employment in the lower echelons of Business etc etc. Medicine and Law were prestige fields and were largely reserved for the High School graduate. For us elementary graduates, there was no Banking and Finance, Management, Mass Communications, Consultants etc etc. But with our limited opportunities, some of us burst through the barriers and became giants of achievement in this country. They were the poor man's sons and daughters, a great many with enormous ability and determination and despite the limitations, they triumphed mightily.

Examples of such giants which come readily to mind are the late Professor Laurie Reid and Professor Aubrey Phillips of the University of the West Indies, Rhodes Scholar Dudley Thompson, eminent lawyer and politician, Rupert Bent, Chief Education Officer, E. H. Cousins, Chief Education Officer, G. H. Owen, Principal Education Officer and later Principal of Mico Teachers' College, B. St. J. Hamilton, Principal Education Officer and later Permanent Secretary in the Prime Minister's Office, S. W. Fagan, successful Principal and academic, later top ranking officer of the Ministry of Education; these were all outstanding performers in our education system. We can add to this eminent group, Isaac-Henry of St. Andrew Technical High School, Ben Francis of Vere Technical High School, Haridath Maragh who broke into Medicine and Eric Frater in Law.

On the feminine side we can readily name Mrs Mary Morris-Knibb, the first woman to be elected to the Kingston and St. Andrew Corporation Council, Mrs. Edith Dalton-James, Mrs. Lucille Morrison, Miss Rhodd of Central Branch Primary, and many others. There were others who branched out into other fields: Willie Henry into Agriculture, Willie James, Noel Walters and C. T. Lewis, into 4H-Clubs, Eddie Burke, Las Murray and a few others who went fully into the community development programmes of Jamaica Welfare. We did forget Reg Murray, brother of Las, and an outstanding educator who worked with the defunct Federation of the West Indies and then with the Jamaica Government.We could go on and on and name so many others who were great successes in various fields.. The poor man's sons and daughters and their Jamaica Local Examinations - may Jamaica lift its hat high and cheer them most lustily.

What of the Probationer who chose to pursue a Teaching career? Where did he go from his Third Year certificate? If he wanted to be a trained teacher, then he would have to seek entry to one of the Teachers' Colleges, namely, Mico for men, and Shortwood, Bethlehem and St. Joseph's for women. The system also made provision for those who could not get into a Teachers' College or those who preferred to do the Teaching course outside of a College. The Teachers' qualification examinations could be done externally. So a Probationer could sit the First Year Teachers' Examination and if he passed he would now be subject to a practical examination in his craft. If he were successful in both the sit down examination and the practical est, then he would become an A3 teacher. That meant that he had passed fully the First Year Teachers' Examination and he could now study for the Second Year Teachers' Examination. If he again passed both theory and practical, he became an A2 teacher. He could now prepare for and sit his Third Year Teachers' Examination, theory and practical, and if he were successful, he would now become an A1 teacher. So, here you now had a teacher who had qualified, successfully doing the prescribed examinations, outside of a Teachers' College. Usually, the external teaching student had a tougher time qualifying- he did not have the facilities and opportunities available to his brother or sister within the Teachers' College. The great majority of our Principals and teachers of note were College trained but there were many externally qualified Teachers who were superb too. An interesting reminder is that in those times, a teacher who was an A1, was not necessarily a brilliant, top grade teacher. It simply meant that he or she had passed all the required qualifying examinations for teaching, whether in Teachers' College or externally, and he now had the status of a fully qualified teacher, for life.

I worked as a Probationer at Nazareth from late 1948, through 1949, to the end of 1950. This was part of a most productive period in the life of this Maidstone community. There was quality leadership in the persons of young Teacher Reice, Mrs. Reice and the young Rev. Neville Neil, pastor of the Moravian church there. All three people were young and energetic and committed to community development. They inspired enthusiastic response from the community and were assisted by a cadre of active local community people. Jamaica Welfare Ltd. was busy pushing its programme of community awareness and development in Manchester, and Maidstone became one of its shining centres of activity. Teacher Reice and Mrs. Reice were tireless workers and gave so very much of themselves to the community. There were regular visits from various officers of Jamaica Welfare Ltd. Mrs Marjorie Kirlew was a favourite of our district people. There was Eddie Burke, of earlier 'Newsy Wapps' fame, dapper and full of energy and a real people person. I can remember the young Eddie, just returned from a study trip to Britain and Scandinavia, spending a short holiday with the Reices. Here was this man dressed in short-sleeved shirt, well laundered khaki short pants, brown shoes and tall khaki-coloured socks neatly folded just below the knees. In the schoolroom he told us of enjoyable and educative experiences he had in Denmark and Sweden - he even demonstrated a few gymnastic exercises he observed in schools in the Scandinavian countries.

Eddie bubbled with energy and enthusiasm and he infected so many in the community. He had been an elementary school teacher and was one of the many who were recruited into the work of Jamaica Welfare Ltd. And an inspired worker he was. The redoubtable D. T. M. Girvan was another Jamaica Welfare visitor. B. St. J. Hamilton also graced our cool hills and made his contribution. We experimented with the Cooperative Movement and viewed films on the Movement in Denmark. Las Murray, brother of educator Reg Murray, and later to become Member of Parliament for one of the Hanover constituencies, was an excellent lecturer with the Film Unit and took us through these films expertly. We established our Cooperative Buying Club which did quite well and received much community support. Then there was the Study Club which fostered groups meeting together and dealing with community issues and well organised Friday evening recreational and games sessions. Picture a games evening in the classroom, a wide circle of villagers seated, and the game is 'Parson's Puss'. There is great hilarity as the adjectives describing parson's puss are given. 'Parson Puss: an abominable puss - a God-fearing puss - an unparliamentary puss - an argumentative puss. Great was the healthy fun generated at these sessions of young and old villagers.

Teacher Reice organised and trained a Community Choir. It was made up of mainly young people, with a sprinkling of older folks. This choir brought renown to our community and copped first places at our Parish Community Festivals, held at the Porus Community Centre in Manchester. This was an annual competitive get-together which took in all the communities in Manchester, who were involved in the Jamaica Welfare community development thrust. There were groups from Nazareth/Maidstone, Mizpah/Walderston, Huntley, Coco Walk, Old England, Brokenhurst, and several other areas in Manchester. On that Festival competition day, we all loaded up on our trucks, from our various corners of the parish, singing and chanting on to Porus. Here the various community groups competed in choral singing, drama, folk dancing, elocution, preparation of dishes and a few others. The quality of the presentations varied as some communities had more experienced leaders than others. A case in point was Coco Walk - it was a young land settlement community in South Manchester, inexperienced, but was never afraid to compete with the more mature and experienced teams in the parish.

I cannot forget this particular Festival day at Porus, when the Choral Singing competition came around. The choirs all sang and the Maidstone Choir and the Mizpah Choir emerged at the top of the pile but the single judge could not decide which of the two choirs should have the first place. The single judge, the late Mr. Eglon Fairweather, requested the two choirs to again sing. Mizpah Choir, under the baton of Teacher Hill, took first turn and sang mightily. Then came Maidstone's turn and Teacher Reice took us impeccably through our paces. Everyone of us in the Maidstone Choir was sure we would win, so confident we were in Teacher Reice's direction. Then we waited impatiently on Mr. Fairweather's decision. When it came, we jumped for joy - we had won. And when Mr. Fairweather further announced that the best alto voice he had ever heard in the countryside was in our Maidstone Choir and that he wished to speak with her later, we felt we were on Olympus with the gods. That night Melrose Hill rang with our victory songs and laughter as our truck bore us back to our dear Maidstone. Even our truck driver, "S- blank", as we called him, because he had only one eye, got into the jubilation and his exaggeratedly polished gear shifts over the Hill were regarded as a compliment to our day's achievement.

A final episode from the Porus festival days reminds us of how times move on and how times change. This was the period of the mid 1940's, going into the early 1950's, and our beloved icon, Louise Bennett was emerging as the princess of Jamaican dialect. There were many, many Jamaicans in all walks of life who would not accept the new respectability being gained by our dialect, so effectively pioneered by the young Miss Lou. For them, what was not expressed in Standard English, was not expressed at all. The dialect was for the lower classes, the tongue of those who were not expected to be comfortable with the King's English. However, it was customary that at the end of a Parish Community Festival Competition at Porus, there would be a concert in the evening, at which all the winners of the day's competition would perform. It would be chaired by a prominent personality and there might be visiting guest performers. In this particular evening's concert, Miss Louise Bennett was the special guest artiste. As she presented her pieces, she received enthusiastic applause from the audience.

But there was one middle-aged gentleman who stood up right by the platform where he could be easily visible and even speak to the performers. Whenever Miss Lou presented a piece and received the ovation of the audience, this gentleman would wait for the return of quiet, then give out, "Give us a real good one now." Miss Lou would disregard the request and go on to the next act. At the end of that act he would again request, "Give us a good one now". This gentleman, for the whole duration of Miss Lou's performance, stuck by the platform, but he received no response. He did not get his 'Good one'. This man, in his own way, represented that section of the Jamaican society which resisted the 'legitimization' of the Jamaican dialect. To many of that period, Miss Lou was an upstart, bent on undermining the English Language's place as 'the language of the society'. How times have changed. Dialect has found its way into the hearts and halls of the great as well as the insignificant, and Miss Lou has become a national treasure.

It was a time of great activity and pride in our community and Teacher Reice and Mrs. Reice worked as if their bodies were veritable machines. There was the Food For Family Fitness or 3F Campaign. Here were introduced new food preparation methods, new food combinations, a greater appreciation of food ingredients, etc. The Nazareth/Maidstone 4-H Club was founded and led by Mrs. Reice and was a tremendous success. It harnessed the energies of us young people and guided us into the areas of vegetable cultivation, small-animal rearing (rabbits, goats, poultry), handicraft, cookery for the girls, conducting of meetings and practice in public speaking. Our Annual 4-H Parish Achievement Day, usually at Grove Place Agricultural Station, was always a day of excellent performance from our Club. We enjoyed our turns as Parish Champions and also had the distinction of one year as All- Island Champion 4-H Club. 4-H leaders like W.A.James, C.T. Lewis, N.B. Walters and B.F. Webber were so committed and presided over a great period of 4-H Club development in this country. Former Jamaica Independence Festival Director, Hugh Nash, is an outstanding product of the 4-H Movement in Manchester.

I cannot by-pass other community organisations which functioned at the same period and made a difference in the life of our districts. There was the old but vitalized Jamaica Agricultural Society branch, doing much to service the needs of the local farmers. Its first cousin, the Citrus Growers Association branch, was founded and run by Teacher Reice. In the citrus season many small farmers were made happy with ready cash coming in from the cooperative sale of their orange crop. A People's Cooperative Bank managing committee met every month and provided low- cost credit for many farmers of the community. Last, but certainly not least, was our Community Council, comprising membership from all our community organisations. It acted as a kind of watchdog, and was held in great esteem by our people. On more than one occasion we entertained visitors from other developing nations who had come to observe and learn from the work of our Community Council. All in all, this was a great period in our community history - a period of committed and inspiring leadership in a community that responded eagerly to that leadership. It was a period of achievement and tremendous community pride in a community which found new impetus and new life.

Chapter Twelve

My Choice: To the Mico

The year 1949 was an interesting and reasonably happy year for me. I was well settled in my Probationer teaching job ; I was residing at home and I did survive on my very, very light pay cheque which I received at the end of the month. I enjoyed good relations with the students as well as the parents and I was involved heavily in community activities. Our community of Maidstone was certainly on the map and we had no time to think that these glory days would not last for ever. We were so proud of our vibrant community and I wanted just to continue living there. But as the year wore on, questions as to my future course began to arise.

Sometime in September, while on a visit to Mandeville, I stepped into Brooks' Exlda Store to purchase a pair of shoes. I looked at a pair on display and thought them to be just the pair for me. They were attractive and apparently well made and were not at an exorbitant price. But before I could summon the attendant, reality struck. It now dawned on me that as reasonably priced as this pair was, I just did not have that money. I now had to search for a suitable pair at my suitable price. I ended up with the cheapest pair in the store. As I stepped out of the store I felt as if a whole new revelation was opening up before me - I could not continue to be satisfied with a salary of four pounds and fifteen shillings per month. I was saving little or nothing - what if I became sick? For the entire trip in the taxi back to Maidstone, I mulled over my situation. The unwanted thought even came to my mind that in making my choices I might find it necessary to leave my beloved Maidstone.

Then on a certain evening, about two weeks later, as I approached the village square, dressed in my new pair of 'cheap shoes', I met my very good friend, Edward. Edward was a good fellow but could be blunt and sometimes indiscreet with his utterances. We walked on together for about twenty five yards then, looking down at my shoes, he blurted out, "Keith, you buy 'nother a dem cheap shoes?" I was so hurt, but I did not make a response to him; we simply continued walking along. Over at the church, Rev. Neil had earlier made a public appeal to the young people to consider offering for the full time ministry of the Church. I readily concluded that the Church was not my calling and gave no more thought to the appeal. Many weeks later, a middle-aged mother, Miss Iris, was walking on the parochial road, past my home, when she called out, bidding good morning to my grandfather.

I was standing by the roadside and as Miss Iris came up to me she bid me good morning, and then, "Mas Keith, is what kind of work you going to go into in the future?" I replied that I had decided on Teaching, and in the coming January would begin studying for my Teachers' Examinations. Miss Iris almost keeled over in shock, "No, Mas Keith, you certain 'bout whey you a say? The other day when Minister did ask fi young people fi train fi parson, all a we think 'bout you an say you is just the one; you certain say a dat you want?" I assured her that my mind was made up and I did not want to become a minister. She was sorely disappointed and as she moved on she asked me to think about it again. I was not aware that my district people thought so well of me and as I watched Miss Iris going away further in the distance, I smiled. Deep down I was grateful that my district folks approved of me and felt I was walking a healthy road. But here I had to disappoint them - I had made my choice.

I must note that at this time there were a number of other male Probationer Teachers working at various other schools in Manchester and I occasionally met some of them in Mandeville, usually on a Saturday. On such occasions we swapped much information on our schools, our principals and their strong points and weak points, progress in studies and our areas of disgruntlement. One or two of these young men had plans to move from Teaching into other areas of more lucrative rewards. It was in this Probationer group that I met a Mico Second Year student who encouraged me to apply to sit the Mico Entrance Examination in early 1950. Someone had floated the idea to me earlier but I was lukewarm in my response. Then, when my Mico acquaintance urged me to try, I was all fired up. He spiced up the encouragement by relating two very humourous Mico episodes, and assured me that the Examination would pose no problem for me. By the time I arrived back at home from the Mandeville trip, I knew exactly what I would do.

At the appropriate time, I did make my application to the Mico to sit her Entrance examination, and was accepted. In early 1950, there was an event in Kingston which greatly facilitated my appointment with the Mico. The Ministry of Education planned an Education Course for all Manchester teachers, from Probationers up to Principals, to take place sometime before Easter, 1950, in Kingston. And the Mico Entrance Examination and selection process would take place within that same period, which was very fortunate for me.

The appointed time for the Teachers' Course came and we all trooped into Kingston - Probationers, A3's, A2's, A1's, Principals. The Course would run for about four weeks. Probationers and A3's had their morning sessions at Mico Practising School, and then would move up to St. Joseph's Teachers College for the afternoon sessions. A2's, A1's and Principals had all their sessions at St. Joseph's. There were demonstration lessons for us Probationers and A3's at Mico Practising by various experienced Principals, including Teacher Pearson from Pike Elementary School in Manchester, who introduced himself to the students as the 'son of a pear'. Mrs. Bair, Principal of Mico Practising, also took some of the sessions with us. Young Ben Francis also did some demonstration teaching for us. But the highlight of my sessions at Mico Practising was my contact with the young Ben Francis. Ben was a recent graduate of Mico College and was now on the staff of the Practising School. He was a big man, in the bloom of young manhood, handsome, well groomed and well spoken. He exuded self-confidence and immediately won the admiration of the teachers. Dressed in well ironed, long sleeved shirts, with beautiful matching ties, he was like a shining knight to me.

But the best was yet to come. On one particular morning, Ben did the demonstration lesson on the English poet, William Wordsworth. The students used the text, "The Story of English Literature", and Ben took them expertly through the material. We were entranced by his rapport with the students, their eager but disciplined response, his mastery of the material and how effectively he passed it on to his students. At the end of the lesson, for what seemed like a whole minute, there was silence among us. It was as if some time had to elapse before we came back down to earth: so transported were we. There and then I made my now full commitment to the teaching profession. Ben Francis was the model for me and I told myself I had to be like Ben, not as handsome, but in all the other areas. All through my teaching years, whether in Jamaica or overseas, Ben's picture never left my mind - to me he was the ideal mentor. Ben Francis had a very successful career and later became an outstanding Principal of Vere Technical High School in Clarendon. There is also a rural cricket competition for schools which is named for him.

For my month's stay in Kingston, I again boarded with my old friend, Miss Fannie, in Allman Town. Also staying with her for the period of the Mico Entrance proceedings was Durrant, a young fellow about my age and a graduate of a Kingston private high school. He also would be trying for Mico and we quickly became friends. On the morning of the Entrance examination, we had our breakfast early, dressed, and in good time, with Miss Fannie's blessings, Durrant and I walked leisurely from 10 East Race

Course, our residence, up to the Mico. We arrived early and so had time to survey the surroundings and meet some of our fellow aspirants. I estimated about one hundred of us young men assembled that morning, the overwhelming majority of us fresh from the countryside. Durrant was very articulate, was well attired and immediately attracted the rapt attention of the 'country boys'. When they discovered that he had been to high school in Kingston and had passed the Senior Cambridge examination, they seemed to have regarded him as someone very special. Remember, at that time high school Education in Jamaica was a privilege, not a right, hence we can understand why these young 'country fellows' crowded around Durrant. Durrant realised and enjoyed his period of eminence and gladly exploited it. He animatedly reeled off episode after episode of his high school experiences, his successful battle with his Senior Cambridge papers; he cited noted examples of Cambridge high performances with their many distinctions and many credits, unfortunate examples of the 'Fatal F' (Fail), exemptions from London Matriculation, etc etc and he went on and on. The young fellows around him listened in silence, seemingly awed by this 'accomplished' high school graduate. Durrant enjoyed his 'period of glory' immensely and no doubt entered the examination room in very, very high spirits.

As we moved into the large classroom for our test we were assigned personal numbers and these numbers had to be attached to all our examination papers. My number was 104. The examination proceeded and we all bent to work in earnest, determined to do our best. I well remember our last paper which was Spelling. Mr. Grant, one of the College tutors, and an Englishman, called out the words to be spelled. I had no difficulty with the words but some fellows faltered and asked for certain words to be repeated more than once. One of the trouble words was 'repertoire'. Mr. Grant's accent seemed to have bothered some and they kept asking him to repeat. He became clearly annoyed, and gave out, "You did not hear the word? Say you don't know it."

For some strange reason, I was dissatisfied with my performance in the examination. I had easily mastered the Spelling test but I felt that the rest of my examination performance was below the required standard. Durrant was cheerful and optimistic but I was disappointed and not very hopeful. We were to return to Mico two days later to get our results. On the day after the Entrance examination, I returned to my Manchester Teachers' Course and had a very quiet and uninspiring day. I could not get the Examination out of my mind. I told myself that I had failed and there was hardly any point in my going back to Mico to hear the certain 'failed' result. The day for the release of the results came and I was not hopeful at all, but

Miss Fannie kept on encouraging me. It was wonderful how much faith she had in me and she pushed me to go. With Miss Fannie's encouragement, I perked up and Durrant and I ambled our way back to Mico.

All of us gathered in the large classroom and waited anxiously. The first two numbers called were those of the two fellows who were placed on the reserve list from the previous year's Entrance examination. Next to be called was my friend Durrant. The crowd was not at all surprised as Durrant had made such a great impression on them on the Examination morning, that they must have felt that this was his natural, predictable result. But a short time after, the seeming miracle came; my number was about the third or fourth to be called and I was so astonished. I, No. 104, jumped up and began my walk from the big classroom, on to the corridor, and into the interviewing room. This walk was not without a measure of embarrassment as the shoe on my left foot cried 'whee, whee', loudly as I walked, and it was 'whee, whee' all the way from the classroom to the interviewing room. Curiously, I did not see any amusement on the faces of the fellows as I went by them; neither did I detect any on the interviewers' faces. Mr. Newman, the Principal and leader of the interviewers, put me at ease and began the questioning. Surprisingly, to me, the questions were not many and they seemed quite interested in my St. Simon's sojourn. Mr. Grant, the Vice-Principal, stared hard at me, from head to toe, and soon the Principal looked at his colleagues, gave an almost imperceptible nod of his head and gently told me I was free to go. That almost imperceptible nod of his head to his colleagues must have said to them, "Gentlemen, I think we can make something out of this shoe-squealing country fellow."

As I returned, shoe-squealing, to the classroom, some of the waiting fellows quietly greeted me, 'Hi, Teacher'. At the end of the interviewing period, about twenty- five of us were selected and we were instructed to report the next day to the College doctor, Dr. H.E.T. McDonald, at a Duke Street address, for our medical examination. We were also to return for our final instructions at a later date. That afternoon, Marescaux Road witnessed not only the steps of many an unsuccessful and disappointed young man but also the triumphant steps of that happy twenty- five. Durrant and I arrived at home, beaming, and Miss Fannie rejoiced with us. Later, after dinner, when I was alone, she came into my room and sat beside me. She again congratulated me but soon became very serious. Then she reminded me of my earlier self doubt and how I nearly ruined my opportunity. She pointed out that here was a great life's lesson to be learnt by me: self-confidence and determination were keys to success. How I thanked her. All through my working life her words of wisdom never left me. We remained such good friends right down to her death many years later.

And so we favoured twenty- five duly had our medical examination and now waited to return to Mico for our final instructions. In the meantime, I rejoined the Manchester Teachers' Course and was roundly congratulated on my success by all my friends there. A lady teacher even brought her aspiring nephew to see me, hoping to get information from me which would help him in preparing for the next year's Mico Entrance Examination. On the appointed day when we should return to Mico to hear our medical results and get our final instructions, I attended the usual Mico Practising School morning session, and then later went on to St. Joseph's for the afternoon session. I planned to leave in good time so I could walk down to Mico College for my appointment there. But the day's sessions were interesting and somehow I completely forgot that I had a later appointment. The sit-down session ended a little earlier and as we were busy clearing the hall of chairs in preparation for a bit of entertainment, it suddenly flashed in my mind that my Mico appointment was that evening. The clock was showing 3:50 p.m. and I was to be at Mico at 4 p.m.. I threw down my chair and ran out of the hall, out through the gate, raced down Old Hope Road, down through Cross Roads, down Marescaux Road and into Mico. I reached with three minutes to spare. I was hot and sweaty, but so grateful that the Good Lord had snatched me from the jaws of disaster.

So we twenty five gathered in the big Mico classroom to hear our medical reports and receive final instructions. When the Principal arrived to begin proceedings, one of our colleagues had not yet come. When he did arrive, about fifteen minutes later, Mr. Newman, the Principal, was annoyed at his lateness, and demanded an explanation. Our colleague spoke up, "I went on a visit to the University, Sir". Mr. Newman looked hard at him and said, "Mr. Grandison, I don't think I want you in this College". But luck was on Grandison's side. The Principal's secretary, who sat next to him at the table took pity on Grandison and lifted an imploring glance up to the Principal's face. The Secretary was very dear to the Principal and her imploring glance seemed to have melted his annoyance. "All right, Mr. Grandison, I'll give you a chance, but I am going to watch you very closely". We all breathed a sigh of relief at Grandison's escape. Later, as we broke up at the end of the session, someone asked Grandison why he gave the Principal that 'University' reason for his lateness, suggesting he might have dug up a less risky one. Grandison held his head high, and with a slight lisp replied to his questioner, "Well, I spoke the truth, didn't I?"

My medical report directed me to have my tonsils out; otherwise, I was hale and hearty. The Principal informed us that we would be put on a Pre-College Course for the remaining part of 1950. Certain books, other work material and tests would be posted to us and we would work on our own.

The completed tests had to be posted back to the College and we were kept informed of our grades. Having received all of our instructions and all relevant information which the College deemed we should be given, we were dismissed by the Principal and we headed for our several abodes. My Manchester Teachers' Course was now drawing to a close and I took in all the remaining sessions. With the Course ended, all of us Manchesterians returned to our dear old parish, tired, but all the better for our Kingston experience.

I returned to my Probationer's post after the Easter holidays and it seemed then that I had acquired additional status. My district people congratulated me at every turn, even a few of the older students questioned me if it were true I would be going off to Mico. One student from Third Class told me that her mother informed her that when I 'finish' Mico, I would become a real teacher and earn 'plenty money'. I now got down to work on my Pre-College Course. I found the Mathematics difficult and help with this was scarcely to be had in my area. I enjoyed the Latin exercises and successfully carried out some reasonable Science experiments which were prescribed. When I got to Mico in early 1951, I discovered that the powers there had been well taken in by my experience at St. Simon's and decided I should be able to handle Course material of a greater difficulty, hence my more difficult Mathematics assignments and a little higher level Latin programme. All of us Pre-College students had received a list of clothing requirements and I decided to get them together gradually.

Sometime later in the year, possibly about September, good fortune turned my way. An adjustment was made in the staffing at school and I now would be paid the full Probationer's salary of nine pounds and ten shillings per month. So, in one stroke, my salary rose by one hundred per cent. I was very grateful to my Principal. I went on buying the things I needed for College and by November I was quite well stocked. One of the College requirements was a white-drill suit. All of us came equipped with it. We later had to wonder why Mico required us to bring these suits as we wore them only once. I remember I purchased, as my dress shoes, a pair of black and white. The toe area was black but had its top surface punctured tastefully with holes which were filled with white polish, using a match stick. It was a beautiful pair and was only worn on Sundays, to church and on any other special occasion.

One amusing but quite embarrassing episode for me, took place sometime during this preparation period. On a particular Saturday I travelled to Mandeville to continue my buying. In the late afternoon I had completed my shopping and now looked to returning home. All my purchases were neatly packed in a 'flat-side basket' and I headed for my bus.

People from my area were slowly moving to the bus and I saw that it would not depart before another twenty- five minutes. So I placed my basket on my chosen seat and decided to stretch my legs for a few minutes and then return. As I left the bus I spied in the distance, young Pamela, sitting in a car not too far off. Pamela was a nice young Miss, about nineteen years of age, and I liked her very much. She lived in a neighbouring district to mine, attended my church not too regularly, and I never had much opportunity to 'know her better'. So when this opportunity presented itself, I eagerly grabbed it. My chat with her was so enjoyable that I quickly forgot about my waiting bus. I chatted and enjoyed myself and the time flew. After about thirty-five minutes it suddenly struck me that I had a bus to board. Lo and behold, when I glanced in the distance where the bus had been, there was an empty space. The bus was gone. I hurriedly took leave of Pamela, hoping I would spy the bus and run to catch it. At the same time I kept hoping that Pamela would not wise up to my embarrassment. But the bus was no where in sight - what was I to do? The 'flat-side basket' with all my day's purchases was lying in that bus, and, as I thought dreadfully, might even by now, be appropriated by some dishonest passenger. I could not think straight. I walked on quickly and put myself behind Sewell's Store, so that if Pamela was driven past that location, she would not see her badly troubled suitor.

I stood for a while and tried to see a way out of my predicament. I decided to take a ride on a later bus to Mile Gully, where I would have disembarked from my lost bus and then do my six mile journey up to Maidstone. By the time I reached Mile Gully I had worked my plan out. I would stay overnight in Mile Gully, meet my bus on its return trip to Mandeville, in the early morning, and see if luck was on my side - that my 'flat-side basket' would still be on the bus. I had a fitful night's sleep and came out early to meet my bus. The bus came through at about nine o'clock and made its usual stop. I rushed up to the driver and asked if an unclaimed basket had been found on the bus. He pointed to a shelf at the rear of the bus - there lying safe and intact was my 'flat-side basket'. I thanked him and I thanked him - I could not believe my good fortune. Of course my folks at home never got the full story - just enough to admit that a slip of judgement allowed the bus to go off with my precious purchases and I had to sleep over to retrieve them.

Chapter Thirteen

Mico: Grubs, Senior Men, And Super Seniors.

And so the New Year of 1951 came and in early January I boarded the train, headed for the Mico Training College, in Kingston. I had my faulty tonsils extracted at the Mandeville Hospital and had gone through my preparations as well as I could. Now, after heart-felt send-off functions from church and school, and god speed from Grandpa Morris and my uncle and all my friends, and with a 'grip' tightly packed with all my belongings, I was on my way to the city. I was a bit apprehensive moving into this situation - new setting and environment, new faces and personalities, new regimen. How would I settle in? I was anxious but not overwhelmed. We twenty- five had to sit a final test based on the Pre-College Course we had worked on and so the passage into the College was not yet fully complete. Again, Durrant and I stayed at our old friend, Miss Fannie. We did our final test and two of our number did not make the grade. One of these two completed his First Year Teachers' Examination, externally, and joined our batch at the beginning of our Second Year.

With this final examination behind us, the gate was now fully open to us. On the College's opening date, Durrant and I bade goodbye to Miss Fannie and made our way up Marescaux Road to Mico. It was mid-afternoon and our new colleagues gradually drifted in, all with their packed suitcases. There were a few senior students who stood by and watched us with rather unfriendly faces. Very soon we found out that they were the 'Advance Guard' of the Second Years, possibly stationed to 'size up' the incoming new students. Before nightfall all of us new ones were in, had been directed to our dormitory, and now, having deposited our belongings there, went downstairs. There we met mayhem. The Second Years, now in full force, stormed at us, making their faces as menacing as possible. I remember Bob Bennett from British Honduras and about six feet seven inches in height, long and slim, hawking down at me like an enraged vulture. I was a bit unnerved by the onslaught but maintained my cool and took it in good spirit. We were labelled 'Grubs', the Second Years were 'Senior Men'', and whenever a 'Senior Man' approached a ' Grub', the 'Grub'' should tremble like jello. We were put down in every way. Later we were taught to parse 'Grub'. From my imperfect recollection I recall that the

'Grub' was 'hopeless case', of 'vindictive mood', in a 'past tense', 'neuter gender', 'non-person'.

That first evening, shortly before supper, the 'Grubs' were rounded up and herded into the courtyard behind the main building, and on an improvised pedestal stood the Second Year student leader. The Second Years ordered us to bow down to him several times, then we were rushed to the showers with our white-drill suits. We were told supper would shortly be served in the dining room and we had to be properly cleansed before entry. We were rushed to disrobe and get our bodies all soaped up. When we had all soaped up and were ready for that invigorating shower, there was no water. The Second Years had locked it off. Then they rushed us to get into our white suits and not to be late for supper. I must add that this was the only occasion when we donned the white suit. It was never again worn by any of us throughout our three years at the Mico.

Our first Mico meal, despite the confusion we had been through, was well eaten up. I had become very hungry, and no doubt my fellow 'Grubs' also experienced the pangs. The Third Year students were more quiet and seemed not very interested in us. One of them, who was very well attired with a nice long sleeved shirt, beautiful tie and impressive bearing, sat at one of the Third Year tables. He impressed me so much that I thought he was a young tutor who chose to sit with the Third Years on this evening. He had a handbell with which he drew attention and proceeded to read out a few notices. Then he sat down and continued to mind his business. We soon discovered that he was the President of the Student body or 'College Officer' as students called him. The Third Years or 'Super Seniors', who possibly had been as 'vicious' in their Second Year days, were very detached in these confusing days and played the respected gentlemen. Most of them proved good fellows and we came to respect them greatly; after all, they were almost teachers. At this first meal, the Second years ate quickly and then left the room, and when we were given leave to go, we found the 'Senior Men' waiting for us outside. In the dining room one of the notices read had informed us about our 'Godfather', a Third Year 'Super Senior', who would be in charge of us until we elected our own batch Student Leader. He would be responsible for showing us around, giving us the various rules of the College and seeing to it that we settled down to the College regimen.

As mentioned earlier, we left the dining room to fall fully into the hands of the Second Years. We were pulled and pushed all around, upstairs, downstairs, on the grounds, bowing, kneeling, "Yes Sir", "No Sir", "Grub, say after me ------." The 'Grub' who had taught as a Probationer Teacher was reminded by 'Senior Men' that he had not 'taught', "Grub, you 'marred' those poor children". My colleague, Durrant, had a tough time. Every 'Senior Man' wanted a bite out of him. You see, during his later high school days in

Kingston, he would always be present to watch the Evelyn Cup matches on the Mico Cricket grounds. There he would meet many of the present 'Senior Men', who would have been First Years and 'Grubs' then. The First Years, by virtue of being 'Grubs', had the more menial jobs of rolling the pitch, and during cricket matches had to take the water or 'pug' (lemonade) to the players at the break. It is said that on these occasions he teased and 'ragged' them and said many annoying things to them. When they discovered that he was aiming to get into Mico the year after, they simply waited for him. On this first night, a sympathetic Third Year student rescued him and hid him until morning. On the second night he was again hidden.

Durrant, during these hectic hours, must have rued the flights of his tongue to those 'Grubs' during his cocky high school days. On the first morning of our presence on the Mico campus, we had our first meeting with our 'Godfather'. He was quite friendly, but there was a certain distance preserved. No doubt he was ensuring that we knew our place and kept it. We had to remember that we were 'Grubs', non-persons, totally ignorant and had to be patiently taught. Later, when he knew some names, we were addressed as 'Mr. Morris', 'Mr. Hewitt', 'Mr. Davis.' Some fellows, after the'Godfather' period was over, about six weeks, accused him, not to his face, of persisting with the use of the 'Mister' label, to preserve the distance between us and he. However true that might have been, he did his job well. He deftly took us through our paces. He brought in the knife and fork into one of our sessions; in another, he brought in the spoon and the porridge bowl and soup plate. We all knew that this was a massive dig at the social graces or lack of social graces of the new 'country boys' - 'Grubs' are 'hopeless', they know nothing and they have to be so carefully and patiently taught. But we took it all graciously - we had no other choice and we knew that after a short period, things would settle down - we would not be 'Grubs' for ever.

It was noticeable, in the first few days, after coming to the end of a session with us, 'Godfather' would say to us, "Now, I think the Second Years would like to see you for some unfinished business. Go and see them now." We later learnt that he was a master 'ragger' during his Second Year days and that was probably the reason why he was given the job of 'Godfather' to us. He became my very good friend. He took me visiting with his family in Jones Town and I got to know his siblings and parents. After he graduated we kept in close touch and our friendship never flagged, insomuch that years later, he was best man at my wedding. But the 'ragging' period soon ended, 'Senior Men' again became normal men and all now had to buckle down to work. Many enduring friendships were now built. Many of these once 'hostile Senior Men' now proved beautiful fellows and were worthy colleagues every step of the way. A great many people nowadays may not approve of 'ragging', but we thought at the time that it was a capital way of cutting down certain rather bumptious personalities, a few notches. I know of one of my batch mates who was made a much wiser and better man from his period of 'ragging'.

This period had its many awkward and uncomfortable and annoying moments but one can also look back on real hilarious moments. How can one forget the 'Grub' concert, which we had to put on, to 'entertain' the 'Senior' and 'Super Senior' men. For that 'Concert' I carefully prepared to recite John Keats 'Ode On a Grecian Urn'. On that night when my item was called, I stepped up on the platform to deliver my gem, such a beauty I would give to them. This was a poem I had carried over from Teacher Reice's glory period at my old school, so I dearly treasured it. I am now on the platform and I hold my head high. Then I begin: "Thou still unravished bride of quietness, Thou foster-child ...." I could barely finish the first line when there was a terrible roar, half of the 'Senior Men' jumped out of their seats and demanded that I get off the stage. They laughed and they guffawed. I had insulted them and they demanded humble apologies from me for bringing Keats to a new low. I was dumbstruck; how could they not appreciate one of the gems of our language? But reality suddenly came back to me - it was a 'Grub' concert and everything 'Grub' had to be made to look bad. But, it was great fun and I smile every time I remember it.

Mico Training College

Mico Training College, in 1951, was enjoying its last years as a bastion of men. For some time the College had offered the First Year Teachers Examination Programme, to Probationer Teachers, male and female, and during my three years there, there were always these Probationer groups doing these Courses. I guess they were regarded as external students. They were non-residential and had their classes apart from the regular College students. But as we could see, the days of all-male dominance were numbered. Women entered the College as regular students in 1954. Up till then, the graduate of the Mico College was a 'Mico Man'. From 1954, we had to begin using the term 'Miconian', as now the Mico graduate could be either male or female. The student body was relatively small, with barely one hundred on roll. However, the number did go up to one hundred and seven during my final year. There were men from every parish in Jamaica, but mainly from Manchester, St. Elizabeth, St. Ann, Westmoreland and Trelawny. There were about seven from the then British Honduras and one or two from the Turks and Caicos Islands. The student body included a number of ex-servicemen who had seen service in World War 2. They wore their medals proudly on the Empire Day and King's Birthday national holidays.

The President of the Student Council or the 'College Officer' led the student body and he was highly respected. In addition, each of the three batches, First Years, Second Years and Third Years, had its Senior Student, who led and represented the batch. The Students' Council was made up from office holders like the three House Captains, President of the Literary and Debating Society, the Senior Student of each batch, the Sports Secretary, the Cricket Captain and the Football Captain. This body, as noted earlier, was presided over by the 'College Officer', and adjudicated on cases mainly involving the First Years and Second Years. The 'more natural victims' were the First Years, but I remember the case of one 'Senior Man' who ran afoul and was sentenced to one week's postal duty. Note that going to and from the Cross Roads post office, morning and evening, was one of the 'natural jobs' for the 'Grubs', so one can imagine this senior Man's humiliation; but this senior Man from Montego Bay, quietly accepted the Council's judgement and carried out the sentence willingly. I cannot recall a Third Year man being embroiled with the Student Council. After all, they were 'gentlemen' and 'Three-quarter teachers'.

Mico's teaching staff was small in 1951. Captain Arthur Newman, a veteran of the British Army and war service, was Principal. He had his quirks and he may not have been loved by the student body but we all respected him and knew that Mico was a dear part of his life. We referred to him as "Ceps", from the Latin word 'Princeps' or Chief. His Vice-Principal was Mr. Arthur Grant, another Englishman who taught Mathematics, English Literature and Latin. His nickname was 'Pythy', for Pythagoras, the Greek mathematician. He sported a stern exterior but he had a heart of real gold. Our Religious Education and Child Psychology tutor, an American Quaker, was also a first- rate locksmith off campus. Our Education Methods tutor was the lone woman on the staff and had a Master's degree. The College's Science programme was handled by Mr. McKie, whom we worshipped as a very great scientist. He was also a super artist who in half of a minute, could sketch your features on the chalkboard, most accurately. Geography and History were taught by Mr. Glave, who also acted as Sports Master for the College. The flamboyant Mr. McNab also taught some English Literature, especially to the Second Years and we regarded him as an expert on Milton's 'Paradise Lost'. Mr. McNab, Mr.McKie and Mr. Glave were more junior tutors and non-degreed s past students of the College.

Our incomparable Music tutor was the young Mr. Lloyd Hall, GRAM, ARCM. Student-tutor relationship was good and the only incidents of serious student protest were on two occasions when the dining room served defective meat which overturned the stomachs of droves of students. On those two occasions, an onlooker would have been most amused - men who had never even jogged for months were suddenly doing the distance between the upstairs dormitory and the toilets downstairs on the grounds, about one hundred and ten yards away, in nine point five seconds flat. I heard men calling out, 'Mama, Mama'. Oh those two nights! I had to do my hundred yards too, but I couldn't help being amused at all those mighty, strong men being reduced to almost whimpering, and exceedingly weakened by their repeated 'losses'. On these two occasions the poor Matron had to endure the venom of her dear 'nephews'. Ordinarily then, we would have been thinking that a 'running belly' naturally could invade the territory of the student, but not that of tutors. However, we were duly informed a short time after our experience by one of the younger tutors that they had their 'sprinting practice 'earlier. But they had kept it so quiet that we never had the slightest suspicion.

Equipment at the College was amazingly limited then. Able students who reared to dig deep into the Science programme, had not even a test tube, much less a laboratory to work in. Science was theoretical; we used to say among ourselves that some of these fellows knew the text, "Biology for Medical Students", almost from cover to cover, but, alas, there was no lab for their practical work. We know well the suffering of many of these fellows when they went on later to do Science at the University of the West Indies. A few even had to go off in desperation to North American universities where they usually did well. College food was reasonable, both in quantity and quality, and I had to learn to enjoy it as I usually never had any money to go to the Tuck Shop. The

Tuck Shop was quite well stocked and a Third Year Student had overall management. Various students, not First Years, took turns to sub-manage it week by week. Final Year students were allowed to invest in it, and they usually received a handsome profit, which always came in handy to help out with their Graduation expenses in December.

Our religious life was not neglected. We were required to attend our individual churches each Sunday. The overwhelming majority of us belonged to the traditional churches: Anglicans, Methodists, Moravians, Baptists, Presbyterians, Congregationalists, Disciples of Christ, a few Catholics and a small sprinkling of the new 'American-originated persuasions'. For the various religious groups, Church Monitors were selected. Third Year men they were, and they were to ensure that their Church brethren attended their respective churches regularly. My first Moravian Church Monitor was Manchesterian, John Williams, who, on our first attendance at the Redeemer Moravian Church, North and Duke Streets, took us new Moravian students directly to the vestry and introduced us to Mrs. Mary Morris-Knibb. Mrs. Morris-Knibb was an outstanding educator and social worker, the first woman ever to be elected to the Kingston and St. Andrew Corporation, an eminent Moravian and a cornerstone of the congregation. She was the founder and Principal of the Morris-Knibb Preparatory School, which she passed over to the Moravians before she died. I recall that after greeting us, she referred to the fact that Mico students no longer wore jackets on their daily business, and that this new freedom subtracted from their dignified bearing. An interesting bit about the Anglican students was that the more 'hoity toity' ones attended St. Luke's in Cross Roads, while the 'lesser ones' attended St. Matthew's in Allman Town. In those days if a student placed a sixpence collection in the plate, he would regard himself as having done very well.

There was service in the College Chapel every morning, which was compulsory for every student,and late evening short devotions which always had its smaller number of faithfuls. The special monthly Chapel Service was a must for all, and the preachers were invited from the various Protestant Churches. Occupying the pulpit on a number of occasions also, were the Principal, Mr. Newman, who was an active Methodist lay preacher, also our Religious Education and Child Psychology tutor, a Quaker and an ordained minister. Several of our students could do very well on the organ and they provided the music accompaniment at our services. A Student Christian Movement group was active in the College and from time to time exchanged visits and religious programmes with other such groups in the city. The religious life of the College, then, was healthy, a nurturing which was so important for these young fellows, many of whom would in a short time have to be lay readers and catechists in communities all over the countryside.

One cannot forget the rich musical life of the College. We had as our Music tutor the eminent young musician, Mr. Lloyd Hall, who also taught at Shortwood College. We had great music. His ordinary music classes as well as his Music Appreciation classes were superb and we were exposed to much of the classics. How well I remember listening to the 'Erl King' and almost crying when the evil 'Erl King' got hold of the little child, who thus died. In Mendelssohn's 'Fingal's Cave' or the 'Hebrides Overture', we listened intently and picked up the roar of the waves at the Cave's mouth. For weeks the common hum of many of my batch mates in the classroom and bathroom were the opening notes of 'Fingal's Cave'. Mr. Hall's record collection was immense and he made us benefit from it. I recall on one occasion he brought in noted Jamaicans violist, Jim Verity, and violinist, Tom Murray, British Council representative in Jamaica, with him at the piano. The trio gave us a beautiful mini-performance in the large classroom. The late Vin James, noted Jamaica bass singer and choir conductor, practically made his debut in the large classroom at one of Mr. Hall's music evenings. Mr. Hall organized our Annual Eisteddfod, in which the three Houses competed in Tenor, Baritone and Bass singing, Digging and Folk Songs, Elocution, Short Story Writing, Musical Composition, Parody Exercise, Impromptu Speech Making and Sketching on the Chalkboard. The Eisteddfod Competition produced some very good performances. It was an education with great enjoyment and it generated a wonderful House spirit.

Members of Lushington House, Mico 1953

The House System was vibrant; the three Houses, Bishop, Buxton and Lushington, competed in the areas of the Annual Athletic Sports, Cricket, Football, Gardening and the Annual Eisteddfod. During my First Year days, my House, Lushington, had a poor year in Athletics, in Gardening and in one or two other areas. We kept our spirits up and made it known over and over, that 'Lushingtons may lack brawn but they are rich in brains'.

The student body had much to keep it active and in touch with the outside. Apart from a full academic programme, there was Scouting, Midsummer Boys Camping, Debates with Shortwood, and we had at least one with the University of the West Indies, lectures from eminent visitors and visits to factories and other business places in the Corporate Area. Add to these Mico's participation in the Evelyn Cup Cricket competition. There were also the inter-house cricket Competitions, there was volley ball, Table tennis and some softball. The College was never dull for the student who wanted to be up and doing.

Referring to educational visits outside the campus, I recall this occasion when we were invited to a public lecture to be given at the Friends Centre in Cross Roads. The topic of the lecture was, 'What is wrong with Jamaica's Education', and the speaker was the then Director of Education, Hon. Harold Houghton. A very representative Mico group was present. When Mr. Houghton ended his lecture, the floor was thrown open for questions and comments. Out came a young man who kept Mr. Houghton on his toes and seemed to have had a good insight into the topic. He held the floor, and other would-be contributors found it difficult to get their pieces in. Eventually our Child Psychology tutor, who was the moderator, had to step in and the others got their chance. Later, we were to learn that this impressive young man was named Edward Seaga and he had recently returned from school in the United States. Three other noted visitors who gave us very informative talks were Mr. Robert Lightbourne, then Chairman of the Industrial Development Corporation, Councillor William Seivright of the Kingston and St. Andrew Corporation Council and Dr. T. P. Lecky, eminent animal geneticist and developer of our noted Jamaica Hope cattle breed.

1951 was the year of Hurricane Charlie which devastated sections of the island. In that hurricane the Mico building lost much of its roof. The students were then on their Midsummer holidays and we were anxious about what would be the fate of our Christmas and examination term. Part of the roof of my home in Manchester was also blown away and I had felt the water raining down on me through the now exposed rafters, so I could empathise with my dear old battered College. Our dormitories were all on the upper floor and thus our sleeping quarters would be out of use for quite some time. We simply had to wait for information from the College. This came not too long after the hurricane, when the College communicated with all her students and directed that each student should arrange with his local primary school to undertake a measure of teaching practice, until the College was able to reopen. I duly made my arrangement with my local school, Nazareth, and I had my period assisting with the Lower Division of the School. I cannot recall how long this period was, but when we were called back to Mico, we arrived to find a number of tents pitched in the area which had been occupied by our large garden plot. This area is now the site of the student residence, Mills Hall. A number of us were assigned to each tent and we settled down to life under canvas. The Principal, being an old army man, settled down comfortably in his tent, and the junior tutors, McKie and Glave, also had their tent. It slipped me to mention that Mr. Newman's residence had also lost its roof and he was houseless like the rest of us.

The entire student body settled down willingly and complaints were few. We were wakened each morning at the peep of day by the 'Wakey, Wakey' call of Mr. Glave who saw to it that every man piled out of his bed promptly. We thought he liked the job a bit too much but then we remembered that he also had seen war service, so camp life was nothing new to him. All our classrooms were on the ground floor of the College building, the dining room and kitchen were functioning very well as also bathroom and toilet facilities. So, as students, we could not complain of being at a great disadvantage and we went about our work and play without much inconvenience. In time the College roof, along with that of the Principal's residence, was restored, and we were able to return to our dormitories, and the Principal, to his residence. Our tent residence was another of the many enriching experiences which we had at Mico and it reminded us that setbacks and hard knocks will come, but we have to face up and deal with them. The Mico administration had demonstrated this in response to our hurricane troubles. The hurricane damage and the consequent tent- dwelling period did not hamper our College programme and our preparation for the December final examinations. My First Year colleagues performed beautifully and garnered six Honours passes.

Teaching Practice has always been a landmark experience for the student teacher and their approach so often differed from student to student. Some students, often the inexperienced who had never been before a class, approached with dread; some students, even though they hadsome experience with classes were never comfortable with a tutor watching. There were others who, from the beginning, were more comfortable and adjusted readily. Then, we had the few, who were very good and maintained the B+

or A grades throughout their College career. But it was a gruelling six- week period, with research, making lesson illustrations, writing daily lesson plans and a half a dozen other things to do before you faced the class on the morrow. The work was relentless but at the end of it all there was the student here and there, who shed a tear or two on parting with his class. It was commonplace to see weeping pupils who could not see how they would live after their beloved 'stew-up' students parted from them. There were so many Practice Teaching stories, both pleasant and unpleasant, and one famous one I can recall was that of the 'Serious Student'. Some years before our time a certain student was sent to a particular school to do his teaching practice. He was very anxious about the discipline of his class and he was convinced that he had to be very 'serious', no jokes, no smiles and 'laughy-laughy'. This went on for the entire teaching practice period, until the morning of his last day, and then, apparently feeling he could now relax, he laughed at a smart-aleck comment made by one of his students. This was the trigger; the class burst out, "Lawd, student laugh; look, him a laugh". Students on teaching practice were supervised by tutors, who checked the lesson plans and visited the classes to guage and assess the student performance. We were graded from A at the top, down to D, which marked a rather poor teacher. A stock encouragement which was always given to the fearful student was: "The only way you can fail Teaching Practice is if you thump down the tutor". No one was ever that 'bright' to test it.

In those years, the First Years were sent to various schools in the Corporate Area. I was placed at Holy Family Primary, a Catholic school in downtown Kingston. The Second and Third Years were placed in schools in the countryside. In my Second Year, my batch, along with the Third Years, were placed at schools in St. James, centred around the Anchovy area. My group of four was placed at the large Anchovy School. Arnold, one of my group, and the pianist, entertained us in the mornings before breakfast, and set us off in the right mood for our classes. We were well treated by this strong Baptist community and a good, understanding headmaster and we had a memorable and productive stay at this school. The Third Years were spread out over the smaller schools in the region, like Roehampton, Leithe, Bickersteth and one or two others. My Third Year Teaching Practice was done in St. Catherine. We were sent to some small schools around the Linstead area, while the big Linstead Primary accommodated some of the Second Years. Two colleagues and I were placed at Yorke Street Primary, and there were others at Bermaddy, Victoria, Time and Patience, and two other schools whose names I do not recall.

I remember that very hard- working trio who virtually 'took over' Time and Patience for the six weeks, and did a great job in the classroom and with the infrastructure outside. One of this trio had to conduct a funeral. As this colleague later related, at the beginning he was literally frightened, but he managed to pull himself together and, as his colleagues and a number of villagers assured him, he had done a good job. Again, we were in a strong Baptist area and we received the best of Baptist hospitality. I recall that special Sunday of the Harvest Festival when nearly all of the Mico students in the schools around, gathered at the Jericho Baptist Church for the big service. Jericho Baptist was the main church of that Baptist region, hence the specially 'big occasion'. The Mico gentlemen were warmly welcomed and each school group had to bring greetings to the gathering. The region's Teachers Association, meeting in Linstead some time later, made us very welcome. It was a very lively occasion, with our Second Year man, McLean, giving a very well received bass rendering of the 'Erl King', taught a little earlier on by Mr Hall, our Music Tutor at Mico. We had some happy memories of our six- week stay in St. Catherine.

One cannot neglect to comment on our little College chapel. During my years there, it was becoming packed. In my final year when our number reached one hundred and seven, it had reached its capacity. But my mind goes back to those lovely chapel services and other special occasions, the hymn practices led by Mr. Hall and the vocal rehearsals for our Eisteddfods. Can you imagine one hundred male voices - treble, tenor, baritone, bass, all blended and lifted in praise? Those fellows sang for the joy of singing and they wanted to sing. The strains of "Let all the world in every corner sing," John Bunyan's "Who would true valour see, Let Him come hither.", "Pleasant are thy courts above", still echo in my memory. It was beautiful. That little chapel still stands on the Mico campus, but the student body is now so large that it had to surrender its pride of place as the centre of the religious life of the College. We trust that this precious little building will be preserved.

Now for a few comments on my batch of fellows. As noted before, twenty- four of us entered the Mico, with about twenty- one of us coming up from the countryside, and were the sons of small farmers. Two of our number had Senior Cambridge certificates, the rest of us had only our Third Jamaica Local Examination Certificates. This was a collection of the poor man's sons, fellows with small opportunities but big in brain power. Several maintained outstanding academic performances throughout the three years, and the majority later served the nation with distinction. At the start of our Second Year, our batch had swelled to thirty- two as several fellows who had completed the First Year programme, externally, joined us. These new fellows who joined us were referred to as 'Augmenteds', after a musical term from our Music classes. They integrated well into the batch, but there was a special bond that existed among that original twenty- four.

I look back with pleasure at these various personalities, their different styles and distinctions. There was Mervin, the 'philosopher' and solid Latin student from St. Elizabeth, and my close friend. Financially, we two had harsh times, but he never hesitated to help me out of his meagre store. In 1951, in our First Year, the great American violinist, Yehudi Menhuin gave a recital at the Carib Theatre. Mervin and I determined not to miss it and we saved up our scarce shillings. On that night we saw no other Mico student there, and for weeks we patted ourselves as the two most 'civilized and musically sophisticated' students in the entire student body. There was quiet and gentle Lambert, another St. Elizabeth man, superbly focused and one of the most academically disciplined and organised characters one could ever find. This was backed up by enormous brainpower and his Honours results attest to this. Noel was also from St. Elizabeth and was possibly the most gifted of us all. He played nearly every sport in the College but was at the head of the class for his entire College career. He was a tremendous intellect and master of the spoken language. He had Honours results for his three years at Mico.

Durrant, my friend from Trelawny, had to be cut down a few notches during the 'ragging' period, was glib of tongue and the champion bass. Erudite Arnold was musician, public speaker and a brilliant mind. He later blossomed into ardent churchman and choir director. Gerald, the youngest of the batch, was quite a 'boasty' fellow, but was well liked and was a good brain. Hubert, or 'Sarge', a product of Holmwood and the Cadet Corps, was an avid gardener, classical music enthusiast and a real hard worker. I am certain he has that record with Chopin's 'Nocturne' tucked away some place. Greville or 'Munche', from Hanover, was a big man with a big voice and was great company. He loved his 'smoke' and no one could enjoy a joke as mightily as he did. Milton, a Manchester man, also liked his 'smoke' and a bicycle. He was a quiet worker with an agile mind and ready wit. Roy, from St. Thomas, was the clown of the batch and you could never be angry with him for any long time. Well we remember that Evelyn Cup cricket match at Mico when Roy was batting. When he was hit in front at 'that crucial area' and fell to the ground, we all thought, "Here again is Roy with his clowning". We impatiently ordered him to get up and continue batting but he did not respond. When other players rushed to his side we realized that he was not clowning after all and he was really hurt.

I have to mention Renford from St. Catherine. He was nicknamed 'Caput', from his big head. His father was a baker and for some time he sent a big bun every week for his son. That bun was divided up among his batch mates and we made certain we were always present during this share-up period. 'Caput' was a businesslike and responsible young man and became Tuck Shop managing director during his Third Year. He was a very good brain and was the first from the batch to matriculate, towards university. Weddy, from Westmoreland, placed first in the island in the Third Year Jamaica Local Examination in 1948. He was bright, but, please, don't ask him to explain an exercise that is giving you a bit of trouble. You will end up even more confused. Leon or 'Nemmy', was the consumate gentleman. He dressed with taste, was dark and handsome and his language was smooth and polished. Mac, or 'Skibo', from Portland, was our batch Senior Student, a good leader and highly respected, but we never could gauge how old or how young he was. But for the three years he led us well. Ashbel or 'Butter', from Westmoreland, was very well muscled and quiet but, as an academic, he was a powerhouse. He never flaunted his Senior Cambridge certificate - a man of humility but of great substance. Reggie or 'Grendel', from Manchester, was short but thick and again well-muscled. He was a devoted Scout who attended the Jamboree in Jamaica and later grew a family of academically outstanding sons and daughters. Our outstanding young student teacher was Euton, from Westmoreland, who earned his Grade A in Teaching Practice, a joy to watch with his little young people. These are some of our number, which is not to say that the others were not noteworthy. We all had our strengths and our weaknesses but we interacted and worked together and each made his special contribution in this our period of training.

The Third Year batch that we met when we entered College in 1951 had its colourful characters. Armstrong, or 'Sammy', struck us as a bit of a dandy. He was always dapper and dressed well, with beautiful ties. He was also a respected Latin scholar. McIntosh, or 'Transcendental,' was literary, and he got his nickname at a debate against the Shortwood ladies, in which he used 'this very big word' on the poor ladies. Woody Miller was most highly respected by us. He was one of those fellows in his batch who had passed the old London Matriculation examination in his Second Year and was a solid scholar. We First Years saw him as a very serious and focused young man who would make a very successful educator. Eddie Owen from Dunrobin, Manchester, an ex-serviceman, tall, with a purposeful walk, would never refuse a bet and never remained in an exam room until the end of the allotted time; but he never once failed. He was also the Tuck Shop Managing Director. A.B. Knight was a born mathematician and held top place in his batch for all three years. Alvin Lisle was another London Matriculation man, was bright, a cricketer, and joined the Mico staff for a year after he graduated. 'Mongoose' Williams, a quiet St. Ann man, went away to the United States some years after graduation, studied, and later became a Professor at Howard University. We never found out why he was given the name 'Mongoose'. There was nothing 'mongoosish' about him. John Williams, Roy Walters, Basil DePass, Henlin, Titus and Roy Atkinson were all good fellows and we respected them. Oh! We have forgotten gentle Astley South from Manchester, the top teacher in his batch - always an A performer before his class, very organized and also an Honours graduate. We end with Alfred Farquharson, dignified and solid St. Elizabeth man, who in later years served as Custos of his native parish.

That Second Year group that 'welcomed 'us First Years and ragged us solidly was the largest batch to have entered the College, up to that time. They numbered over forty and for their three years had to remain in the 'Big Classroom', the only classroom that had adequate space for them. In the election of 'College Officer', in January 1951, this large batch used its strong voting power to block the election of the 'favourite'. We heard it said that the 'Favourite' was not liked by this batch and it used its numbers to ensure the election of an alternative candidate. A number of these fellows stood out and our batch relations were very good. I recall the 'Classicists', Dwyer, Gregory and Dawkins, who were opposed to the 'Romanticists', who would be the bulk of the rest of their batchmates. Both groups knew their Palgrave's Golden Treasury of Poems well, and many were the exciting arguments and conversations between the two 'schools', each pushing its preference for its poetic style. Of course, the overwhelming majority of the student body would be 'Romanticists', so the tiny 'Classicists' were facing a colossus.

I remind that this was quite sometime before the flowering of Caribbean literature and we fed on English poetry, via Palgrave's. Lennie Wray and Vane Waller were men of the Humanities and excelled in the use of the language. Lennie was the A teacher of his batch. I remember an amusing little incident between Waller and my batchmate, Claude, just when we were coming out of the ragging period and were getting closer to the Second Years. Waller was strutting around, with his head held high and using a few 'big words' to impress the 'Grubs'. My batchmate, Claude, said to him, "Waller, when all those big words in your mouth finish, what you going to do?" Waller, still strutting with his head high, replied, "Grub, do you know of the waters of the sea? They are inexhaustible. So is my vocabulary." Poor Claude smiled and kept very quiet. Dawkins was the great mathematician, Mullings from St. Elizabeth was bright and a hard worker, avid gardener and was Lushington's Garden Captain. He later developed voice trouble and had to leave the classroom. He later became a top notch Civil Servant. Bob Bennett, Joel Arnold and Peter Enriquez were from

British Honduras. Bob, a great footballer, was six feet seven inches. Peter lectured us on the world of the Mayas. Bertie Lewis was the great athlete - was College goalkeeper and Evelyn Cup wicketkeeper. He went on to Boy's Town and played on their Senior Cup team. For a great part of his career he was involved in social programmes and Youth Work. Hutchinson or 'Hutchi', tall and dapper, from St. Mary, became Cricket Captain. After overseas study, he returned to Mico and spent the rest of his career at his alma mater.

There was E. Gordon from Montego Bay, slick on the dance floor, sang a beautiful, soothing tenor and was adept with his artist's pencil. His namesake, Sterling, was a good academic, conversationalist and debater. Later, he became Principal of York Castle High School. I remember others like quiet and studious Gordon-Rowe, the youngest of his batch, 'Hercules' Graham, a great sol-fa man, with Herculean strength and John Hughes, Westmoreland man, big and bespectacled and his House's anchor man on their Tug-o-War team. As is expected, his large frame had to have 'very ample' feet to support it. R. E. Powell from St. Elizabeth, was serious and focused, a real hard worker. He was one of the first of his batch to attain his first degree. He spent long years on the staff of Bethlehem Teachers' College. Joe Earle was a bright young man, focused and straight talking. He later gave great service to Jamaica's education via K. C., Jose Marti, Calabar, AAMM Credit Union etc, etc. We remember well E. St. Leger Young, ex-service man, ex-travelling salesman, no-nonsense, experienced and the very 'senior' man in his batch, dimunitive Redway or 'Chief' (Chief of the Pygmies), Dennis Gooden, the Clunie cousins - a good collection of men they were. It gives one a certain touch of sadness when I think that I lived with these colleagues for one or two or three years and there is a number of them whom I will never again meet, once we part at the graduation gate. But, maybe, that is inevitable.

I must at this point, make reference to a realization which was brought forcefully to me from my Mico experience. When you are young, out in the countryside, and are busy sitting your Local Examinations and passing them at every sitting, and success is riding high on your wings, when you may be the toast of your district or hamlet, then you could end up being convinced that academically, you are a real 'hot item'. But when you arrive at a place like Mico or The Jamaica School of Agriculture and in later years, the University, and join the groups of other 'poor man's sons and daughters', from all over the country, when you witness the performance of some of these sons and daughters and the extent of brainpower brought to bear, then you may be brought to admit that, after all, you were really 'not that hot'. So many of these Mico men were great intellects, and though starved of opportunities, they rose to the very top. Let us suppose these fellows had enjoyed the privilege of secondary education, where would be the limit for them?

But my third and final year did arrive. I had gone through the stages of 'Grub', then 'Senior Man' or Second Year, when we had our turn to get at the incoming 'Grubs'. Now I was a Third Year man or 'Super Senior' or 'three-quarter teacher'. The year was an interesting one and I had to take on a significant measure of responsibility. I became Captain of the Lushington House and with it went a seat on the Student Council. There were several important activities for the year which were based on the competitive House System, and we were kept very busy. The first of these activities was the Annual Athletic Sports which the Bishop House won running away. This was to be the only victorious taste for the Bishops as the Lushingtons came mightily into their own and won the Annual Eisteddfod, the Garden Competition, and the Cricket and Football Competitions. An amusing recollection of this Eisteddfod was the winning of the Tenor, Baritone and Bass solos that evening by the 'Grub' Abbot Anderson, and the consequent fury of my friend Durrant, Captain of Bishop House. For the two previous years, Durrant had been the unquestioned king of the basses, and now, to be dethroned by a 'Tenor Grub', was more than he could take. He retired to bed immediately after the event, and for days, fumed at the 'Injustice'. Altogether, it was a great year for the Lushingtons, and the wealth of talent present in the House during this year made my task as House Captain much easier and enjoyable.

The year 1953 was soon drawing to a close, and my batch, along with the usual stepped-up end-of-year examination preparations, had to make arrangements with the Final Year ladies of Shortwood College regarding our joint Graduation exercises. Our graduation agenda included the joint Valedictory Service which was held on the Sunday immediately preceding the week of examinations, and the joint Graduation Dance, held on the Saturday night, ending the week of examinations. The Final Year student found himself extra busy at this time as he had to be attending rehearsals of the joint Mico-Shortwood graduation Choir. It was usual at this time for the joint choir, under the direction of Mr. Lloyd Hall, to contribute one or two pieces on the Valedictory programme. Maybe our graduating friend would be a member of a committee which had to meet with the Shortwood ladies for further planning on the Graduation agenda. Then, if he chose to dance the Graduation Waltz with a Shortwoodite, he would have to be attending those dance practices. But, the Final Year Mico man still had more concerns. For Graduation he had to be well outfitted - certainly a new suit, from fabric agreed on by his batch. All thirty of our suits were made by our tailor friend, Trevor, on Sutton Street in downtown Kingston. Maybe our friend would step out in a brand new pair of shoes, maybe a new white shirt and tie. He would have to finance all of this, and in addition, might have to take care of taxi fares to and from the dance, with funds enough to cover drinks and eats for himself and his lady, and other costs of the night.

Financially, this was always a tough period for the Final Year man. One has to understand that many of them 'eked out a meagre living' throughout their student days and when their Graduation came around, they yearned to really enjoy what they had earned. After all the sacrifices and often deprivations, they wanted to enjoy 'a little splash'. A lot of debts were chalked up at this time, but can we fault them? I had my full share of 'meagre living' and was sure I deserved my 'little splash' at the end, but, financially, I was in deep trouble. However, I was most forcefully reminded that 'the Lord moves in mysterious ways', and timely help came to me at this time of need and anxiety. Edward, my classmate through Primary School and one of my partners in that very early 'love quadrangle' I related earlier, had gone off to farm work in the United States and we lost contact for a long time.

Then in late September, when I was at my wit's end how to finance my Graduation expenses, a letter arrived from Edward, enquiring if I needed any money. I promptly replied, informing him of my situation, and that I would greatly appreciate a loan. Edward replied quickly and he enclosed a United States money order which gave me nearly twenty pounds sterling. In addition he said I should not worry about repayment now, but later, when I had established myself and was able. I was so grateful to my old school chum, and my letter of acknowledgement was so profuse with thanks that I suspect he was embarrassed before he reached the end. I was convinced that our Good Father in Heaven had a hand in this - He had inspired Edward, at the very right moment when the need was so great, and I was rescued. Edward and I remained so close for many years after he returned from his stint in the United States. Later on he migrated permanently to that country but as Edward was not a man for much letter writing, our communication was not often. He died in New York a few years ago. Regrettably, I could not attend his funeral. Here was a great friend, sincere and caring, and I owed him a debt, not in money, a debt which possibly, could never be fully repaid.

But to return to the graduation story - our Valedictory Service was held at the Scot's Kirk, in downtown Kingston. It was a solemn service - Mico-Shortwood choir rendered a stirring anthem, followed by a sermon which bid us goodbye, godspeed and invoked the blessing of the Almighty on our future endeavours for our children and our nation. I left the Church with a double feeling - I felt uplifted that I had virtually completed my term at Mico and the world was waiting to welcome me with open arms. But there was, at the same time, a touch of sadness. I had come to revere Mico and the Mico tradition and now I was parting from the hallowed halls of that great institution. As I stepped from the church on to Duke Street, there were three of my batch mate friends a short distance away, animatedly talking among themselves. I waited for my bus and I watched them. That comradeship would soon be broken and we would be scattered all over the country - how many of us would keep in touch? Here, my bus arrived and I had to jump out of my sad thoughts.

Our final examinations started the very next day, Monday morning. Sometime later in that week, our Principal, Mr. Newman, arranged a special communion service for the batch. We gathered early that morning, before daylight, in the chapel, and we sang lustily. The Communion was administered by Rev. John Stewart, then pastor of St. Paul's Presbyterian Church, Lockett Avenue. At the time, I thought Mr. Newman was real fatherly to arrange this final, quiet service for us. As I watched him at one point in the service - the tall man bending low, prayerfully, I thought to myself, "Is he going to miss us?". Well, he had seen so many Final Year batches make their departure - should he remember this batch, specially?

This Graduation saga will not be complete without further words on the Dance. As the custom was, if the graduating Mico man wished to dance the Graduation Waltz with a Shortwood lady, he would have his name placed on that special list. When the list was complete it was sent on to the Shortwood ladies, who would choose their waltz partners. With the choices decided on, the practices would then begin, usually at Shortwood. I was not an accomplished dancer, just reasonably competent, and I decided I had to be a part of this waltz. So I had my name placed on the list. I had no real friend at Shortwood, just a few acquaintances. I waited, hoping I would be chosen, and knowing fully well I would have to take who came my way. At last the day of decision came and the fellows hurried to the classroom notice board to view the returned list. I was met at the door by exuberant 'Ferno' who gleefully greeted me, "Lord, G. K., you come out big. You lucky cuss you." I literally bounded to the board and was virtually hurled back by what I saw. There was my name, in clear, unmistakable letters, paired with one of the prettiest girls in the ladies' College. I was really stunned and it took me some time to regain my balance. My batchmates naturally accorded me that extra bit of respect and must have wondered about that hidden talent which I had not shown them over the years. The full story behind the choice is hilarious, but will not be told in this place.

And so this weekend came. Examinations were now over and in the next several hours we would be heading for our Graduation Dance. The waltz practices had gone very well and now we were ready for our 'little splash'. The Dance was held at the Bournmouth Club in East Kingston, with music supplied by Eric Deans and his orchestra. It was a merry night and things went smoothly. Onlookers said the Waltz was quite well executed and I know for certain that I did not step on my partner's toes even once. I am certain that she did not in the least regret her choice. The batch of 1953 had now passed out.

We returned to College that Saturday night, rested on Sunday and put our belongings together, for we had to vacate the premises on Monday morning. At mid-afternoon on Sunday I wended my way down to my Dance partner's residence in Allman Town. Before we parted on Saturday night, I had extracted her permission to call on her at that time, and I spent a beautiful two hours. Monday morning came and we said our many goodbyes. There were so many shoulders balancing tightly- packed suitcases, heading for the gates. As I went through the Marescaux Road gate and crossed over to the other side of the street, I turned to take a last look at the Buxton Tower. Its clock would no longer toll its ten o'clock lights-out for us. In the life of that batch of 1953, it was the end of an era.

Chapter Fourteen

The Trained Ploughman
Goes To Work

January 1954 marked my entry into the world of work as a trained teacher. I had accepted a position on the staff of my old school, Nazareth, and had looked forward to resuming on that old familiar hunting ground. When the job offer was made to me, one of my close batch mates had warned me that a prophet had honour, except in his own country. But by then I had considered that aspect fully and decided I would make a go of it. My stint there as Probationer had convinced me that there was nothing to fear in this area. I did think, too, of the economy of living at home. My mother's marriage had failed and by then she was back in her father's home; so the domestic situation, at home, in one way, had improved. Grandpa Morris was pleased to have his grandson back in the house, at least for now, and he was very supportive. My first paycheck was eighteen pounds sterling, which went up to nineteen pounds when my success in the final examination was established. I was now a young, trained teacher, graded A1, and ready for the fray.

By this time, the community had lost the services of Teacher Reice and Mrs. Reice. Teacher Reice had procured the headmastership of a much larger school in the parish, and furthermore, he was soon to be promoted to Education Officer in the Ministry of Education. At Nazareth he had started his climb up the academic ladder by successfully sitting the London Matriculation examination. His climb from this point was rapid. In not too many years he had attained his Doctorate and was appointed to a teaching position at the Caribbean's highest and most prestigious educational institution. Our community has always looked back with tremendous pride and gratitude, on the great years he gave to us. Maybe, it is instructive to note that it was a long time before Teacher Reice's old position in our community was reasonably properly filled. One of his successors stayed for less than four months.

Long years after this, I met a lady teacher who knew this successor, and she said he told her that at Nazareth, he would not have been able to deliver on all that they expected him to do. So he thought it wise not to tarry in that community. This tells us how high was that standard of excellent service given to our community by the Reices. When I arrived from Mico, the situation was somewhat stabilized and a promising young headmaster was in place. But he already had his Bachelor of Arts degree, was quite innovative and we could see that the Education Officers thought much of him. So we kept our fingers crossed. After barely a year at this school the call did come and he was appointed Education Officer. The community was fortunate that his successor, not with a Bachelor's degree, was a good worker and settled down there in the community for several years.

The community welcomed me back and I ploughed into my work at my old school with energy. I worked closely with the Headmaster in the Upper School and learnt much from him. I had very good relations with the other teachers, as also with the students. Parents were, in the main, cooperative, and always had a good word for me. I was sometimes a bit embarrassed by the fact that some of my classmates from our old schoolhouse on the hill, insisted on addressing me as 'Teacha'. Even old folks who knew me from my days in 'nappies', were addressing me as 'Mas Keet' or 'Teacha Marris'. But I never stood on ceremony with my district people. What was important for me was that I earned their respect, and I worked to maintain that respect.

Apart from my regular teaching job, extra-curricular duties received their full share of my days. The Jamaica Local Examination classes or 'Teacher's Private Class' were still a very important part of the work of the school and I naturally took on my share of the tuition. I tutored students of the 'Private Class' in the mornings from 7:30 until about 8:45, with regular school starting at nine o'clock. Then in the afternoon we would get back to it from about 4:20 until 6 p.m. During the period approaching Summer and early Summer, when the evenings were long, we could go on to near nightfall. I had no complaints about the early mornings or late evenings, as I looked on it as simply a natural part of the job and I worked with enthusiasm. Added to this, one could not have gathered anywhere else a more beautiful bunch of young people. Those students were eager and so cooperative and they encouraged us to do even more for them. And then it gradually opens to you that if your students do well, so will your reputation grow. I was not much of a cricketer but I busied myself with organizing the older boys into a respectable cricketing unit. We had much difficulty in raising funds to purchase balls and bats but the enthusiasm was there and we even organized one or two matches with neighbouring schools.

Our district had always maintained an active Jamaica Agricultural Society branch and I now acted as its Secretary. We had a tough time attracting young people into the group, though the area was a solid farming one. But there was a faithful core of oldsters who kept the Branch humming. They attended their Branch meetings, Branches Associated meetings in Mandeville, worked with the Agricultural Instructor and in that year of 1954, led ably by the school's Headmaster, put on a successful Agricultural Fair on the school grounds. 4-H clubbing was also active and I gave my services as a Project Leader. The Community Council and the Parents Teachers Association were vibrant groups and a special part of the life of the community. I recall that the Parents Teachers Association had two very lively meetings where the subject of corporal punishment in schools was discussed. The school's headmaster was not in favour of that kind of punishment and actively discouraged his teachers from using the rod. But he was challenged by parents as to the wisdom of such a policy. He was reminded of the biblical pronouncement on the matter and while they were not in favour of excessive or cruel use, they felt that there was still need for the rod. Children were children and adults have a duty to correct them when they go wrong. Our good headmaster stood his ground; the parents felt he was going too soft on his students and that would send a wrong signal to them. One parent who was quite irate, made the comment that if we put away the rod, then we might as well put away the Bible. But the headmaster retained their confidence and cooperation though they had their differences on this matter. Our Moravian church was at the core of our community life. I honoured our Moravian tradition and what it stood for and I continued active in the service of my community church. I was living and working in an area which had always experienced a varied community life and I readily chose to continue to be an active member.

A bright spot for me early in that year of 1954, was my journey into Kingston to receive my Teachers' College Certificate. On Friday, May 14, at 8 p.m. Shortwood and Mico held their United Presentation Ceremony, at Ramson Hall. On this occasion, the Colleges presented their graduates of 1953 and awarded their certificates. The graduates, in those times, were not awarded Diplomas, only Certificates. It was a short but impressive ceremony, presided over by the Lord Bishop of Jamaica. The certificates were handed out by Lady Foot and the evening's special address was given by the Governor, Sir Hugh Foot. His address centred on Nigeria, newly independent member of the British Commonwealth. Governor Foot had served in Nigeria and he spoke of the tremendous potential of that new West African nation. His speech mirrored the great faith he had in that region and the hope that Nigeria would fulfill its glowing promise. He had great faith in us too and in a sense, we were like Nigeria, full of potential and he hoped that over the years we would fulfill that potential. Thirty three of us received certificates. There was no get-together following the function and after greeting each other and much friendly banter, we broke up and went our several ways. I knew that there were batch mates there whom possibly, I would never again set eyes on. And so it has happened - a few of them I have never again seen. Some have since died, a few went abroad for further studies and never returned, others who remained here have retired and I run into one or two occasionally. But that is the way of the world - we all have to spread out and find our individual niches in various parts of this universe.

The sad event of this year, for me, was the loss of my grandfather. In September he quietly passed away. He did not suffer; he had led a remarkably healthy life and never had to consult a doctor. His was an active and productive life, and at ninety- two years of age his body must have given out and it was time for him to go. Early in that week he had visited the village square and on his return had remarked how tired he felt. He took to his bed, experienced no pain, but he progressively grew weaker and weaker. On Sunday morning, at eleven o'clock, he breathed his last. For me, Grandpa's death was a great blow. He had been father, grandfather and mother to me, much closer to me than my uncle or even my mother. He taught me so much and created that home environment which fostered that love for learning and achievement. Community leader and consultant, amateur historian, farmer and expert apiculturist, skilled carpenter, faithful churchman, he was a man for so many seasons. I never cease to be ever so thankful for the blessing of being his grandchild, growing up in his household and being shaped for life by his teaching and example. Now he sleeps with his fathers and may he rest in peace.

The new year of 1955 opened quietly and I now began my second year of work at Nazareth. I was comfortable in my job and I spiced up life with the occasional weekend visit to Kingston. On these visits to the city I stayed with my dear friend, Miss Fannie, and made contacts with two or three of my batch mates who were based at city primary schools. There were a few other Mico men whom I knew very well and would run into on my saunterings down King Street. The General Certificate of Education examinations had recently been introduced into Jamaica and a few of these Mico men were busy studying for this new examination. We will be reminded that the Mico man, then, was awarded a Certificate, not a Diploma, and that the Certificate did not help him much if he had intentions of moving on to higher studies. In the 'old days', that Mico man would have to sit the London Matriculation or the Cambridge Higher Schools examinations to qualify for entry into university or possibly private study leading on to a first degree. This explains why Mr. Newman, the

Principal of the Mico, each year picked out several very gifted students and had them tutored for the London Matriculation examination.

The result was that for several years a number of these Mico graduates would leave College with their Teaching Certificate and the London Matriculation Certificate, thus giving them a jump start into the academic field. Mr. Newman was really thinking ahead when he gave Mico students the opportunity to do the Matriculation examination and he had to withstand opposition to this move, from influential quarters. He was reminded that Mico's job was to train primary teachers, not to prepare candidates for the Civil Service. The last Mico group to sit the London Matriculation examination came from the batch of 1951. Woody Miller is the only member of that Matriculation group who is still alive in Jamaica. The first Mico group to sit the General Certificate of Education examination was selected from the batch of 1952. They tackled the Advanced Levels and came away with Advanced Passes in Mathematics and Zoology, Ernest Dawkins in Mathematics and Joe Earle in Zoology. The selectees from the batch of 1953 did not attempt the "A" Levels, one reason being the difficulty of securing that level of tuition from outside, but they did very well with their "O" Levels. Nunes, Genus and Lambert are survivors of this group - about four of them have died.

What we came to realise was that by the mid 1950's, there was a great wind of change blowing in the teaching fraternity in Jamaica. More and more of the younger teachers realised that they had to upgrade their academic qualifications and aim for entry into university, either here or abroad. The Teachers' Certificate awarded by the Teacher Training Colleges laid a foundation but was not near enough for entry. Hence they had to go the route of the General Certificate of Education examinations, doing "A" Level and "O" Level subjects until they matriculated and were now qualified for entrance to a university. So by the late 1950's there was a wave of studying. Young teachers, especially those in the urban setting, were busy attending Evening Extension classes, and St. George's College evening Extension School was a great boon for them at this time and it had the much needed facilities. Others were taking Correspondence Courses from Bennett College, Rapid Results College and Wolsey Hall, Oxford, all in Britain.

There were recent reports of examination successes filtering around and they served to encourage and enthuse. I recall the successes of 1952 Mico graduates, Sterling Gordon who secured "A" Level passes in four subjects at one sitting, and Earl Powell who attained his Bsc. Econ., within a short time. Both young men were full- time teachers and had to study part time; it was hard work but they showed that it could be done, and we were inspired. Maybe this new drive could be rightly termed a sort of mini-revolution. I must not neglect to add here that the Jamaica Ministry of Education now began to increase the number of scholarships awarded to practising teachers for undergraduate work at the University College of the West Indies. By the time that the Government of Jamaica launched its new Junior Secondary Schools, in collaboration with the Government of Canada, a number of these new schools were headed by teacher graduates of this 'new era'.

When I started 1955, I had already decided I would complete two years at home and then move out to new fields. By Easter I leaned towards an urban situation and began to make soundings as to possibilities. By then I was smelling the aroma of further studies and I knew that a Kingston base would be to my advantage here. There was one further pull factor which will be dealt with at a later date. However, I was in constant contact with two of my urban batch mates who were making plans to change their jobs. Our plans had been that if either of them succeeded in changing his job, then he would do his best to ease me into his previous job. My two friends did change their jobs but the Managers of those two schools had other plans and I did not get either of the town jobs. I was disappointed at first but I soon came to see that it was fortunate for me that I missed out, as moving at this point would have faced me with a few complications. I was firm, however, in my decision to leave home at the end of my second year, and I now concentrated on seeking a teaching job in Kingston for January 1956.

In the summer holidays of this same year, 1955, I attended an Industrial Arts Course (then called Manual Training) at the Kingston Senior School (now the Kingston High School). I had never been good at this part of the teaching vocation, but the Ministry of Education was now giving added financial incentives to teachers in this area of work and I wanted to make another try at it. Hence a good 'brushing up' in the workshop would do me fine. I also wanted to listen and observe for job opportunities for January. Again I stayed at Miss Fannie's residence in Allman Town, from where I could walk easily across to Senior School in the mornings. The Course lasted for four weeks and I worked hard at it, but my best was just not good enough. I recall on one particular day during the Course, three of my batch mates paid a visit to our workshop. One of them, Gerald, came across to my work desk and spent some time with me. When, after about twenty minutes, he was parting from me, he looked at me and became unusually serious. "G. K.", he said, "Let us stick to things of the mind." Gerald had said it all and I immediately saw the wisdom of his advice. He had been the youngest in our batch and a 'boasty little fellow", but he was quite a good judge of character and competence. Almost needless to say, I never earned any of that financial incentive offered by the Ministry to Industrial Arts teachers, and Gerald's advice stayed with me.

The General Election of 1955 provided an unforgettable experience for me and two local friends. In that Election all three of us were actively involved. Dunkley and I worked as Presiding Officers in a nearby district. Our Polling Stations were in the same house, while my second friend, Lee, worked as an Indoor Agent in Dunkley's Polling Station. The day was uneventful and polling was moderate, with no incidents. When the polls closed in the evening, we made our counts, fixed our boxes and dispatched them as we were instructed. With these chores completed, we were now free and we walked the distance back to the village square in nearby Maidstone. This is where the night's drama began. This part of the Northern Manchester constituency was a solid People's National Party area and had voted most strongly for the Party's candidate in the past two General Elections. We all expected the new People's National Party candidate, Dr. Glendon Logan, to sweep the area. He was very popular and his meetings in the district were very heavily attended. One of his camp assistants, aptly called "Honey Mout," was the song leader and he could quickly whip up the crowd into a vociferous throng. People jumped in great fervour as he led them in singing of 'the licky, licky govament'[33] and 'the gully govament', referring to the then ruling Jamaica Labour Party Government. We strongly scented a People's National Party victory, island wide, and we, as Party supporters, were joyful on that election evening. We were certain that our Party would achieve its first General Election victory and form the new government. But I have to slip in this thought at this point: suppose that Labour Party Government that we jeered and made fun of, had not been a 'gully govament', how would the Corporate Area have dealt with its now frequent flooding situation? That same 'gully govament,' in its wisdom, constructed the Sandy Gully drainage system, and we have to eat our 'Gully words'.

When in late evening we three friends arrived in Maidstone square, we were in high spirits. We had no thought of our dinners nor of going to our homes at such an early hour. We jumped on a waiting truck, owned by a man from Devon, a large village near Christiana, and which had been used to transport voters during the day. The three of us, without much thinking, and in our Party rejoicing, decided to head for Christiana, the headquarters of the constituency. About two cars from the area had conveyed boxes to Christiana and we heard that other cars from the district were in that town and we were certain we would easily secure transportation back to our

33 "Will take gifts and favours from anywhere, of questionable honesty, of low principles."

district. We felt it would be nice to be there in Christiana, at the very centre, and celebrate victory. The truck stopped in Devon, and we three hoped that the halt there would be brief, as we were anxious to get into Christiana. But the driver did not return to the truck, and we waited and waited.

It was very dark and we kept low and quiet as we now remembered that Devon, for us, had a bad name as a Labour area. As we cowered in the darkness, we heard comments by Devon young fellows about those 'fool fool people up inna di hill de',[34] referring to us in the hills and that part of the constituency. 'A dem dweet, a dem mek we lose.'[35] Through all this we dared not venture out to find the truckman. When we were there for almost an hour we decided we had to find the driver of the truck. We crept out and eventually found him standing with a small group of men in a shop. He stepped out to us, and when we asked him if he were not heading for Christiana, he emphatically said no. He said that the People's National Party had won and he would not venture into Christiana, into that victory mood there. It was then that we realised he was a well known Labour supporter and he felt it might be foolhardy to drive into an area of People's National Party jubilation.

Our wings dropped. We now decided that we had to get back home as best as we could. We knew that there were about three cars from our area in Christiana. Perhaps we could wait by the streetside and hail them as they passed through on their way home. It was dark but we had to be lucky. We did spot two of the cars but our luck ended there. We hailed them but they did not recognize us and they picked up speed, unwilling to do any lingering in Devon. Well, this was it. We were in a real mess and for some strange reason we set out on foot for Christiana. We arrived in Christiana at twelve, midnight, and found everywhere closed down. We stopped briefly at the police station and got a smattering of election news. We were now ravenously hungry as we had not eaten since midday. Dunkley, a small shopkeeper, had neglected to take any money with him that morning. Lee, the second man in our trio, had less than three shillings in his pocket. I turned out to be the rich man on spot as I had a pound and a few shillings with me. Perhaps the hand of Providence had intervened because I did not expect any spending that day, but for some unknown reason I had tucked the pound note into my pocket. The moment's priority was to find food.

And so these three hungry men set out to find food. We walked around for sometime but everywhere was closed. As we continued walking,

---

[34] "Those foolish people up in the hills."

[35] "They did it. They made us lose the election."

dejectedly, we eventually came upon a 'coldsupper'[36] shop, the owner just about to start locking up. In better days or nights we would not have countenanced such an establishment, but tonight, driven by acute hunger, we gladly sat down to be served. The proprietor must have been exceedingly pleased to see these three men so enjoying his food - they ate as if they were inspired. My pound paid the food bill and we then addressed ourselves to the sixteen mile walk back home to Maidstone. We departed from Christiana some time after one o'clock in the morning and we finally reached Maidstone at daylight. Interestingly, I did not feel as tired as I should have been after such a long walk. Dunkley and Lee were older than I was and they might have felt it more. But we had walked at moderate pace, took all the short-cuts, and we chatted and joked, so the miles did not seem as tiresome. I think we were chastened but we ended up wiser men for the experience we had been through. Dunkley and Lee must have settled down to a good long sleep when they reached home, but for me there was to be no such rest.

After a short time at home I was informed that the minister and his family, the school principal and his wife, the neighbouring school's principal and his wife and one or two young teachers from Mandeville, were heading for Alligator Pond beach, to spend the day. I was invited to join the group, and soon we were on our way. We had an enjoyable day, with good food and drink, good conversation and plenty of political discussion. We were ardent but quiet party supporters and we felt our Party's success merited a measure of celebration. About two weeks later, a goodly lady from neighbouring Galway district threw a special victory party at which the two newly elected members for the two Manchester constituencies were present, Dr. Logan from Northern Manchester and Mr. Winston Jones for Southern Manchester. I recall that Mr. Jones ended his evening's thank-you speech with the promise: "Ladies and gentlemen, we shall not let you down."

Time was speeding and I was now approaching the end of my two year stint at my old school. I had made several job applications but none had yet borne fruit. Also I had made a number of exploratory trips to Kingston to personally push my quest for a city job. Then in early November I was summoned by the headmaster of a school in East Kingston and offered a teaching job, to begin in January 1956. A few weeks later I was contacted by letter from the Manager of the new Tower Hill Primary School in St. Andrew, offering me a position on the staff of that school, soon to be opened. I had already given my word of acceptance to Windward Road and so I respectfully declined the Tower Hill offer. Things had worked out very

---

[36] "A small shopkeeper's shop, which sold cold cooked food."

well for me and now I was all set for my new city job. I was now leaving my home district and was about to launch out on my own, away from immediate family, other relatives and life-long friends. On my last worship day there, the community bade me farewell and gave me their blessing. In my thank you reply, for the first time I expressed how I felt about that community, that community that saw me grow up, and nurtured me for so many years. I assured them I would never forget, nor let them down.

Chapter Fifteen

My Move Into The City - Windward Road And Calabar High

I started my new job in the city in early January 1956. I arranged to board with my old batch mate, Durrant, who had recently married my childhood Kingstonian friend, Marjorie. They had a spacious apartment in Bournmouth Gardens, and quite near to my new workplace. Bournmouth Gardens was still a very desirable residential area and I was very comfortable in my residential situation. Windward Road School, or 'Range School', as it was called by the older folks in the area, was a relatively young school and was built on the southern edge of lands which were said to have once been part of the Camp Range lands. The school had, at that time, an enrollment of a little over four hundred students, with a staff of fourteen teachers. The headmaster, Mr. N. B. Falconer, was an amiable gentleman and not very far from retirement. Miss Clarke, the Senior Assistant, was next to the headmaster. Today she would be known as the Deputy Principal. She was hard-working and committed and occasionally got on the wrong side of teachers, but could never be accused of any ill-will.

There were two headstrong lady members of staff, but overall, the staff worked hard and cared much for the children they taught. The Headmaster, Mr. Falconer, was very much liked by the community and led a vibrant Parents-Teacher group. The children loved him and it was always said that he knew the name of virtually every student attending his school. This might not have been exactly accurate, but it said very much about his standing in the community. He was a great believer in children learning to save from an early age and his Savings Bank group collected every Monday afternoon. I would say that Windward Road School was one of the less flamboyant schools in the Corporate Area at that time, but it had a solid programme. We worked quietly and got good results.

As the lone young male on this staff, I was expected to direct the organised sports activities of the students. The school had a good record in Athletics, having won the Corporate Area primary schools athletic championship on more than one occasion. We maintained the active athletic programme and gave very good account of ourselves at subsequent championships. Lucas and Kensington Cricket grounds were nearby and those two Cricket Clubs allowed us to stage our annual school sports on their grounds. These were the times when we had the good fortune to make the acquaintance of young cricketers like Easton 'Bull' McMorris, George Prescod, and a few others. The school had a good cricket team and played many a match at the old Kingston Town Moor field.

I recall our junior small boys' football team and our journeys to the Town Moor. There we had some memorable matches, with some hilarious moments, watching the 'little boy football.' For some unexplained reason, the boys never took on to the game of Softball, leaving it to the girls to field quite a strong team in that sport. I cannot recall if there was a competition for the Kingston primary school teams, but that girls' Softball team from Windward Road School played and won many a game on the Kingston Senior School diamond. I cannot forget our star pitcher, Claudine, who was big in size and who would burst into tears when taunted with her nickname, "Big Sid". You see, "Big Sid" was the name of the pet bull kept at Up Park Camp and was present at some of the military parades there. Those were the days when we could take our children off campus safely and enjoy our events. There were no knives or any other offensive weapons. The students played their games, interacted well on the field of play, had much fun, and win or lose, they returned home in mighty good spirit. These were students I enjoyed working with. Most of them were from homes with moderate or small means and there were very few disciplinary situations. They were cooperative and encouraged you to do the extra for them.

Another enjoyable area of my work at Windward Road Primary was the operation of a small but active 4-H Club group there. In my teen years at home in Manchester, I had been a keen 4-H member, and at Windward Road Primary I decided to try out the 4-H idea in city conditions. The 4-H Organizer for Kingston and St. Andrew gave us much help and the little group found projects that were suitable to the urban environment. They planned and attended their meetings, attended 4-H parish events, organized events such as hikes high up on the Wareika Hills, above the school, and pursued their individual projects. One ardent young clubbite, Barbara Matthews, was a leader and grew into a keen role model in the area and was greatly respected in that area of East Kingston. But I cannot forget that first group of students that I was given charge of on my arrival at the school. The most senior class in the school was named Form 4, and I was given Form 3, the next most senior. This was a class of about twenty eight. I have always regarded them as the best primary group I have ever handled. A large percentage of them were bright and talented and never failed to produce beautiful work. Most were always well groomed, well mannered and had a very positive attitude to their school and work. So many of those faces are still fresh in my mind; they were such a great group of young people.

The landmark event of my second year at Windward Road Primary was my marriage in June 1957, to Vinnette Smith, a member of the staff of Trench Town Primary School. Vinnette and I had been contemporaries at Teachers' College, she at Shortwood and I at Mico, and I had the pleasure and good fortune of dancing our graduation waltz with her. I was convinced then, that her great interest was to dance the waltz well and enjoy her graduation exercises, then go on with her life, unencumbered. I remembered a pet comment always uttered by a female member of Teacher Reice's 'private class:' "Opportunity comes but once. Hold on to it and don't let it go." Well, this was my opportunity and I had no intention to let go of it. I was not going to allow her to just go off into the sunset, unencumbered. So I launched my campaign that very graduation evening and the first victory obtained was her permission to visit her at her home the next afternoon. There I met her foster father who was a loyal old Manchesterian and who had never lost his love for things and people Manchesterian. It turned out that, as a small boy, he knew my home district, my grandfather and my great aunt, and he commented that my grandfather was 'such a nice young man.'

All this made the playing field even more level and I pressed on with my suit. The letters passing between Maidstone and Allman Town, where she resided, became more and more frequent. At home I was convinced that people understood that I simply wanted some fresh air and needed to get out at intervals - that they would not know that there was another vital interest. When I said that I needed to upgrade my qualifications and the facilities for such studies were much more available in the city, I thought that this explanation for my more and more frequent visits to the city was foolproof. Then the shocker came. On October's month end, just after my birthday, I took my trip to Kingston. I returned home on Sunday evening. On Monday evening, just before nightfall, as I returned home from school, I met Miss Ruth, a close neighbour who had just ended a visit with my mother. As she came close to me, she said, "Den, Mas Keith, I hear you just come back from town. How is the young lady and when you going to bring 'er down 'ere to show wi?" I was dumbfounded. How did she know? Sometime later, when I had got over my surprise and some embarrassment, I had to remind myself, 'Mas Keith, maybe you are not as smart as you think you are, and you certainly underestimated the worldly wisdom of your district folks'.

With my coming into Kingston, the romance grew abundantly and by the end of 1956 we were seriously considering getting hitched. I loved and adored this young lady, Vinnette, and on June 29, 1957, we were married.

She brought into my life humour and laughter, beauty and grace, music and a great respect for the finer arts. Our young household was one where music occupied a special place. She played the piano competently while her father did his bit with the piano and violin. Many were the duets which resulted and which soothed the ear of many a passerby and neighbour. Vinnette delighted in choral work and she never failed to train student choirs wherever she worked and her groups always performed with honours in the music competitions of the period. In addition, she sang with one or two well known Corporate Area choirs, and then for many years with the St. Andrew Singers, led by her former music tutor at Shortwood, Mr. Lloyd Hall.

Vinnette was one of the early serious fans of Louise Bennett and ably performed some of her dialect pieces at various social occasions. She never tires in telling of that occasion, when she did two pieces from Miss Lou's poems and the popular and well- liked Governor, Sir Hugh Foot, was so impressed that he walked over to her seat, sat down with her and they had a brief conversation on the intricacies of understanding the dialect. But she was also a great teacher who got the best out of her young charges. She has remained a humble and sincere friend to so many; and to cap it all, her housekeeping was immaculate, and the food which came from her kitchen was unsurpassed. Vinnette has been an ardent Methodist all her life. I have never had even the slightest thought of forsaking my Moravian faith, so when we got married we made a pact that we would share and respect each other's faith; I am comfortable in a Methodist church and she is comfortable in a Moravian congregation. The arrangement has worked beautifully and our two children factored in - the older boy was christened Methodist while the younger was christened Moravian. 'Manasseh' went to the Methodists and 'Ephraim' stayed with the Moravians. Of course, our older son, Paul, was born in early August, 1958.

Our Principal at Windward Road Primary, Mr. Falconer, retired in early 1957 and was succeeded by Mr. H. B. Dixon. Mr. Falconer right away entered, for a spell, St. Peter's Theological College, and was soon ordained as an Anglican clergyman. With Mr. Dixon's coming, we experienced a difference of management style in the administration of the school. Mr. Falconer, the much older man, was more conservative and was sometimes regarded by the younger teachers on the staff as being too soft on certain issues. But he was loved by his students; they knew they would have a listening ear to their problems and that he knew their community intimately. Mr. Dixon was a far more proactive person, and his presence was always strongly felt in the school. He could be impulsive and on more than one occasion found himself in rather warm waters with parents. However, he never lacked faith in his students and believed that they should have healthy fun alongside their labours in the classroom, hence the fun days the school had at Doncaster Beach nearby. Also he did so much to encourage the musical side of the school programme. Though differing in some of their approaches to the management of their school, these two men were good headmasters. They had much to teach the young teacher and I learnt a great deal from them.

But another very significant landmark in the life of this country was the first sitting of theCommon Entrance Examination in 1957, whereby the Government awarded 1400 new places to the country's high schools. For the first time in the history of this island, the children of poor parents had a firm chance to get a high school education. We have mouthed the ideal of "Free Education For All" over a long period of years but we are still miles away from realising it. The new Common Entrance Examination was "Common", open to all, open to the poor and unprivileged. It was a small start but the door was opened. Here was the Government, clearly exhibiting a new political will, beginning the slow and arduous job of righting this wrong. There were great obstacles in the way: scarce financial resources, insufficient classroom space, lack of qualified teachers, poor equipment, age old prejudices, etc., etc. There was the immediate criticism that the 1400 places awarded were too few, but the Government had to start somewhere, and the hope was that in each succeeding year, there would be a substantial increase in the number of awards. Some people questioned why there should be an examination at all, but we had to be realistic. We have limited classroom space and limited funds and we can afford to award only a certain number. How do we then select this number? A just and reasonable examination seemed to be the answer.

Whatever we may say against the system, it was a mighty move in the drive to develop our people via education. This Common Entrance system grew with us, into the present Grade Six Achievement Test (GSAT), a change of name but not of much substance. We still have not reached the goal of secondary education for all our young people but we are making progress, too slowly, but we will not look back. So much tremendous talent in our young people has been unearthed by this drive for universal high school education, and every year the GSAT performances remind us all of the gold mine of talent possessed by our children, just waiting for the opportunity to shine. And so Windward Road Primary found itself in this Commn Entrance field, relentless and most competitive, with entry to high school being the prize. Mr. Dixon, on his arrival in 1958, reorganized and placed my friend, Marjorie, in charge of the group which came to be called 'the scholarship class'. Over the years the school has worked hard and many,

many of her students have won the path into the high schools of this country.

Mr. Dixon laboured on as headmaster until December 1960 when he made his exit. The principalship of Kingston Senior School (now Kingston High School) became vacant and he was appointed to the position. Kingston Senior School was a much larger school and, at this time, was still regarded as one of the prestige schools in the Corporate Area. We viewed it as a kind of promotion for him. We were sorry to lose him but we sent him off with our blessing. I also said goodbye to Windward Road Primary in that same December 1960. I had secured a position on the staff of Calabar High School and would report for work there in January 1961. The school had lost its two male members of staff at one shot. I had spent five good years there - now I would move on, some years older, but a wiser and possibly a more mature man.

In January 1961, I began working as a Junior Master on the staff of Calabar High School. Now it was a well known fact that a primary school teacher in those days, would not normally be able to transfer to high school teaching with his bare Teachers' College Certificate. He would have had to do some serious upgrading to qualify for such a change. Well, how was it that I was now heading for Calabar? I will have to acquaint the reader with my academic efforts between 1956 and 1959.

One fundamental reason that I gave when I decided to seek a teaching position in Kingston was that I needed to start studying to improve my academic qualifications, and Kingston was the place that would readily facilitate this. Thus, even my boarding arrangements were made with that in mind. Durrant, my old Mico batch mate, and his wife, Marjorie, were anxious for me to stay with them. As Marjorie put it, her husband was ready to begin further studies and she wanted me to come and be his study partner. I agreed that this arrangement would be to our mutual benefit and I took up residence with them. As mentioned earlier in this piece, this was a period of 'study-mania'. Young teachers from near and far were studying and studying, and even some middle- aged teachers were cashing in too. And so Durrant and I ordered our correspondence courses from Wolsey Hall, Oxford, in England. Both of us stuck to the Humanities and so we did not have to chase after science facilities. In the mornings, we went off to work at our schools, and then in the evenings after work, we got to work on our Courses. In my case, I would take my Course lessons to school, and whenever there was the opportunity, at Recess time or at lunch, I would 'snatch a read'. Durrant and I worked very well together and soon we had two Advanced Level subjects tucked under our belts. Our aim was to get our combination of subjects so that we could matriculate and be ready for university entry.

By the end of 1959 we had our required subjects; I had successfully completed four "A" Level subjects and Latin and English Language at Ordinary Level. I recall a bit of embarrassment at the English Language sitting. Here was I, by this time a reasonably experienced primary classroom teacher whose level of English Language command was good and much above the average "O" Level student's. Yet I had to sit in the same examination room, amid a large collection of little more than teenage candidates. Because, at that time, however old you were, however good your language was, and however many "A" Level subjects you had, if you were headed for the Humanities at the University College of the West Indies, you had to have your Pass certificate for "O" Level English Language. This was a must and there was no way around it.

Some years later, after I had gained my Bachelor's degree, this experience came vividly back to me. I was teaching at an eminent high school in Kingston and that school had just employed a bright young Mico graduate to teach "A" Level Economics. This young man was very good though he did not have an "A" Level certificate in Economics. Some months later after he started work there, he came to me with this problem which he said was eating at him and asked my advice. He said that he wanted to secure his "A" Level certificate in Economics but he feared that when he stepped into the examination room, one or two of his present students might be there too, writing the same examination. How embarrassed he would be! And what if he failed? I advised him not to think of any failure, that he actually had much more than was necessary to pass the examination. I reminded him that he could not choose his examination room; he needed that "A" Level certificate and he had to get it. So, go into that room and care not who is there or who is not there, his students or not: just sit and write that paper. When he was through, he should walk leisurely from the compound and head for home. And that was that, and no apologies to any man. And he should remember, too, that it was to his everlasting credit that he was taken fresh from the Mico, without that "A" Level certificate, and sent to teach, successfully, "A" Level Economics to a reasonably sophisticated Sixth Form. He did accept my advice, wrote his paper and easily gained top marks. He did not encounter any of his students in the examination room.

Thus, by the end of 1959 I was armed with four "A" Level subjects and two at Ordinary Level and was ready to join the junior ranks of a high school staff. Durrant had done well, too, and would go off to University in America later. For the next year, 1960, I remained at Windward Road and looked around for a high school teaching job for the next year. Calabar

High School accepted me and I was assigned classes in Forms One to Three. I had already made application for a Teacher's Scholarship to the University College and I knew that my tenure at Calabar might not be very long. However, I began the job with enthusiasm and was determined to give of my best. By this time I had graduated from my dear old bicycle and every morning you would see me chugging along on a light, second-hand motor cycle, from Allman Town where I lived, through Cross Roads, Half Way Tree, down Dunrobin Avenue and through Calabar's gate. I quickly developed a strong loyalty to the school. Calabar had not won Boys Championships for some years, and this year, 1961, it was felt that the school's time had come again. I recall the school's coach, Herb McKinley, making this comment in the staffroom, in answer to a question on the school's chances in the 1961 Championships: "I don't think we have a bad team this year, you know. We should do some good things at Sabina this time."

Calabar went on to win Champs comfortably and great was the celebration in the school chapel on the following Monday morning. I was so moved by that scene on this morning. I wonder if Claude Robinson, then Deputy Head Boy, remembers that congratulatory speech he made to the throng that morning, and the reference he made to that special 'Old Boy''. He said he had been speaking to that 'long, long standing' Old Boy about the victory, and the Old Boy said that in all his long years at Calabar, he had never seen anything like it. Of course all the senior boys knew who was that special Old Boy and what he was 'special' for. The chapel barely contained the resultant laughter. And on that morning I made my vow that I would never, never root for any other school at Boys' Championship, and to this day I have kept my vow. A little later in the year I had the pleasure of meeting the great Jesse Owens, whom coach Herb had persuaded to visit the school and address the boys. As I watched Jesse at the podium I again saw him in my mind's eye, racing on that Berlin Olympic field, now heavier, but not overweight. I reflected on how time moves on. Now, those glory days recede further and further into memory.

Calabar had a mixed staff, male and female, with Jamaican, Caribbean and English nationals. This was my first experience of a staff where unity was not present. There was serious dissatisfaction with the leader's management style and his interpersonal relationships. The senior boys got into the act; the large glass window at the front of the leader's office was broken one night, and sand was poured into the petrol tank of a car belonging to a Jamaican staff member who was thought to be a strong supporter of the leader. At the time, if you were a casual visitor to the school, you would hardly have sensed such a climate, but it was there. I was appalled one morning when I unexpectedly came upon a junior Jamaican staff member roundly polishing off the leader. I remember this staff member saying to the leader, "I am going to see that you leave this school and go back to where you came from." Of course the leader was an English national. I did witness two other occasions when there were sharp exchanges between the leader and staff members, but despite these, I could not complain, personally, of any disregard or poor treatment accorded to me.

As a new junior staff member, I did not have very much contact with the leader, but on two occasions I had to see him in his office and he was the perfect host. He was most approachable, he listened and he was understanding. When I was awarded the Teachers' Scholarship to the UCWI, he was informed early by the Ministry of Education and he summoned me to his office. He heartily congratulated me and enquired what Course I would pursue at the University. When I told him that I was serious about doing an Honours degree in the subject of my choice, he discussed with me the General Degree and the Honours Degree. He warned me that with an Honours Course, I should endeavour not to gain a Third Class degree but to aim at a First Class Honours Degree or at least gain a Second Class. He gave a few tid bits on University life and then sent me off with his good wishes. But he never got on well with much of his staff. The word which went around quietly at the time, never loudly, was that on this staff with which the leader had to work, were two experienced senior members who had applied for that very leader's position but had been bypassed in favour of this English national. In all this, I kept my place as a very junior member of staff. I heard much but I made certain I did not get involved in any of the cut and thrust or lining up on any side. I was there to do a job and I meant to do it.

Chapter Sixteen

My Three Years At Mona

As I said earlier, I was awarded a Teachers' scholarship to the University College of the West Indies and I departed from Calabar at the end of September 1961. Thus I entered the UCWI in October 1961 to begin three years of study leading to the Bachelor's degree. The Ministry had awarded me a Category B Scholarship, which did not allow for the payment of any salary to the Scholarship holder. The Category A Scholarship, provided for the payment of one year's salary to the holder: six months' full pay and six months' half pay. I did make representations to the Ministry, citing that I was married, with one young child and bills to honour, and asking for a possible upgrading of my award to Category A. The Ministry officials were unsympathetic and advised me to hold off until the following year when I quite likely would receive a Category A award. I was very disappointed and felt that the Ministry was saying to me, in well disguised language: "Be grateful for small mercies." But I thought over the matter - no one could guarantee what would happen the following year. Maybe, I would not even get any award. Hence, I felt I could not let go of my Category B award. It would be difficult but somehow I would have to make it. My wife was working, on that 'princessly' Teacher's salary, my boarding and tuition and the cost of some books would be covered by the scholarship and if I lived even more frugally, then I should survive. This scholarship was then worth Three Hundred and Twelve Pounds sterling. I went into residence at Chancellor Hall.

The choice of Hall of residence depends largely on your friends there, and the reports that they pass on to you. I had several friends who had lived in Chancellor and they all painted a wonderful picture of life there. When I arrived with my belongings I was positive I was entering the best Hall on the campus. The early indoctrination was very effective. Taylor Hall was referred to as "that other place." Irvine Hall was a decent place but you did not pay much attention to her. I recall a Second Year Chancellorite from Antigua who, at one point, looked disdainfully over at Taylor Hall and uttered, "Oh, that place over there? I don't go over there, you know." But out of all this in the Halls, the new student quickly builds up a fierce loyalty to his particular Hall, and one may say that it remains with him for life.

There was a certain amount of moderate 'ragging' of freshmen students at that time but Chancellor's Warden, Dr. Francis Bowen, kept a close eye on the proceedings and it was known that he was not enthused with it.

The first few days could also get quite hectic as the hustle and bustle of sorting out subjects and courses and getting registered, plus the whole newness of the atmosphere and environment could be taxing to the freshman. I have never forgotten that morning when I returned to my room feeling so stressed and not very hopeful on a certain matter. That certain matter was my request for a transfer from the General Degree Course, covering three subjects, to an Honours Course, where you specialize in one area. Most of my acquaintances assured me there was little chance of my getting that transfer; it just was not done. I was determined that I had to do the Honours Course, and if that was denied, then it would amount virtually to a death sentence.

That morning, in that state of mind, I threw my window open and stretched out on my bed. I had an eleven o'clock appointment with the Department heads when I would hear the verdict. I decided to just lie quietly for half an hour and then go down for the appointment. Then about five or seven minutes later I heard a bird singing in the tree just outside my window. The Singing sounded so specially sweet this morning, that I got up, went to the open window and peered to locate the sweet singer. There, on a limb on the far side of the tree, sat Miss Nightingale. She must have seen me but she continued to sing. She sang and she sang, like she was singing her heart out. I was transfixed; as a rural boy, I would have heard dozens of songs from birds, but this one was extra special. I listened and drank it all, and then I sensed that my mind was more settled and there was a peace as if descending over me. I did not leave the window until it was time to leave for my appointment. Miss Nightingale continued her song and as I descended the stairs from my room, I could still hear her. As I reached ground floor I stepped out near the root of that tree and looked up again at my dear Miss Nightingale. 'Sing on, my love', I whispered to myself ; "Was it a vision or a waking dream?" I silently quoted from Keats, as the song gradually faded in the distance. Not surprisingly, my interview went beautifully. Professor Goveia was most charming and after checking my marks in the University Entrance Examination, graciously approved my transfer to the Honours History class. On a number of occasions, on visits to Chancellor Hall, I have stepped behind to the back of Block C to have 'last looks' at that accommodating tree which sheltered my 'nightingale love', so many, many mornings ago.

The freshmen of this 1961 intake was a talented and bright set, from all over the Caribbean and Br. Guiana. The Barbadians boasted about their prestige high schools, Harrison College and Cumbermere, the Br. Guianese their Queen's College and the Trinidadians their Queens Royal College. We Jamaicans did not bother to boast as our prestige ones were right here for all to see. But we were really impressed when Barbadian Velma Headley, a Harrison College old boy, told us that his old school had the occasional PhD on its staff. Over the years I keep wondering if a more talented group of young people have ever graced the halls of this our University. The years 1960 - 1964 certainly sent us a great lot of the region's most mighty young minds. So many of them have blossomed and bloomed and served the Caribbean and the world with distinction. Some of them with whom I lived in Hall, some with whom I attended classes, others, male and female, who were of the same time period, come readily to mind.

Members of Chancellor Hall 1961

There was Carlyle Dunkley, Chancellor's Hall Chairman, Historian, later Trade Unionist and Minister of Government. Henry Lowe, final year science student, was serious and focused. He has blossomed into an outstanding scientist, researcher, lecturer and entrepreneur. His leadership of Blue Cross of Jamaica sharply underlines his unswerving commitment to readily accessible health care for all. Barry Wade, another scientist, First Class Honours, was awarded the Silver Musgrave Medal for his work in Marine Biology. He has become one of Jamaica's outstanding environmentalists. Walter Rodney, brilliant Historian, was greatly revered as a tremendous intellect but was not fully trusted for his political views. H.

Orlando Patterson was already practising his research skills and did some research on Hall life and personalities. "Patto," as he was nicknamed, has been one of our brightest sons, Ivy League Professor, very successful author and world renowned social scientist.

There were the Fletcher brothers. Peter became a Professor in the medical field, and Richard, First Class Honours in Economics and Rhodes Scholar, later served as Minister of Government here. Kennedy Simmonds, medical student, later became prime Minister of his native St. Kitts. Ken Dennison, medical student from Br. Guiana is now an eminent opthalmologist; Earl Wright, now prominent psychiatrist with the Ministry of Health; Arthur Geddes, later Government geologist; Alvin Thompson, from Br. Guiana, father of Obadele, the sprinter, later History Professor at Cave Hill; Harold 'Define your Terms' Lutchman, again from Br. Guiana, later eminent Caribbean Economist; and Trevor Munroe, First Class Honours in Economics, Rhodes Scholar, early Communist, University Professor, Trade Union leader, politician and sociologist.

We look too, at Patrick Bryan, another outstanding History Professor and specialist on the Latin American region; Isaac Dookhan, my classmate, another Br. Guianese, author of 'Pre-Emancipation and Post-Emancipation Histories of the West Indies' texts; Charles Thesiger, a beautiful darts player, medical student, later Head of Psychiatry at the University; Ren Holness from Mona Heights, now a great success in the medical field in the United States; and Franklin Knight, irrepressible History student and my classmate, has carved out a large niche in North America. He is a much-published Johns Hopkins History Professor, prize-winning author and journalist and renowned specialist on Latin America. Rae Davis, scientist and educator, retired President of the University of Technology; Wayne Reid, outstanding engineer and public servant, co-head of JENTECH; his classmate Noel DaCosta, outstanding engineer, industrialist and public servant; Edison Gift, Trinidadian, later High Commissioner to Jamaica and noted public servant.

How can one forget Haslyn 'Pinhead' Parris, from Br. Guiana, musician and mathematician, later to become one of Forbes Burnham's right- hand administrators. Lawrence Carrington from Trinidad, a French Honours graduate, and Gordon Rohlehr from Br. Guiana, a brilliant English specialist, have both made enormous contributions in their specialist areas at our regional university. Two other medical men also spring to mind: Orin Barrow from Br. Guiana was an outstanding steel-band man. I cannot recall how many distinctions he gained when he sat his medical finals, but they were many. He has had a distinguished medical practice in Jamaica. Albert Lockhart is an ophthalmologist, scientist, researcher and co-discoverer of a drug for treatment of the eye. Then my two closest cronies in hall: Horace Neita, fellow historian, classmate, sharp thinker and ardent Excelsior man; and Winston Morrison of Kingston College, French Honors student, accomplished Latinist, quiet and reserved, but a stimulating colleague. Both these my cronies later migrated and distinguished themselves in Canadian classrooms. Last but by no means least is Kenneth Octavius Hall, now Sir Kenneth, Rusea's old boy, Historian, Administrator, later Principal of the Mona campus of the University of the West Indies, and a former Governor-General of Jamaica.

These personalities named above, all came from Chancellor Hall, my first love. But that is not to say that the other Halls then, namely Taylor Hall, Irvine Hall and the ladies' Mary Seacole Hall, did not produce eminent graduates who went on to great things. I can think of Robert Pickersgill from Taylor Hall, now Peoples National Party Chairman, attorney and long-serving member of Jamaica's Parliament; Norman Girvan, one of the most gifted of the Caribbean's economists; Fred Hickling, eminent Professor in the psychiatric field; Roy Anderson, my classmate and one-time Taylor Hall Chairman, now a High Court judge; Joscelyn Leo-Rhynie, again my classmate, now a prominent attorney and Queen's Counsel; and Howard Cooke, noted Hall footballer, now a judge of the Court of Appeal. From Irvine Hall came Patrick Robinson, now a respected judge of the International Court of Justice at The Hague, Netherlands; Colin Palmer, another Jamaican and my classmate, now Dodge Professor of History, and widely published, at Princeton University; Leo 'Sheriff' Oakley, classmate, from Montego Bay, man of the Fine Arts, outstanding teacher in western Jamaica who later served as President of the Jamaica Teachers' Association; Cedrick Harper, the 'strong man' from St. Kitts who stayed in Jamaica and served his distinguished alma mater for long years. He now serves as High Commissioner to Jamaica for his native St. Kitts.

The ladies' Mary Seacole Hall also produced her complement of stars. I recall Erna 'Stick' Brodber, who was one from that formidable Excelsior contingent and has well established herself as an eminent historical sociologist, a gold medal novelist and is honoured worldwide. There was Gloria Lanaman, large of physique and brain; Elsa Fairweather, later to become Elsa Leo-Rhynie, wife of Joscelyn and Principal of the Mona Campus for a period; Barbara Bailey, now one of the gender experts at the University; and Ena Campbell, a brilliant French Honours graduate, and Anthropologist, but is better known as an accomplished Spanish translator and Latin America/Caribbean specialist and was University Professor in the United States for many years before returning to her native Jamaica. Daphne Morrison has had an illustrious teaching career and has headed her old school,St. Hugh's, on more than one occasion. Maureen Warner stayed on in Jamaica, later married Garvey Scholar, Dr. Rupert Lewis. She is a well known Africanist and has done sterling work in Creole Language and Culture. Her latest book, "Archibald Monteath, Igbo, Jamaican, Moravian", has been a great success. I also remember Joscelyn Lonque from British Guiana, a perfect lady, consumate pianist and a brilliant French Honours student. Back in Guyana, she has had a very productive career. Oh! 1960 - 1964, a great bunch of young West Indians - and they have produced.

The University College then, was small in numbers. The graduating body of 1964 was the last batch of graduates which would receive University of London degrees, except for some medical students whose course stretched beyond 1964. The University College of the West Indies would gain its independence from London University in 1965 and would, from then, award degrees of the new University of the West Indies. As a small and young university, academic standards were high and the entry requirements were geared to maintain quality inflow. Later as the University grew, features of the North American system were adopted and further growth led to a significant broadening of the entry requirements. We old alumni, may sometimes yearn for the good old days of very high academic standards, but we have to remind ourselves that as we democratize higher education and make it available to more and more of our society, a broadening of those standards will take place. This does not make us any less proud of our young institution of higher learning and we are grateful for the opportunity our generation had, to make good use of its services.

When my undergraduate group began in 1961, certain changes were creeping in, into the English climate of the University College. For example, my class started out attending lectures clad in the undergraduate red gowns, as did some other groups on the campus. Then one morning, about midway in that first term, about half a dozen of my class were strutting down to a lecture with our red gowns over our arms. Then we met Carlyle Dunkley coming up from his lecture, and he stopped us: "What! Are you still wearing those gowns at lectures? No! That is not done." This was a signal for us and we gradually forsook the gowns. None of the University authorities said any word on it and we simply shed them. Among the staff, the wearing of academic gowns to lectures also gradually declined but a few lecturers persisted. I recall a lecturer who had been a Trinidad Scholar in his time and had trained at Cambridge University. He remarked to us that his best years were his Cambridge years and we regarded him as remaining quite English. He kept to his lecturing in academic gown but he was a very good lecturer and you did not dare to miss his lectures.

We of the Department Of History, had a few of the then most eminent figures in West Indian History scholarship. There was Professor

Elsa Goveia, a great scholar; Dr. Roy Augier, now Sir Roy, from St. Lucia, a tremendous Caribbean History scholar and a hero for so many of us aspiring young historians; Dr. Douglas Hall, later Professor Hall, outstanding economic historian; and Dr. Keith Laurence, specialist in 19th Century English History, Trinidadian, later to transfer to the St. Augustine campus. Dr. Arthur Lewis, world economist and later, Nobel Prize winner in Economics, was our Principal for a period. We also enjoyed the services of one or two Fulbright Scholars on short stints from North America.

Life in Hall could be very interesting. It was also a great learning experience as it was still in the early years of West Indians getting to know and understand other West Indians. Jamaica and the Eastern Caribbean are far apart and it was the University which did so much to pull us together. Relationships among these various islanders were very good, and though, here and there, there might have been a comment with a tinge of criticism of Jamaica and Jamaicans, it was always taken in good spirit and with open minds by us Jamaicans. We did not forget that the well-known aggressiveness of so many Jamaicans would certainly not sit well with other West Indians; also we felt that some of our Eastern Caribbean brothers and sisters could be suspicious of Jamaica as a result of how she behaved in the failed Federation experiment. No doubt some would arrive with a not too sweet a taste in their mouths towards Jamaica. But despite these, the relationship among these young West Indians was excellent and we know of so many, many marriages which have taken place. Many of these other islanders did not return home, have settled in Jamaica and have made a tremendous contribution to the building of this young nation.

We also can give high marks to our Halls for feeding us well. The Halls of residence maintained their own kitchens and staffs and served good quality meals to their members. In Chancellor Hall we were served a solid breakfast in the early morning, then a solid lunch at midday. At seven o'clock in the evening, formal dinner was served, and all participants dined, clad in their academic gowns. And, lest we forget, we were served tea or a cool drink, with biscuits, at four o'clock. We ate some great steaks and chicken at these evening formal dinners, and the serving was done by selected students. So you can see that our stomachs were well looked after and no one needed to hit the books on an empty stomach. That three- hundred-and-twelve-pounds sterling scholarship satisfied my tuition and boarding, and at the beginning of each term I received, roughly forty five pounds towards the purchase of textbooks. Today, when I see the vast sums which a University education now demands, I breathe a quiet prayer of thankfulness for being on that road when 'the world was cheaper and less complicated'.

Speaking for myself, living in my University Hall opened my eyes to many things and gave me a wider view on a number of issues. I think back on my early years growing up in rural Manchester and journeying to Mandeville on so many occasions. The few doctors there were all white or near white, and when we had need to consult them, we sat in the waiting room and viewed them virtually with awe. We saw them as living in a different and higher world to which we ordinary ones could not aspire. They were special human beings. If they made a blunder with your body, even a fatal blunder, who would ever think of suing them for malpractice? When I went to University, I slept in a room next to that of the medical student, we mingled in the bathroom, we sat and argued together at the meal table, there was the medical student lying on my bed reading his textbook. One particular young medical student who lived off campus would often come on my floor after a session in the lab and would be reeking of preserving fluid. I hated the smell, but he was my friend and he needed somewhere to rest his legs, so I put up with the disagreeable smell. There were medical students whom I thought were coarse. One medical student's room was so filthy that it was avoided by others and it was said that he would not bathe. But all this is to say that this experience showed me that medical students were ordinary people like us, with our failings and strengths, and living in our world. Sure, they were moving into a prestigious and high- paying field but we had the chance to see them as they were and most were good, normal, human beings and as black or even blacker than I am.

Medical students came in all shapes and sizes, colour and creed, social class, attitudes and peculiarities. I can remember a First Year medical student who seemed to often experienced headaches whenever he settled down to serious study. He lived on the floor below me and I could always hear his tell- tale steps coming up to my room to get his Phensic tablet. I could never make out why he did not get his supply of Phensic since he had a certain dependence on them. Another Jamaican medical student was not much liked. He was regarded as rather rough and somewhat anti-social. But this very young man graduated as a doctor and enjoyed a very successful practice somewhere in the Corporate Area.; a much sought after doctor he was. A third medical student I remember, came from the Eastern Caribbean. He had gained his first degree in science from a Canadian University, and then had gained entrance to our University to study medicine. But he was not very bright and had a struggle with his studies. He was always cheerful, however, and over and over he repeated, "When I flunk out of here, I'll go home and teach." This was so distasteful to us who were teachers and we were sure he had little respect for the teaching profession. He did flunk, as we expected. We don't know if he became a distinguished ornament in the teaching service of his native island.

How well I remember Renison Chung-Kit from Trinidad, a young man whom I regarded as a future great doctor - well groomed and attired, courteous and well mannered, a disciplined hard worker. See him at one a.m. in the morning, pacing to and fro by his room, his fingers moving up and down as he quietly digested what he had just studied. He was always the budding doctor whether he was taking blood from a few of his Block mates, sounding you for your heart beat or pricking some finger tips for some little experiment of his. Yes, medical students were, like us, packed with strengths, failings, idiosyncrasies, peculiarities. And, to cap this all, I skip back to Kennedy Simmonds, distinguished son of Block C, Chancellor Hall, who was soon to sit his medical finals when I entered Chancellor as a Freshman, 1961. He took a Jamaican bride, returned home to St. Kitts, practised medicine, then entered politics, and later became Prime Minister of his country. Hats off to you, Kennedy.

Men and women in Hall had much serious work to do if success was their goal. If an Honours student did not aspire to more than a Third Class pass, then he could do a modicum of work and get his Third Class pass. If he aspired to a First Class, then he would have to work triply hard to attain his goal. But despite the pressures, undergraduates enjoyed their play time. We Jamaicans tended to feel that the Eastern Caribbean students enjoyed their play time much more than we did. In the early 1960's, Carnival was still new to us in Jamaica, and when we watched the seeming abandon with which the Trinidadian or the Grenadian or the St. Lucian jumped his Carnival tune and belted his calypso, we concluded they had certain vibes which we did not have. The Students' Union was open every evening and the student could use the opportunity to unwind, to wet his whistle properly or to have lively conversation with his fellows. Fetes were regular at the Students' Union and many were the students who would never miss a fete. A Jamaican student friend of mine who was doing an Honours Course always commented that in his years at this University, he never, never missed a fete. But, he followed up, he made certain, without fail, that for Monday, Tuesday, Wednesday, Thursday and Friday, he put in a real solid amount of work, so that on Friday evening when he turned up for the fete, he had nothing to regret, and he did not have to worry that he had work left undone. In other words, his conscience was clear and he could enjoy himself. That was a wise balance indeed.

Every now and again, you could witness measures of wild behaviour by young students. Picture the young nineteen or twenty-year-old, coming straight from high school into University and leaving home and the jurisdiction of parents for the first time. For some it was a heady experience, and the immediate desire was to enjoy this new freedom to the full. Generally, after a time, most settled down and became 'good citizens'. They found out that "Vanity of vanities! All is vanity."

Competition between the three Halls of residence with males, in various games, generated a great deal of fun and excitement. The inter-Hall football championship was held for many years by Chancellor and the finals was usually between Taylor and Chancellor Halls. In my freshman year, the finals between Taylor and Chancellor, for me, was an experience never to be forgotten. The preparations and the spirit, the carnival-like atmosphere, the mild costuming, the colours, the merry procession down to the playfield headed by the lone steel pan expertly played by a Trinidadian, the merry laughter and chatter. Oh, poor Taylor Hall! We will give them the usual thrashing but we will not humiliate them. Ah, the match begins and there is a keen tussle. Look at the players' faces; it is like a life-and-death struggle but neither side can find the back of the net. There is Taylor's lanky Howard Cook with the ball up and down, in and around, but he can't score. Then later, sometime later, Chancellor's Peter Fletcher gets hold of the ball and scores. Pandemonium! The game resumes; both sides press hard. Chancellor's Whitelocke in goal stands solid and safe. Chancellor holds on grimly and the match ends: Taylor nil, Chancellor one.

Our procession reforms and we march triumphantly up the hill, back to Chancellor to continue the victory celebration. Interestingly, the following year the football final was between Irvine and Chancellor. In this great inter-Hall rivalry, Irvine had always been, to us, a lesser quantity. But in this year there was a revival, a surge of new spirit, and a strong driving force in this new surge was Leo 'Sherriff' Oakley, the proudest of Irvinites. In this year, 1962 - 63, Irvine dethroned us and it took us quite some time to recover from the shock. There was inter-Hall competition in Field Hockey, Athletics, Darts and one or two other events, but none generated the overwhelming enthusiasm that the inter-Hall football did. It was good, clean fun, we enjoyed ourselves, poked fun all around and when all that was over, we went back to work.

A very pleasant and memorable experience for me at the end of my freshman year was the staging of the historical pageant, "Jamaica, From Slavery to Independence", written by Neville Bramwell, a final year English Honours student, and directed and produced by Hugh Gentles and Peter Maxwell, themselves final year students. It was a fully- University production and presentation and the cast came from undergraduates, tutors and just one or two off-campus personalities. It was a spirited enactment of the Morant Bay riot of 1865 and was presented as part of the 1962 Independence celebrations. It was a real team effort, with tremendous enthusiasm and drive from the whole cast. Noel Vaz, Extra-Mural Tutor in Drama, gave invaluable help in launching the venture. English Lecturer Bill Carr played a prominent part in the cast as part of the white elite, and William Gocking, the University Library head, gave a moving performance as George William Gordon. Bearded Vic Patterson, Architect with the Ministry of Education, effectively played the part of Paul Bogle. Gemmy Morris, a final year science student, took expert care of the dance segments of the production. Sir Roy Augier was the official narrator for the evening. The performance, put on on the grounds of the University College, was well received by an appreciative crowd and we gave a good account of ourselves.

I can well recall that night when, on the way home from the performance, some of us had to travel down Monroe Road, beside a part of Beverley Hills. It was the same night of the opening of the Independence Celebrations at the National Stadium, and we climbed up on Beverley Hills to a spot where we could get a fair view of the Stadium. We were just in time to see the lowering of the Union Jack and the raising of the new Jamaica flag. For us, watching the proceedings from afar, it was a source of great pride. We straightened for our new National Anthem, and as we watched the fireworks demonstration afterwards, we thought of our young nation, full of potential with a good future, given wise leadership.

In tune with the celebratory spirit of this August month, a request came from Morant Bay for the pageant to be presented there. We were all fired up for the Morant Bay staging of the pageant as it was felt that the town had a special right to have a staging done there. We were accorded a hearty welcome by the Custos of St. Thomas, Hon. Isaac Matalon, and in return we gave Morant Bay a stirring show. We thoroughly enjoyed the trip to St. Thomas and playing to that appreciative audience. When our cast, after its two performances, dispersed for our holidays, we were proud that our stage production had made a significant contribution to this period of birth of our new nation.

These experiences opened up, for me, a wider horizon and engendered a greater awareness of the world around us. I think, too, that university experience encourages in one a greater appreciation of the variety of gifts and talents around us and a sincere admiration and respect for quality performance. So many of our colleagues with whom we study, with whom we eat and play and converse, are people of enormous talent and brainpower and we learn to appreciate and honour them for their superior output. I recall a particular student in my Hall, who I was convinced, had the filthiest mouth I had ever heard. Yet, as an intellect, he was an enormous heavyweight and moved away easily with his First Class Honours degree. It was amazing how, after a test or examination, he could unerringly predict what his scores would be. Certainly, he could be most obnoxious, but in the end, we had to ascribe to him the honour which his performances earned.

Chapter Seventeen

The Working Graduate, And Migration To The North

My three years of concentrated reading of History ended in June 1964. My Honours Class of twenty one failed to garner a First Class Honours pass, but copped eight Upper Seconds, some Lower Seconds, one or two Thirds and one failure. It was a good class overall. My classmate, Colin Palmer, always referred to us as "a good class, but rather lazy". Of this class of student historians, I know of three becoming prominent History Professors overseas, two who have become eminent lawyers, (one of whom now sits in the Jamaica High Court), several who went into classrooms here and abroad and, for the others, we have very little information on them. For me, those undergraduate years were three of the best in my life. I had no plans to pursue graduate work then, and I headed back to the classroom. I was a married man with a wife and young child and I had not earned for three years, hence the haste to get back to employment.

I secured a position as history master on the staff of St. George's College, in Kingston, under the headmastership of Father Leo F. Quinlan, S.J., and I began my stewardship there in September 1964. One of the changes which had taken place during my three years at University was the change of the school year. When I entered the University in 1961, the school year began in January. Now, three years later, the school year began in September. St. George's, then, was one of the most prestigious of Jamaica's high schools, not yet co-educational and with an all-male staff. The composition of the school population was striking: a large Chinese group, quite a number of Syrian-Lebanese, a few Jews, a sprinkling of white Europeans and North Americans, and a majority of Negroes. A few students drove their own cars, and some were dropped off by opulent parents. The end of the school day would see a host of cars coming in to pick up well-off students. Very high performance was spread across all the racial groups and no group specially dominated when the prizes were being awarded. The inter-relations between the racial groups was good, and overall, discipline among this large population of teenage boys, was good. The troubles, then, were mostly tricks played in class, attempts to get around teachers, chatter and noise at the wrong time; rudeness, or dangerous aggression were rarely encountered. In fact, at this period in time, St. George's was still in the era of 'peace and love', and quite some time before the onset of violence in the schools and the age of the knife, ice pick and the gun.

Academically, St. George's College was still in its heyday. Annually, it took in a good crop of material from the Common Entrance Examination and these boys had the training and direction of a top notch staff of natives and expatriates. We should be reminded here that St. George's was a Jesuit-led school and it reflected the high quality of academic performance for which Jesuit schools are noted. A large part of the staff consisted of Jesuit clergymen, most of whom came from North-Eastern United States. There might have been one or two Scholastics, who were advanced trainees for the Catholic priesthood and who were doing a period of teaching before completing their theological training. Father Richard Ho Lung was an active Scholastic during this period and gave real glimpses of his future energy. Then there were the young Catholic laymen, also from North-East United States, who, after getting their degrees from possibly Boston College, would come to this school and do a period of teaching. Sometimes, up to three or four of them would be here. Hundreds of St. George's past students of the period, will remember the expert tuition in Mathematics which they received from Mr. Rupley. Mr. Rupley, unlike most of the other of these young men, settled in Jamaica for a long time and gave his expert guidance to many, many boys.

The boys of St. George's College for many years boasted that their school had the best science laboratory in the island, that they had the best science staff of all the schools, and that their Upper School Mathematics teacher, Adrian Chaplin, was the best of the best. The Physics, Chemistry, Biology, English and Spanish areas were headed by highly experienced and dedicated Jesuit Fathers. Old students like Ronnie Thwaites and Trevor Munroe will still sing the praises of Father Caroll, their celebrated Sixth Form History teacher. The Middle and Junior staff had the young Father Lawrence Burke, later, Archbishop Burke, John McKay, later headmaster of Campion College and Ronnie Thwaites, who did a short time there before he went off to Oxford University. A bright group of young Mico men rounded off the faculty. It was a very good staff and the consistent top examination performances attested to that. In these years St. George's College enjoyed a substantial chunk of the top scholarship awards made each year based on examination performances. Staff morale was very high and both students and staff had a tremendous pride in their school and its high place in the educational thrust of their country.

I spent four very productive years at St. George's College and had the privilege of teaching some very talented young fellows. I had succeeded, as History Master, the celebrated Father Carroll, hence when I arrived, I naturally came under close scrutiny from both staff and students. I had grown up on a diet of English and European History, with little Caribbean. When I came to St. George's I did some English History with the Sixth Forms, but the very main fare for my Fourth and Fifth Forms and nearly half of the Sixth Form programme, was Caribbean history. Thus I had to learn Caribbean History. I did learn my Caribbean history well and developed a love and deep appreciation for that section of our History programme. At that time, Sir Roy Augier was one of the pre-eminent authorities on Caribbean history and the Caribbean text that he co-authored with Hall, Gordon and Reckord, was the mainstay of our study material for the Fourth and Fifth Forms. This was some years before the outburst of Caribbean History scholarship. This later tremendous research in this field now provides the Caribbean History student with enormous resources from which to work.

Despite the short resources of those times, we did do consistently well and many of these young historians went on to excel. Dwight Nelson, Trade Unionist, and now Minister of National Security in the Bruce Golding-led administration, was a member of my first Upper Sixth Form group. So was young Michael Nunes Jnr., a very good History student, always earning B+'s for his essays but never worried about going up to the A. Patrick Whittock was quiet and hardworking and later became a successful banker. Down through the years there were other excellent performers whom I can recall. There were the Wilmot brothers, Swithin and Hugh. Swithin is now History Professor at the University of the West Indies. Hugh was a beautiful student in every way, a teacher's dream. He was a top class intellect whom I rate as one of the best three I have handled in my whole teaching career. There were the Williams twins, Chully and Charles, both now prominent attorneys; Patrick Lewis, who always declared himself to be a 'Coromantin', a trickster in class but a good brain; Aggrey Irons, an excellent student and person, heading straight for medicine but produced delightful History essays and Anthony and Fred Kennedy, cousins. Fred became Principal of his alma mater for a period in the early years of this century. Howard Mitchell, now a practising attorney, has made quite a name for himself as a public servant. I remember too, Smedmore Ziadie who always claimed to be a Sephardic Jew, a talented student who became famous later on in matters other than academics. There were many others whom I can't pinpoint now but I always had a good crop of young men who worked well with me and performed mightily. And lest I forget 'Pluto' Shervington, musician from that early period. I could never get it into his head that History could be useful but he has certainly secured his niche, not in the field of History, but in the development of our music.

I look back with so much pleasure on those four years at St. George's, working in a stimulating environment and reaping the good fruits of our labour. Our Headmaster, Father Quinlan, was a great human being, a very hard worker who whenever we urged him to take some rest, would assure us that when he goes to Heaven he will get plenty of it. Father Feres, head of the Lower School, was jovial and a good friend. Father Feeney, veteran head of the Spanish department, was very interested in public affairs. I remember his 'Gleaner' article, 'Jamaica as a Haven', in which he traced the history of Jamaica giving refuge to so many personalities, including Simon Bolivar, expelled Haitian ex-Presidents on their way to exile, Cubans fleeing the Castro Revolution on their way to the United States, and a number of other examples.

There were also Father Bowman (Prefect of Discipline), Father Hennessey, Father O'Toole, Father Heffernan, Father Ryan, (head of the English department). Adrian Chaplin, mathematician extraordinaire and head of the Maths department, old boy of the School, spent his whole teaching career at his alma mater. C.A.P. Thomas, former headmaster of Tichfield School in Port Antonio, also worked in the English department. The boys had it among themselves that when you scored 60% on CAP's English paper, you had done remarkably well; so demanding he was. The younger staff included tireless and enthusiastic Vincent Chin, mathematician and geographer, 'Tabs' Tabois, gentleman of Spanish,'Nemmy' Nembhard in English, 'never absent, never....'; Ren Crawford, Nigel Haye, who later 'deserted' to Kingston College, Eustace Wilson, mathematician and ardent conversationalist,'Step Light' Livingstone, a quiet worker and 'General' of the school's Cadet group The rest of the younger staff were all good fellows and we worked harmoniously together.

Being a member of the faculty of St. George's College in these years meant hard work and the non-stop drive for excellence but there were the lighter moments when staff could relax, especially the lay staff. Some of the Jesuit priests were more extrovert than others and could be very jovial. One of these lighter occasions I can recall, was the visit of the then Governor General, Sir Clifford Campbell, to the St. George's campus. The day had a holiday atmosphere and a cricket match among staff was arranged with Sir Clifford bowling the first ball of the match. Father Bowman, the Prefect of Discipline, opened the bowling for his team. He had a run-up of about twenty yards and generated pace of about a good thirty miles an hour. He did get a wicket or two and he enjoyed himself immensely. Young Father

Lawrence Burke commanded great respect as he sent down his clever leg breaks and googlies. It was a day of great fun for all of us. At one point Sir Clifford had us all ' in stitches' when he confided to us that in bowling that first ball of the match, he deliberately did not send it down at his usual pace and he curbed that lethal in-swinger that he was famous for. He did that because he did not want to take the wicket, first ball, and cause a bit of embarrassment to the team. Sir Clifford enjoyed the occasion so much and made the entire staff very comfortable with him.

When I was about joining the staff of St. George's, I had an experience, the memory of which has stayed with me all these years, and it reminds me that in this life we never know what lies around that corner ahead; you are in the classroom and who knows what that little fellow or that quiet little lady will turn out to be in ten years time? When I applied for the teaching position at St. George's, Father Quinlan asked me to come down to the school, meet him, and then 'Edwin' could give me information on the syllabus and what he had been doing. I could not think who was this 'Edwin'. I duly visited the school, had my discussion with Father, and then he sent me up to the Junior School staffroom where 'Edwin was.' This young Mico man, 'Edwin', sat with me and gave me a full run-down of the History situation in the Upper School, and what he had been able to do. When he had given me all the relevant information and had answered all my questions, he quietly asked me, "Did you do Teaching Practice at Anchovy School many years ago?"

I did do my Second Year Teaching Practice at Anchovy Primary School in St. James some twelve years before and he now reminded me that he was one of my students in Second Class, the class that I taught there. I did not remember him but he refreshed my memory on many details of my stay at his school. Edwin had been to Mico Teachers' College and then taught at St. George's for some time. When the redoubtable Father Carroll left, Edwin helped out with the Sixth Form history. Now he was leaving for the University, and he was being succeeded by his one-time primary teacher. How strangely can the world's wheel turn? You will be pleased to know that this young man, Edwin Jones, had a brilliant undergraduate career. Graduate studies naturally followed and he has ended up as Professor of Public Administration at the University of the West Indies. Edwin has not only been an outstanding academic, but he has served in areas outside of the University and was a member of the Public Service Commission..

The year 1968 saw me making a momentous decision. My father-in-law who resided with us, was advanced in age, and became ill at the beginning of the year. He had to be hospitalised for a short period but his health deteriorated steadily. He died in early April and it was later that

Vinnette and I made the decision to migrate to Canada. We knew that Canada had been experiencing a severe teacher shortage for some years, and a number of our Mico friends who had migrated, kept us informed. Some of our friends had earned their degrees at Canadian universities and chose to accept teaching jobs in Canadian cities. We received reports of how well they were doing, earning decent salaries, buying houses and enjoying good facilities all around. About a year before, we had received reports of a Mico man who had been hired by a Canadian School Division before they had even laid eyes on him; so badly did they need him. So when my father-in-law died and we were no longer tied down by responsibility for him, we made the decision to 'ply our trade' in that northern clime. Our two young sons were joyful at the news and we went ahead with our preparations.

We applied for our immigrant visas as well as teaching permits from about three Canadian provinces. Manitoba was the most prompt and she issued our permits quickly. Where the immigrant visas were concerned, it was a more complex matter and it was much more drawn out. Our plan was that I would go ahead of Vinnette and the boys, get a job for the new school year, then set up house and send for them. But from soundings from the Canadian High Commission I realised that I would not get the immigrant visa in time to start the new school year there in September. I had resigned from St. George's effective August 31 and now I would be jobless for the opening of the new school year here and unable to leave the island without the visa. Here Father Quinlan, that great human being, stepped in and rescued me. He allowed me to continue on staff and assigned me to the Lower School, with the younger boys, for the term. I was so grateful to him. I received that visa in early December and flew out of Jamaica in the first week of January 1969.

I had said my aborted goodbye to St. George's at June's end but circumstances described above, stretched my tenure there by one term. I had served the school for four years and one term. My formal goodbye was done at a beautiful function, a dinner, at the then Flamingo Hotel on Half Way Tree Road, arranged by the Upper Sixth Form history group, for all the Masters who had taught them during that year. It was a tasty and sumptuous meal and a moving occasion. The boys were wonderful and demonstrated such responsibility and maturity. So much of the organisation was undertaken by young Richard Morin, whose family owned and operated the Flamingo. At the end of the evening, the young Scholastic, Richard HoLung, now Father HoLung of the Brothers of the Poor, gave the vote of thanks to the boys, on behalf of the staff members. For me, it was the end of a most rewarding stewardship, not in monetary terms, but in terms of that service given to groups of boys who responded so positively, that comradeship and the stimulation of working in such a community so academically endowed. I ended the experience much richer.

It was on January 5, 1969 that I boarded an Air Canada propeller-driven airliner and headed for Winnipeg. I remember that on the day that I had booked my flight at the travel agent, my face must have clearly showed her that I was a bit apprehensive when she informed me that the plane was propeller-driven. Jet-powered planes were very much around by this time and I had hoped to start my air travels with the new jet. However, she quickly assured me that the propeller-driven planes were just as safe, only that they were slower. Here was I, clad lightly in long-johns which I had purchased in a King Street Hanna store, light socks, long sleeved shirt over merino, sweater, a full suit and a new felt hat, heading into a Canadian prairie winter. I never entertained any fear of this reputedly severe cold - ignorance is bliss. To me, at the time, it would simply be a new experience.

At this point I should pause, and reflect on how I viewed our migration to this north land. I saw myself as embarking on a tremendous, new adventure. Here was I moving into a new and sophisticated society- a great mix of people from all over the world; different customs, institutions, political and educational systems, a huge country with so much to see and learn, and limitless opportunities for travel. For the overwhelming majority of us Jamaicans moving into Canada, the great incentives would be better wages and salaries, better working conditions and opportunities for study and self-improvement. All these I had, but in addition I had a special yearning to be a part of this great civilization that was to be new and different. The historian in me wanted to get at the Plains of Abraham, Niagara Falls, prairie wheatfields, the Royal Canadian Mounted Police and Parliament Hill, see the Trans-Continental railroads, meet the Iroquois and other native peoples and interact with fellow migrants from other parts of the world. From my earlier years of study and with further reading I had built up quite an extensive general knowledge of Canada and I came to regard her as a most desirable destination for the ambitious migrant.

The Canadian High Commission in New Kingston was a very different place from what it is now. They did not yet have their spanking new building, and they occupied rented premises on Trafalgar Road. The atmosphere there was more inviting and far more personal. You were served as if you were important and they wanted to see you comfortable. Nowadays, whenever I have business with them in that new building, after that electronic thing buzzing all over my body at the front gate, and they, as if reluctantly, allow me into that Olympus, I feel merely tolerated. Now I wonder, do they really want Jamaicans in their country?

I find it difficult to be convinced that the absence of even very limited parking space for the public, is not by deliberate design. In 1968 when I dealt with them, the service was so personal, the immigrant officers were so patient and obliging and talked at length with Vinnette and me in their inner offices and not at a window. I remember that particular occasion during the period of the processing of our immigration applications, when the immigration officer informed me that it was highly unlikely that we would receive our visas on time for the beginning of the new school year in September. He patiently explained the situation to me and though I was very disappointed I was not angry at them. When he was finished with me, it happened that he had business to do a short distance away from his building and he walked leisurely with me down Knutsford Boulevard until he reached his destination. Granted, those were far less dangerous and complicated times, but it does say much about the Canadian High Commission of the 1960s.

On the 5th of January 1969, I disembarked from the Air Canada airliner at Toronto Airport. I was lightly clad and had on no gloves, but as I stepped down from the plane I was surprised by the mildness of the temperature. I was seeing snow for the first time and when I had gone a few steps from the foot of the plane steps I bent down and scooped up some loose snow in my hands. As I examined the snow, so much came to my mind - all those poems and stories involving ice and snow that we had read in our school books and anthologies - here was I now gazing at it and holding it 'in the flesh'. I was to learn shortly that this winter was one of the mildest in many years, and Fate would have it that I would arrive in Toronto, very lightly clad, during this mild, mild winter. I was headed for Winnipeg, Manitoba, and so had to change plane in Toronto. I suspected that all immigrants into Canada had to enter the country through Toronto. I had to wait for about an hour before boarding the Winnipeg-bound plane and something significant happened there, before I was in the air again.

When the call came for us to head to our Winnipeg-bound plane, three of us passengers were held up at the gate while the officers there re-checked our documents. Thus, we three were the last to board the plane. I was the last passenger to step into the plane, and strangely, the air hostess could not find a seat for me. All the seats had been taken. I could see that the hostess was puzzled and she went up and down the aisle but could not solve the puzzle. Then she went up to the cockpit area and summoned an older and very elegant lady whom I could see immediately was her supervisor. This elegant lady quickly came down, took my ticket and slowly went down the isle, then she turned and started up again. Halfway up she spotted a young lady and spoke with her for about half minute. Then the young lady got up, took down her hand luggage and smilingly left the plane and I was directed to the vacant seat. I found out she was an employee of Air Canada on her way to her home in Winnipeg. What I never found out for sure was why there was no seat for one who had booked about a month before. Had the airline over-booked or did this young lady, an employee, feel she could simply step on the plane and take a seat? What I was satisfied about was that the supervisor realised that the airline was at fault and this employee had to be 'sacrificed'.

On the plane I sat next to a Canadian lady who told me she was travelling to Regina, Saskatchewan, and she heartily welcomed me to Canada. On landing in Winnipeg, I headed for the YMCA Hostel, where I had pre-arranged lodging for a period. The Hostel was conveniently located in downtown Winnipeg, with male lodgers of all ages, and with me as the lone Black. I was welcomed by the Director who had a nice little talk with me and advised me that the very first thing to do next morning, Monday, was to go to the nearby Hudson Bay Department Store and purchase a good winter coat, an advice which I followed to the letter. The YMCA environment was very healthy. The men were friendly and were always ready to give information and valuable advice. There were three of them, retired men, who actually resided there, who took a special interest in me and never failed to encourage me and make me feel welcome. One of them I specially liked and I offered him my extra bottle of white rum. He was glad for it but he absolutely would not take it for free; he insisted on paying for it. Alcohol use was strongly discouraged in the hostel and I remember when he came to my room to pick up his bottle, he deftly tucked it under his winter coat as he ambled his way down the corridor.

I had my meals at the hostel's cafeteria and was careful to partake of the lower- priced foods as my funds were not unlimited and I was unemployed. I picked up the local newspaper, the "Winnipeg Free Press," every day and thumbed through the job advertisement pages. In those early few days, I operated much about Winnipeg's main downtown thoroughfare, Portage Avenue, and explored some of the side streets in the area. As I ploughed through the rather heavy prairie snow, I thought of the area as being one big white mess, with snow piled up around the business places, offices, residences, the side streets. Oh yuk! But I adapted very well and reminded myself that I would have at least another two months of such before Spring arrived. I could see that Winnipeg was a quiet and conservative city and it fitted into what L. Dudley Stamp had said of it in his geography text, as a grain collecting and shipping centre and railway hub. It was not a great manufacturing city.

I needed to find a job quickly as I had little money and I had to get settled early in order toreceive my wife and two boys sometime in March. I reported to the offices of the Winnipeg School Division No. 1 and was registered as a Substitute Teacher. That meant that if any of their teachers fell ill and had to be absent from work for a day or a few days, then I might be called in to fill in for that sick teacher. The severe winter temperatures took its toll on the teachers, with influenza cases quite common. I received quite a number of calls to various high schools in the city and was paid a stated rate per day. But this kind of employment was erratic and I had to seek permanent employment. I visited the offices of all the school divisions around Winnipeg and filed applications for permanent employment but none was forthcoming. They were all very satisfied with my credentials and welcomed my applications, but always, there were no vacancies.

One good thing which came from this Substitute teaching period was that it enabled me to make contact with about four of my Mico college mates who were teaching at schools in Winnipeg. My first contact was made at a most welcome time and I am convinced that the hand of Providence was active here. I had been out on this particular day on a substitute teaching call and I ended the working day with a bout of flu. I had an early dinner and quickly retired to my room. There I lay in my bed, miserable, lonely and sleepless. Then came a knock on my door and when I opened, there stood Winston Roache, one of my Mico colleagues. I had not met Winston since our Mico days. I had heard he had migrated to Canada but I was unaware that he was in Winnipeg. He had done his degree in Manitoba and had stayed on to teach in a Winnipeg high school. Somehow, Winston received information that I was bound for Winnipeg and that I would possibly be at the YMCA. Can you imagine how glad I was to see him? Sick, miserable and lonely as I was at the time, there could never have been a better tonic for me than the company of another good Jamaican. Winston spent a long time with me that night and told me of the whereabouts of three other Mico colleagues. He also invited me to dinner at his home, with his family, on the next Sunday evening. On that Sunday evening he drove down to the YMCA, picked me up and took me to his apartment where I met his wife and two lovely children. Winston's family and I enjoyed a beautiful home-cooked meal and I had a really happy evening with a healthy and endearing Jamaican family.

In the weeks following I was to come into contact with Vincent Belvett, Eddie Bent and O.T. Anderson, all old colleagues of mine from Mico. All three were well settled in Winnipeg, with permanent teaching jobs in the city. My wife, Vinnette, when she arrived later, found her Shortwood batch-mate and close friend, Enid Mitchell, also well settled and teaching in the city. Enid remained our close and faithful friend for the entire period of our stay in Canada. Over time I met other Jamaicans through the gatherings at the lively Canadian-Caribbean get-togethers. It was here that I met my schoolmate from the hills of North-West Manchester, Irving Dwyer, who worked with the Canadian National Railway. His home became one of my 'Winnipeg homes' and our families spent many, many happy hours together, especially during the later years when we spent our summers in Winnipeg. The Canadian-Caribbean Association catered to people from all over the Caribbean and gave a feeling of home to so many of us.

My first stable job came at the beginning of February. This was a teaching job with the Manitoba provincial government. The provincial government ran a large upgrading Centre at the old Fort Osbourne military barracks in Winnipeg. Here, into this Centre, students, young and up to middle age, from all over Manitoba, were brought for three-month-long Courses. They were offered upgrading in Mathematics, English Language and Biology up to Grade 10 high school Level, and sat an examination at the end of the Course. These were people who wanted to move into better employment and work areas but were held back by poor academic achievement. The government brought them in, paid them a healthy stipend and enabled them to take care of their food and lodging while attending their classes in the city.

It so happened that the officer who headed the project at the Manitoba Ministry of Education was a Trinidadian East Indian and when I took up work there, three Trinidadians were already on the teaching staff. Three of us were interviewed for the job openings: a white Canadian young man, a Trinidadian chap who had just completed his first degree from one of the Manitoba universities, and I. The Canadian took the Biology opening, the Trinidadian took the English Language and I took the Mathematics. I was never very strong at the subject and my Mico classmates would have been amused at my choice. But Biology was not my cup of tea, I was always very strong at English but I never enjoyed teaching it, so I held on to Mathematics. The Mathematics course required here, covered a bit more than basic Arithmetic, much Algebra and much Geometry Construction. I loved Algebra and had always done creditably with Geometry. So I hung on to Mathematics and I was confident that I could take the students up to Grade Ten level. In fact I did quite well with my students and I worked hard. I handled two three-month batches, from February to July and they were all successful in their end-of-course examinations. I liked what I was doing and became very devoted to the work of the Centre.

I found the population of the Fort Osbourne Upgrading Centre quite intriguing. The overwhelming majority were white, there were a few native

Indians and Metis (descendants of French and Indian unions), and I recall one black native Canadian. The staff carried half a dozen of us Caribbean fellows; the rest were white. We maintained a good working relationship among ourselves and some firm friendships were forged. Student discipline was good; the vast majority was focused and took good advantage of this their second chance. But one thing was very striking to me in the early days at the Centre and it took me some time to get used to it. For the first time I was closely involved with so many white students in their homeland. Many of them were imposing personalities, well spoken, men who attended classes in not cheap suits, and women who were immaculately outfitted and impressive. Many drove expensive cars. Yet so many of them, impressive as they may have been, were ranked underachievers where formal education was concerned. As a Caribbean man, just entering that wealthy society, I was really taken aback. This reminds me of the first time that I beheld a white man wielding a pickaxe. This man was part of a work gang doing road repairs on Portage Avenue in downtown Winnipeg. I stood there and I watched and watched. My education was progressing; I was seeing something that the Caribbean plantation slave of the 18th century was never privileged to behold.

I must say here that I moved from the YMCA in mid-January and was boarding with a Canadian lady in one of the middle scale suburbs of Winnipeg. Again, my Mico colleague, Winston Roache, was so helpful and it was he who introduced me to my new landlady, Mrs. Stewart. This was one of the best things to happen for me, for Mrs. Stewart was more than a mother. She was of Irish-Canadian stock, the elderly widow of a United Church of Canada minister and lived alone in a small but comfortable bungalow. There was nothing ostentatious about her or her home. She was completely open and lived a genuine, practical Christian life. Racial overtones were completely foreign to her and she treated me as her third son. She introduced me to her local church, where I was made very comfortable. From her I gathered so much information on immediate local affairs, Manitoba affairs, Canadian history and politics - she was a good and devoted Liberal and in later years when I returned to Jamaica, she regularly enclosed interesting and useful newspaper clippings and other bits of news in our correspondence. Our correspondence never ceased until shortly before her death in 1991. The world had lost a rare spirit, so good and so beautiful.

My wife, Vinnette, and our two young sons, were due in Canada in Mid-March and I had to set about renting an apartment and getting it ready for their arrival. My friend, Mrs. Stewart, gave me useful pointers and helped me to choose. About two weeks before my family arrived, I was safely installed in a moderately- priced two bedroom apartment, a short distance from Mrs. Stewart. I had bought some light winter clothing for Vinnette and the boys and had posted it to them in Jamaica, so that they would be comfortably clad when they met the mid-March Canadian weather. My family duly arrived and I was so happy to be reunited with them. They settled in beautifully, especially the boys who were so intrigued with the ice and snow still on the ground. The family was made very welcome at the Church and Vinnette was drafted right away into the Choir. We made some good friends there and a certain German family was especially kind to us. My ten year-old son, Paul, was drafted into a local junior Softball team and soon became a valued player. Up to then I was very impressed with that little neck of Canada where I was. People were open and helpful - on the streets they readily gave information as to directions. They always wanted to know where I came from and why I chose a cold place like Canada. I felt comfortable among a people who, to me, were not flamboyant, were very tolerant, pursuing their everyday sober business, with little time or inclination to be hostile to the immigrant. Vinnette, though unemployed, was reasonably happy. We hire-purchased a piano and she made plans to do some music tuition in the immediate area. As for our children, Paul was happy at his new school and on his softball team, while five- year- old Rohan or 'Teddy' as we called him, had several little friends on our street and there were the wide and safe sidewalks where they could do their tricycle riding. As for me, I was reasonably happy with my teaching job at the Fort Osbourne Barracks. I had run into many immigrants, a few of them were very interesting people. There was the neighbourhood shoemaker, a German who had fought in World War 2. That German family which was so dear to us, came from Bingen, on the banks of the River Rhine. Our landlord, Mr. Funk, was a Ukranian and very genial. Our family doctor was a Chinese from Hong Kong. I met Swedes, Portuguese, British, Russians, Danes, East Indians, Philippinos and many other national groups. There were the first generation immigrants who would always regale you with amusing stories about the 'Old Country', and tell you about the towering snow drifts of those early years after their arrival in Canada. They were convinced that the snowfalls of the 1960s were far less formidable than what they had to cope with as young immigrants. Their children, the second generation, were full-blooded, sophisticated Canadians and had less time for their parents' 'Old Country' loyalties.

I recall an incident in this early period, involving my older son, Paul, and his school, and which made us very worried at the time. One afternoon in mid-April when Spring was approaching and the snow was rapidly retreating, we received a call from his school that he had not returned after lunch. His mother and I were very worried at his disappearance and couldn't figure out where he could be. He never complained about his school and everything seemed fine with him there. Was he experiencing a problem there and wasn't telling us? In our near panic we contacted the police and a mature-sounding officer endeavoured to assure us that all was not lost. He reminded us that the young fellow was new to the country and so much was new to him that possibly, he might be off to do a bit of exploring on his own. The officer said he felt confident the little fellow would find his way home when he got hungry. If he did not return by nightfall, then we should call them again.

Well, the young man did find his way home. About an hour after his usual time of return from school, he walked in, as innocent as an angel's child. Over dinner we gradually pried out his story. The Assiniboine River flows through Winnipeg and joins up with its senior partner, the Red River, just outside of Winnipeg. The Assiniboine freezes over in winter and my son had heard his classmates talking about the break-up of the ice on the river as Spring came. Apparently he was determined to see some of this ice break-up, with its cracking sounds, and he wandered off to sit by the river bank. We scolded him on his 'french leave' but we were sensible on the situation and I myself later went to see some of this ice break-up. Regrettably, I did not meet that police officer to congratulate him on his practical wisdom and professionalism.

And so Spring came to Winnipeg. After what I had described as 'one great white mess', it was utterly amazing to see how quickly the vegetation came to life as if overjoyed to be released at last. Soon Winnipeg was abloom and I thrilled at the new beauty all around. The lawns were quickly green and immaculate; many of the business places downtown maintained green spaces around their offices and they took great pride in their flower gardens, with the most beautiful flowers. To me, this first spring on the prairies was a wonder. It was as if Mother Nature was reborn and was shining out in all her glory. I fully enjoyed this my first Canadian Spring but I now had to begin thinking seriously of securing a teaching position which paid me a better salary; also, Vinnette was rearing to resume her teaching. My job at the Upgrading Centre went well but the pay scale was significantly lower than that in the provincial School Districts. Hence we aimed to secure, for the next school year, teaching jobs in the provincial School District System where salaries were higher. We sent out many applications to School Divisions all around, in Winnipeg and in areas not too far removed from the city, but with no luck.

What we were now realizing was that Manitoba had got over her teacher shortage and was now trying to avoid an oversupply. We recalled that in April, the Winnipeg Free Press had carried a message from the Manitoba Ministry of Education, announcing that no more one-year grants would be issued to University graduates who had just completed their first degrees and who decided to teach. The Manitoba government could afford to do this as they now had all the teachers they needed. We had entered the Canadian teaching scene about two years late. So we had to settle for a very rural area and we accepted jobs in the School District of Churchill, in Northern Manitoba, on the shores of Hudson Bay. I am reminded of the comments of a Canadian university professor two years later, at a Summer Education Course. He was dealing with Teacher Training and Demand, and he harked back to the years of serious teacher shortage in the province. He said that there was the standard joke at the University that if an individual applied for a teaching job, as long as he could see lightning and hear thunder, he would be hired; so great was the need.

Churchill was Canada's northernmost port, on Hudson Bay and about nine hundred miles north of Winnipeg. It was closed by ice for several months of the year so its usefulness as a port was limited. The Canadian National Railway had pushed a line over a vast expanse of largely barren terrain to Churchill, and the port was also served by small planes, mainly from Winnipeg. Here lived a small population of Chippewan Indians, Eskimos, white Canadians, most of whom were from further south and engaged in a variety of activities. A military base was maintained on the outskirts of the town where military equipment were tested, under the severe weather conditions, by the Canadian and American governments. Many of the workers who came to Churchill were only temporary and few accepted permanent settlement there in that harsh climate. Salaries were generally high as workers had to be given incentives to go there and work for any length of time. All food had to be shipped in and there was no agriculture.

The community had two schools, one, the Duke of Marlbrough School, was operated by the School District of Churchill, and comprised primary and junior high departments. The other school, the Duke of Edinburgh School, established and maintained by the Canadian Federal Government, had junior high and senior high departments. Vinnette and I were employed at the School District's school, the Duke of Marlbrough. She was based at the primary plant downtown while I worked at the junior high level which was based at Fort Churchill, about three miles from downtown Churchill. The Federal School operated at Fort Churchill which was an active Canadian Forces base during World War 2. We lived in Fort Churchill and we rented comfortable quarters in the old army compound. Vinnette travelled the three miles to her school and back on the lone bus which plied between the Fort and downtown. My junior high department was a stone's throw from our residence. Paul, attended the Federal School nearby. "Teddy" was not yet out to school and was baby-sat by a lady who lived a short distance from us.

When we arrived in Canada we had no intention of ever living in such a cold area, but at this time teaching jobs were scarce and we had to eat, nonetheless. So we braved it up to cold, cold Churchill. In late August we packed up our belongings, which included Vinnette's new piano, and much that we had brought from Jamaica. We boarded the Canadian National Railway car and started the long trip to the north. We departed from Winnipeg in late afternoon and would spend two days and two nights on the train before we reached Churchill. The train was equipped with sleeping cars and we were reasonably comfortable. Among the passengers I can recall, were a very pleasant Eskimo young woman and a Hungarian male teacher who was headed for a Physical Education job at the Federal High School. It was travel through hundreds of miles of low forest, then very thinly forested areas, swamps and barren expanses, level land as far as the eyes could see, hour after hour, after hour. The food served on the train was good and the dining car well set out. At last, after such a long railway ride, we glided into Churchill one morning. At first sight the people looked so weather-beaten but we soon got used to their special gait, always bracing against the frequent cold winds. The downtown area was supplied by a large well-stocked general store and one or two smaller ones. Fort Churchill, three miles away, was supplied by another large general store called the Commissary, which dated back to the days of the army camp there during World War 2. Virtually everything one needed could be had there and was shipped in from Winnipeg, about nine hundred miles away.

The liquor stores did very good business as the cold climate and loneliness encouraged drinking. A severe winter could push the thermometer more than twenty degrees F. below freezing point, but people were dressed for the cold and it did not hinder them from going about their business. The typical winter outfit was the thick parka, so made to cover head and ears down to a little below the knees. Underneath the outside workman's parka would be his sleeved merino and warm long-sleeved shirt, long johns and heavy work trousers. With these went heavy socks and winter boots and thick gloves. For the man who worked inside, his equipment was lighter, as indoor heating was readily available. However, if he had to walk a distance to his work or run errands through the snow, he had to be adequately clad. The modern parka was made of synthetic material which was specially adapted and it well resisted the penetration of cold air. Nobody now wore the heavy animal skin outfit of the old North.

We had arrived in Churchill at August end during the short summer and by October we had to be donning heavy wear. Interestingly, when we departed from Churchill at the end of the next June, 1970, we had to be clad in warm sweaters, which reminded us that the summer up there could be slow in warming up. But people adapted well and there was little complaining. A great many of them came up from the southern parts of Canada, attracted by good salaries and other incentives, and intending to remain only for planned periods. Few would become permanent settlers. For many workers in the far north of Canada, it is an area where one can save much money. It is lonely and there are not many attractions to snare away your money. So, for example, if you are a single man and you travel up to the North-West Territory and work there for three or four years, and if you are focused and sensible, you can return to the South with a hefty bank account.

We Morrises adapted well to Churchill's conditions but from the very beginning we made the decision to spend only one work year in this 'God-forsaken, cold place'. We had well heated, well furnished, comfortable living quarters and we did not have to travel much in the severe weather conditions. There was a small Anglican chapel which welcomed us, with a small Sunday School for the boys. We were the only blacks in the settlement but we did not experience any overt signs of prejudice and the students got along well with their black teachers. Our two boys actually enjoyed Churchill and loved to go outside and play in the snow. There was a Pee Wee (small boys) ice hockey team which pulled in the elder soon after his arrival. He learnt to skate quickly and took on nicely to his ice hockey. He loved the outdoors and was always doing his bit of exploration in the immediate surroundings.

Rohan and friend playing in the snow

Churchill is closely associated with the Canadian polar bear as the town lies smack on the migratory route of these beasts across northern Canada. At certain times the bears ventured into the town looking for garbage and scraps, and residents were always warned against leaving garbage outside their residences. A town garbage dump was maintained outside the town limits and the passing bears were encouraged to stay away from the town. The Royal Canadian Mounted Police post was vigilant and monitored the bears' movements when they were in the area.

The Mounties used to go into the schools and advise the children of the bears' habits and movements and how to stay safe. While we were in Churchill, a boy was severely mauled by a bear. It was said that the boy had been tracking the bear and possibly became careless, surprised the bear and it attacked him. The Mounties warned us that as lumbering and awkward as the bear appears to be, it can generate amazing speed and outrun a man on the ice. A bear with a young cub was most dangerous. The port of Churchill does not unfreeze until late Spring and attracts schools of beluga whales which could be seen sometimes sporting in the waters of the bay.

A very good thing I remember about Churchill was the provision made for children's activities. There was the spacious skating rink, well equipped, and the ice hockey club. There was a large gymnasium where floor hockey and basketball were played. Saturday mornings was a very busy time for the youngsters as they could engage in a variety of sporting activities, with dedicated instructors and supervisors. For the adults there were social clubs which were well patronised. Remember, so many of these people were far away from home and were lonely.

My school and Vinnette's, the Duke of Marlbrough School, had a total population of about four hundred. Vinnette taught the First Graders and was excellent at it. Her students were Chippewan Indians, Eskimos, a few Metis and most whites. I must mention here that there was a native Indian village outside the town called 'Dene' Village. This Indian group was not a progressive one. Their houses were dilapidated, their surroundings were dirty and they depended virtually wholly on government welfare payments. Many of them habitually consumed too much alcohol and most were unemployed. Some distance away was located an Eskimo village, called Akudlik. The Eskimo people were more go-ahead, and their village presented a much better picture. But there was no love lost between Indian and Eskimo and they went to great lengths to avoid each other. The Indian and Eskimo children spoke their native tongue at home but Vinnette did an excellent job with those youngsters and the English language. In this school, Vinnette was regarded as a super teacher and the several young beginner teachers on the staff were encouraged to visit her classroom and take note of how she got her job done. Her headmaster was intrigued and spent so much time in her room that she began to wonder whether he was really supervising her or trying to learn as much as possible from her.

Vinnette and her Grade 1 Class

Many are the interesting stories Vinnette tells about these kids in her class - about David Duck, the Indian boy who had extreme difficulty in getting his mouth to form English words; Lanny, the over-helpful little girl, but a dear little soul; and that darling Polish girl, who for weeks did not utter a single word in class - her father even sat with her in class one day and urged her to break her silence, but to no avail. She was clearly learning, but in silence. Eventually, eventually, one momentous day she broke forth and there was no stopping her after that. Her father was so joyful that he invited Vinnette and me to his home and treated us royally. He was so grateful for Vinnette's work with his daughter. Then there was the little Indian boy with the infected ear. Teachers of Indian children every now and again have to deal with this problem. Because of the cold and sometimes inadequate clothing and poor health habits, the inner ear becomes infected. The Indian parent often does not seek medical attention and the child has to carry the problem, much to the discomfort of others around. The smell of that infected ear is most offensive and Vinnette had a difficult time holding her stomach in place whenever she had to get near to that poor little boy. In the end the headmaster came to her rescue and hustled him off for medical treatment.

Author and his Grade 8 Class

In the Junior High section of the School, where I was based, there were interesting times and interesting people. We had a staff of eight in this section and our building was located about three miles away at Fort Churchill. Of this staff, Lou, the Vice-Principal, and the one in charge there, was a six-footer, big and genial but reputed to be unable to hold his liquor whenever he went beyond half-pint. Henry, a World War 2 veteran, taught a small group of Indian remedial students. It was said that for the entire day he never left his seat except to use the bathroom. His class was utterly silent but for his occasional grunts to his students. Russel's great love was alcohol. He never drank on the job but his weekends were often bouts of inebriation. He once, in a drunken spell, threw one of his shoulders out of joint. When he arrived at school on Monday morning, with his arm in a broad sling, he explained that he had suffered a 'muscular spasm'. Mrs. Rendelson was a Dutch woman and had migrated from Holland shortly after the end of World War 2. She told stories about the German occupation of her country and emphasized that they had to become accomplished liars to outwit their German occupiers. Grace Reboff was the Grade 7 teacher. She was in her early thirties and was passionate about the independence of her native Ukraine. I gave her my opinion that there was no chance of her country getting away from the mighty Soviet Union. But, amazing, we have witnessed the crumbling of the great Soviet Union and the Ukraine and other Soviet republics gaining their independence. How I regret I cannot now meet Grace Reboff to congratulate her heartily and apologise for my lack of faith in her country's cause.

We on this staff were so different, individually, but we made quite a good team and we worked well together. I taught Grade Eight, a class of whites and Eskimos. The parents of the whites came from far and near. One boy was from Portugal; about four of them were from parents who were permanent residents of Churchill, and the rest's parents were all temporary and from other parts of Canada. There were about five Eskimo boys and girls in the class. They were quiet and pleasant and were very cooperative. Johnny Patterk's English was quite good and he talked easily. He told me that during the previous winter he had tried his hand at building an igloo but he had failed. This reminds us that present day Eskimos now live in houses built of timber and no doubt much of the igloo-building skills might be on it way to being lost. Simona Issakiarc was my favourite Eskimo student. With her full Eskimo eyes, she was so neat and good-humoured. Towards the end of the school year I asked Simona if she would be going to work when she returned home further north. She looked at me and asked, "Do you mean work for money?" which reminded me that white society's money system and labour ethic were not yet fully a part of their lives.

I must here explain these Eskimo students' presence in Churchill. The Canadian Federal Government is directly responsible for native affairs, both Indian and Eskimo, and native education is one of its main areas of responsibility. Thus a considerable number of boys and girls were brought down from further north to High school in Churchill. These Eskimo boys and girls were boarded at a well-equipped hostel where they were properly supervised and had access to all the amenities. There was the gym nearby with varied recreational activities and one of the most skillful basketball players in the town at this time was Moses Verluk, an Eskimo senior student. In the summer holidays they all returned to their homes, many miles further north.

Churchill in the summer

To most people, Churchill would not be an attractive place to settle and work. But there were people there who were permanent and were well satisfied to spend the rest of their lives there. Such people would always take their trips to the south, usually in the short summer, but would surely be back for the first snow. Some of these people could give much of the Churchill lore and they even had a few notable historical spots to show. They would talk to you about the special difficulties of life in this Hudson Bay port, how they battled with them. They actually loved the place. My family adapted well. Our children enjoyed the snowy conditions but we waited patiently for that school year to end, in order to return to warmer areas. I certainly would not forget the beauty of the Aurora Borealis or Northern Lights, bands or streamers of coloured light sometimes seen above the horizon in these northern latitudes. Oh! So beautiful. Of course it is interesting to note that in those northern areas, in mid-winter, darkness arrives at about 2 o'clock in the early morning. How did this affect the sleep patterns of the residents? The children must have reveled at being able to stay up so much later, or earlier.

And so the school year ended in June and we packed up our belongings to return to Southern Manitoba. We said goodbye to Churchill at the end of June and headed for Winnipeg. It was officially Summer, but we were still clad in heavy sweaters. We again crossed the hundreds and hundreds of miles and after two days and two nights in comfortable Canadian National Railway cars, we arrived in Winnipeg. Disembarking was a motley group of people. Some were teachers who had completed their stints in northern schools and were glad to be out of the North. A few teachers would return north after a long southern holiday. A number would be coming back from very isolated areas, glad to be returning to 'civilization' after ten months of severe loneliness and hardship. Many other workers in various fields would be piling out of these railway cars - so many different people, but all feeling joyful to be back in warm Winnipeg.

Vinnette and I were again unemployed. We had contacted our former landlord in Winnipeg and made arrangements to stay in his apartment block for the summer. From this base we would seek teaching jobs for the new school year beginning in September. We had sent out several applications but without success and by the midpoint of the holidays we were getting quite anxious. Then, one sunny day, as I walked in a section of downtown Winnipeg I came upon an office of the Department of Indian Affairs and Northern Development. A year ago I had met a Mico friend who was teaching in an Indian school, north of Winnipeg, and he had informed me that there were three other Mico men who were employed in Indian schools in Manitoba. Indian schools were usually small, tucked away on Reserves and were sometimes poorly supported by the Indians themselves. Many were in the far north and very isolated. However, we needed jobs and I stepped into the office and enquired. The officer quickly responded and brought out his school list, pointing to a school which needed a Principal and one or two other teachers.

Then he gave me a run-down on the school itself. It was as far north as Churchill, but much more isolated, with no roads going in, and the only contact was by small aircraft. All goods and people went in and out via these little planes. Mail might come in once per month and the nearest clinic was one hundred miles away. The school population was a little over one hundred. But, the salary!! I licked my lips as he spelled it out to me. There was an attractive basic salary, plus a generous Isolation Allowance, plus another allowance. It would all add up to hefty pay packages for Vinnette and me and I was really tempted. When I went home and told Vinnette of the prospects, she was also impressed by the size of the pay packet but she looked further than her pocket. What of the severe isolation? The nearest clinic was one hundred miles away. What if our children became ill, what kind of medical attention would be available? She felt it would be too risky. I had to agree with her and we dropped the idea.

Some days later I visited the second Winnipeg office of the Department of Indian Affairs and again enquired about teaching vacancies.

They had at this time, openings on two Indian reservations for Principals and other staff members. I chose the smaller Reserve, Lake St. Martin,which was about one hundred and seventy miles north of Winnipeg. A first class road ran from Winnipeg to the small town of Gypsumville, which was about five miles from the Reserve. A good second class road then ran from this small town on to the Reserve. I was satisfied that communication with the outside world was good and there was no question of isolation here. I accepted the position of Principal of this small school of about one hundred and fifty pupils, and Vinnette again found herself in charge of the beginner pupils. We again had peace of mind and settled down to enjoy the rest of the precious summer in Winnipeg. I made visits to Mrs. Stewart, my Canadian 'mother' and other good Canadian friends we had made during our previous residence in that city. Then there was that small colony of Jamaicans there and we had some good times at our social occasions at the Canadian-Caribbean Association's get-togethers. Our two sons were happy and the community and the local United Church of Canada congregation organized interesting summer activities for the children. On the Canadian prairies the winters are long and the summers are short and the people endeavoured to make the best use of this warm period, both at work and at play.

The parks and scenic areas were attractive and well maintained, there were holiday trips to various distant parts of the province and country, there were the many lakes and big rivers, summer Sunday evening short cruises by paddle steamer on the Red River, well-received plays staged by drama groups at open-air theatres in the parks and there were ethnic occasions like the Icelandic Festival, the Indian Days and the German festival. The Ukrainians and West Indians also had their festive days. All these festive occasions were in the precious summer and people made the most of it. Our family inevitably took up this spirit. And you must be reminded that Winnipeg was a real melting pot with people from all the continents, with native Indians and Eskimos as well; all these peoples living together in peace and harmony.

Chapter Eighteen

Life On The Indian Reservation

As the end of summer approached I made ready to embark on my new job as Principal of the Lake St. Martin Indian School. We again packed up our possessions and shipped them to the Reserve via a trucking company which operated between Winnipeg and the region around Gypsumville, the small town lying a short distance from the Reserve. We arrived on the Reserve about a week before the beginning of school and were able to settle in reasonably and get acquainted with the Chief and other Indian parents. There was no gushing welcome from the Indians. That was not their way; they were quiet and reserved and would patiently wait to assess these strangers and decide if they deserved their confidence.

The Lake St. Martin Indian Reservation, by Canadian standards, was a small one, about three square miles in area. It was located beside the Lake St. Martin, one of the several considerable lakes that Manitoba was blessed with. The population was about four hundred Indians of the Saulteaux (Sow-toe) group, some of whom did a bit of fishing and ranching. Many of them were unemployed and depended on government welfare cheques. The administration of the Reserve was headed by an elected Chief but there was some oversight by the Department of Indian Affairs. Native education was the responsibility of this federal government department and the Reserve's educational operation was controlled by the Federal authorities. Thus, we teachers on the Reserve were employees of the Canadian Federal Government and not of the province of Manitoba. We note here that by this time, the early 1970's, a few of the more advanced Reserves were being allowed to take control of their primary education, but were still funded by the Federal Government.

Most of the Manitoba Reserves were relatively small, resulting in generally small school populations. The federal government pumped a lot of money into Indian education, often getting less than good results. Regular school attendance was sometimes a problem on some Reserves as some Indian parents were still not yet convinced of the usefulness of the white man's education. On my Reserve, school attendance was good overall, and there were only a few delinquents whom I had to hunt down. But there was some progress for the Canadian Indian. More Indians were going into the nation's high schools. There were now Indian medical doctors, lawyers, and others who had made good in various other fields. The Canadian Indian still had serious problems but there was some move forward by him.

Before we assumed duties at Lake St. Martin, all the new teachers recruited for the Manitoba Indian schools were called to a two-day orientation session, organized in Winnipeg by the Department of Indian Affairs. Here we met officers of the Department and other personalities who had much experience with working in Indian communities and came to know much about the Indian way of life. They lectured us on cultural differences, the Indian approach to education, the Indian child and his growth and learning, and gave advice on special problems of the Indians and general hints on developing an everyday relationship with him. We also picked up much literature on the Indians - their history, facts on Indian development and some notable Indian figures of the present and the past. Thus armed, we all now headed for our Indian communities, confident that we would acquit ourselves well.

My house on the Reserve was a trailer unit, quite well furnished and with enough space for my family. Trailers were fairly common in the area and housed many satisfied families, but we would have preferred a solid, permanent house as we were used to. However, we made the best of it and found ourselves in the end, liking it. Trailers were very suitable for people who were more transient and might not desire to put down roots in any particular place. When they became bored or desired to change their location, they could easily wheel their trailer home and have it pulled to any place in the country.

My trailer home which was set at wheel level from the ground, had bundles of hay neatly and tightly packed all around the foundation, in preparation for the winter. This was to prevent the cold winter air from getting in and ascending through the flooring of the trailer. One had to be careful of fire as a flimsy trailer could be consumed in twenty minutes. About two years after our arrival on the Reserve, an attractive single story three bedroom residence was built, as the residence of the Principal and his family. The other staff members were housed in spacious quarters, attached to the two school buildings. The Federal government maintained these residences and ensured that they were well furnished and had curtains and drapes, kitchen equipment, washing machines and dryers. On every Reserve this would be the usual arrangement: the compound with school and teachers' residences together. Over the fence nearby would possibly be the Band Hall where the Indians gathered for their meetings and functions, and also the administrative building. Some Reserves actually had a few local industries e.g. fish curing and Indian craftwork. Our school compound was sited about three hundred yards from the lake shore.

Our school staff was comprised of Santosh, the Kindergarten teacher from New Delhi, India, and Elsie of Ukrainian stock, was the Grade Two teacher. She was the longest serving teacher there and knew the Reserve well. Jake Heinrichs, of German background, was the able Grade Three teacher. He loved working with that grade and could extract so much out of those Indian kids. Fred Larwood, from southern Manitoba, was the Grade Four teacher, a genial and devoted teacher who had his small herd of cattle at his home in the south. John Stewart, of Catholic-Irish extraction, from Quebec, spoke fluent French and was the Grades Five and Six teacher. He was a widower and the oldest of our bunch. John was witty, loved his weekend pints and could pick up a bit of the Saulteaux lingo.

The Grade One teacher was my wife, Vinnette. She had to deal with the beginner students who spoke only Saulteaux at home, but she worked wonders with them. The work was very challenging but she delved into it with a zest that was amazing. Her classroom was always a showpiece and her examiners were always so highly impressed. A great advantage for her was her musical skill which she used to great effect on the class keyboard. I was the Principal and teacher of Grades Seven and Eight, the top grades in the school. Graduates of Grade Eight would go off to high school, either to the small neighbouring high school in Gypsumville or on to Winnipeg. During my last year there, a Grade Nine class was introduced, without an additional teacher, an experiment which did not last for long. Sarah Beardy rounded off our number. She was a full-blooded Indian young woman from the Reserve and served as Assistant to the Kindergarten teacher. This was our team. Vinnette and I were the novices here; all the other teachers had previous experience of working with Indians. But we put our heads together and got down to work.

My job as Principal covered supervising my seven colleagues and the school custodian, teaching Grades Seven and Eight, in winter keeping a watchful eye on the school's heating system and instantly reporting any malfunction, each month reading the electricity meter and forwarding the reading to the Indian Affairs office in Winnipeg, and keeping a strict inventory of the school's and residences' equipment and furnishings and submitting it to our head office at the end of the school year. I had to nurture and extend the goodwill and cooperation of school and community and ensure that our young Indian charges got the best that we could offer. We maintained good relations with the parents and over time we received their near- full cooperation. We learnt to respect their cultural differences; we came to understand how and why their vision of the education that we were offering to them differed so much from ours. We knew that the Indian people harboured some amount of resentment towards the white society we represented. In fact they were a beaten people, their lands taken from them and their way of life crushed. They were herded on to Reservations and their culture undermined. For a long time they were held virtually helpless in this backwater, written off as listless and lacking in ambition. Many Indians found solace in alcohol and over-consumption of it became a common problem on North American reservations.

For a long time the Indian was pushed to the back of the heap and little effort was made by white society to understand him. One comment we heard over and over again was that the Indian's genetic system just could not deal with alcohol, hence his very quick drunken stupor. But the underlying problem was much deeper than that. However, by the time that we took up work on the Reserve, in the early 1970's, Canadian society's attitude to the Indian was changing significantly. There was now more respect for the Indian as a person, and, as said before, the Federal government was putting much more money into Indian education and actively encouraged Indian participation in the planning of the programmes. More advanced reserves were being assisted to take over the education programmes of their schools. A few Reserves even now included segments on Indian history and culture, and Indian crafts, in their local curricula. These small Indian schools were quite well equipped and the Department never failed to fully honour my requisitions for each year's supply.

Vinnette and I were the first blacks that these Indians had encountered. We gradually gained their confidence and they responded very well to us. We quickly learnt their word for 'Black man' and could readily know when they were talking about us among themselves. If you were among a group of Indians, they would talk to you in English but all comments and conversation among themselves would be in strict Saulteaux. They never thought of such as being impolite. The white man complained much about the Indian's work ethic. The white man's life was strictly grounded on 'time' - when he reported for work, when he left at the end of the work day, when he sat down to eat, when he went to church, when he played - it was time, and time, and time. The Indian's culture never had that and when he took up employment in the white man's world, he found it difficult to adjust. He might report for work on Monday, Tuesday and Wednesday but he may be absent on Thursday. For him, what you did not do today, you simply did it another day. Can you imagine the frustration of the white employer who has a tight deadline to meet? In our working with them at Lake St. Martin, we had to be mindful of certain cultural differences and be understanding.

For example, our new young school custodian started out as an energetic and capable worker and we were satisfied with his performance. But then after a few months he began to falter and sometimes did not turn up for work. As Principal, I had to keep a careful log of his attendance, which was submitted to the Department's office at the end of each month, and all his absences were duly noted and reported. Then he disappeared for several weeks. We learnt that he was on a long drunken binge. However, as the response of governments could often be so slow moving, he continued to receive his full pay cheques. The wheels of our Department at last reached him and his pay cheques were now very drastically cut, according to his previous performance on his job. Somehow he just could not or would not see the justice of the Department's action; that he gets paid for the amount of work that he had done. In his eyes he had been most unjustly and cruelly treated and he directed his anger at me. I had reported him, and in his eyes, I had wronged him. As he might have been thinking, since he could not get at those individuals at the top who had stopped his money, get at that individual who was right on spot and who had supplied the information on him. He carried his dislike of me and even warned me to go back to where I had come from. He did simmer down, however, but the Department eventually replaced him. His was a real strange line of thinking - how under heaven could he think that he could stay away from work, without being sick, and just continue to collect his salary.?

But also, how about that young Indian student to whom you lent that book for him to read at home. When the book is due back he does not bring it; he keeps telling you that he will bring it the next day but the book still does not materialize after many days. You press him to bring the book and when he still does not produce it, you begin to question him closely. After a marathon session of questioning and you painfully put together the pieces of information you extract from him, this is the story you construct. He took the book home gratefully and was determined to read it all and bring it back to teacher. But the same evening when the book arrived in the house, our young student placed it somewhere on the floor, as he did not have anywhere else where he could, as he thought, put it away. Our young student's eighteen month old brother was crawling around on the floor and unobserved, he took hold of the book and when he was finished with it, it was in no fit condition to be returned to teacher. Our young student friend is overcome with rage and grief but in his culture you do not tell to an outsider that kind of situation in your home. You will endure every pressure, every punishment from teacher but you will not 'rat' on your baby brother. In so many ways you see that difference of culture and you have to make allowances. When our errant custodian friend was to be dismissed, the

Department was very careful in how they went about it, and ensured that all the due 'processes' were observed.

The Indian students, in general, were ready to learn and moved well with their teachers. I had some promising students whose performance boded well for the future of their people. One of the best student performers in written English that I have ever encountered was a young Indian girl in my Grade Eight group; also, her handwriting was sheer beauty. But, strangely, this same young maiden was one of the shyest of students and always seemed reluctant to use the spoken English sentence. But, to write it, she was a queen at that. Indian students were often very shy, which is a cultural thing with them. They all begin school, grounded in their tribal lingo, and though, overall, they learn English very well, most do not practise speaking it enough. They will write competently, sometimes exquisitely, but often they do not acquire the confidence in using it orally.

At our first Christmas on the Reserve, our staff staged a well-received Christmas concert in the Band Hall. Parents were pleased to see and hear their children performing - singing, reciting, acting in little skits. It was quite a job to get them to speak out before an audience with confidence but we did a reasonable job and it was a good first outing for them, young people who had so little of this kind of healthy exposure. Then there was the big Christmas Treat for the children, to round off the Christmas festivities, made possible by donations from business people from the area and even from far- off Winnipeg. I recall that at the big Christmas party the son of the Chief agreed to dress up as Santa. At the Party the poor fellow was so terrified that he just stood there, all well decked out and physically impressive, but he never said a word and we had to force a smile from him. At the end of the party my five year old son, "Teddy", came to me all disappointed with Santa. "He never even say, 'Ho, Ho, Ho.'" For an Indian, impersonation of Santa Claus would not be an easy job and our staff understood that.

My two boys settled down comfortably to life on the Reserve. They had good Indian friends, wide open spaces and there were wooded areas nearby where they could explore. Accompanied by their faithful canine friend, 'Oddie', their Spring and Autumn weekends saw many a trek on the safe trails. Paul, now an early teenager, attended the small high school in nearby Gypsumville, while 'Teddy', started in the Kindergarten section of the Reserve school. We spent the summer holidays in Winnipeg and they had the chance to enjoy the beautiful parks and get a taste of the many summer activities. I must make mention here of my first experience of Autumn in rural Manitoba.. The Reserve still had extensive wooded areas with pine, beech and birch trees. As the season progressed, there was a riot of colours as the leaves changed in preparation for their fall. I saw for the first time, Autumn in all its glory, as the leaves changed and then gradually fell as the trees prepared for their winter rest. Oh, it was so beautiful and it took me back to those earlier years when I read those pieces dealing with Autumn, from those class Reading Books and from Palgrave's "Golden Treasury'. At last I was beholding the real thing before my very eyes. I had a majestic view of the Autumn vegetation from my classroom window and I made it the subject of one of my art classes with my students. They produced some admirable sketches and I kept an outstanding one with me for many years.

Winter on the reservation

The seasons in this northland are very marked. Eagerly awaited Spring arrived by mid-April and it was interesting to witness the retreat of Winter. The snows melt away, leaving large areas covered with water which soaks away quickly. These areas of water become the playground of thousands of colourful wild ducks and other waterfowl, while the waters last. Then the lakes and rivers unfreeze, the ice melts away and the boats again resume their passage. But it is most remarkable how quickly the plant life recovers; utterly amazing. The flowers are quickly out and the manicured lawns soon appear. The birds are everywhere and singing and one has to feel that joy of Nature resuming its essential life and energy. Spring moves rather quickly into Summer, which can be as hot as in the tropics. But it is a season that is made the most of - school holidays, time for tours and travel both overseas and over the vast country, Summer classes at the Universities, farmers busy with their crops and livestock and the ethnic groups busy with their annual festivities. The Icelanders hold their days at the little town of Gimli, the Indians have their days at Fort Garry, just outside of Winnipeg and the Caribbean groups celebrate theirs at their Centre in Winnipeg. The Ukrainians and the Germans also have their celebrations then.

The area around Lake St. Martin is heavily settled by Ukrainians who grow wheat, rapeseed and other grain crops, accompanied by some ranching. Some still follow the Russian Orthodox faith and a few of their churches could still be seen with their characteristic architecture. In our little town of Gypsumville, all the business places were owned by them and their farms spread all around the town. The big general store in Gypsumville was owned by the Rawluk family, of solid Ukrainian stock. Alec and Dorothy, the parents, became our good friends and their business supplied our needs on every weekend for the four years we were there. Alec's brother, a crusty old farmer who seemed to have had little contact with the outside world, declared that I was not a black, when he met me for the first time. The picture he had in his mind was that of jet- black Africans in tribal regalia or American blacks, hostile and fierce looking, unkempt hair and possibly, in trouble with the police. To him, the Morrises did not fit into those pictures. But we finally convinced him.

We never spent any of our summers on the Reserve but at the end of the school year we would pack necessary belongings into our medium-sized Toyota Station Wagon and roll into Winnipeg town, where we would rent an apartment and stay until the end of August. Many city teachers took off on long holidays overseas and rented their vacant furnished apartments for the period, so we had no trouble securing good accommodation for the entire summer. I took the opportunity to attend Summer School at the University of Manitoba for three consecutive summers, and gained a second first degree, the Bachelor of Education.

Our sons had much to do and enjoy. There were the parks, river trips on the nearby Red River on a historic river steamboat, and there were little trips to well- maintained historical sites, children's theatres and supervised ball games. The suburban local authorities made great provision for the young and one had to admire people's discipline and their peaceful living together, the respect for the aged, the respect for law and order, the care and cleanliness of the environment, very good health facilities, efficient transportation and excellent roads, a good education system and civilized politics. Of course we were living in a wealthy country with ample resources to achieve such high living standards, but we ask: was it money alone which enabled all of this?

Group of Indian students (Saulteaux)

With and the new school year about to begin, we again packed up and returned to the Reserve for the resumption of school. There would be the clean-up of the residences and classrooms, unpacking and distributing the school supplies which had been requisitioned for the new school year and which had arrived before the summer holidays started. The oil furnaces supplying the heating of the school buildings and the attached residences had to be checked and serviced and any necessary repairs done. School resumed in early September and we headed into golden Autumn. We savoured the joys of Autumn but we also now had to prepare for Winter. The Reserve people would now be busy piling up firewood as they did not have oil or electrical heating. Only the Principal's new cottage had electrical heating. Then we had to look to our Winter clothing. Snowfall was usually heavy on the Prairies and winter temperature could fall as low as twenty or more degrees, Fahrenheit, below zero, so we had to be very adequately prepared.

We had to instal studded tyres on our cars, and ensure that the car's heating system was sound or you could end up with a stone dead car in the cold weather. Soon, Winter would be upon us, with four months of possibly heavy snow, with rivers and lakes frozen. The road to nearby Gypsumville was sometimes blocked by heavy snowfall but there was service from a snow plough based nearby, which would quickly clear our way to get our domestic supplies and mail and getting to church. Many of the Indians owned cars and got around handily. Every now and again, after the snows came, one could see a sleigh gliding by, laden with firewood for the Indian wood stove which provided comfortable heating for their homes. The Indians had no piped water and they received their supply from wells. They had a method of packing around their pumps with hay to prevent their freezing, but freezing did happen once or twice, during my sojourn on the Reserve.

Much activity continued during the harsh weather. Work did not shut down and playtime was well used. The Reserve had a skating rink and my older son was an avid skater. "Teddy" gradually learnt to do some skating but he left the Reserve before he became expert at it. Paul was an ice hockey enthusiast and played a good game. In areas where there were adequate gyms and Community Centres, much ice hockey, indoor floor hockey and basket ball were played during this season. There were a lot of pine trees in the woods on the Reserve and we always went out and cut our own natural Christmas tree. The teachers' residences were heated by oil furnaces which were quite old and did break down on more than one occasion. Whenever that happened, the Principal had to rush into nearby Gypsumville and fetch the service-man. Fortunately, the roads were always open but you had to pray that when you reached the town, the service man was not away on a long service call. There was no telephone service on the Reserve. The winter was long and harsh but no one complained or seemed bored by the long cut-off from the free outdoors. To the Indians, and others, I imagine it was simply an unchanging part of their lives and they coped with it in the best way they knew. We should not forget the well- stocked pubs which did a roaring business with the male population. Well liquored-up Indians was a common sight on these very cold days.

But I had experienced five Canadian winters and I noticed that my longing to be back in warm Jamaica was getting greater and greater. Vinnette sided with me in this but my two sons were not in agreement with us in this. They were in love with Canada, they loved its sports and were happy in their rural location. They revelled in their summer activities in the city and eagerly awaited the occasional shopping trip and visits to Caribbean and other ethnic friends. Paul had two very successful summer camps in

North West Ontario and did not want to give up such. On the Reserve he was a good baseball player and was champion athlete in the immediate area. "Teddy" was also a very fair Pee Wee baseball player and was learning to use his hockey stick. In the classroom he had a great advantage over his Indian classmates and was always at the head of his class. So, both boys were happy and had no desire to return to Jamaica at this time.

However, Vinnette and I looked at the situation from another angle. We wanted the boys to have access to good educational facilities and conditions. We wanted to nurture in them a drive for excellence and we knew that on the Reservation there were factors which did not encourage this. At that time in Canada many of the Indians were still not enthusiastic about the 'white man's' education and on the Reserve there was not the drive to achieve. Also, Paul's small high school did not provide an adequately challenging academic product. "Teddy", now nine years old, led his Indian class but his parents were convinced that it was time for him to leave the Reserve setting and get into the Jamaica Common Entrance stream. Paul, now approaching sixteen, needed to get back to high school in Jamaica and we did not see rosy prospects of moving to one of these areas where the boys would be in a good high school system. We could remain on the Reserve for as long as we wanted, but we did not want our boys to grow up there. The pull back to Jamaica became irresistible.

And so we began our plans to return home, after four years at Lake St. Martin Reserve and a total of five and one half years in Canada. In the Easter break of 1974 I visited Jamaica and scouted around for job openings for the upcoming new school year. I landed a position as Lecturer on the staff of Shortwood Teachers' College, while Vinnette got one at Pembroke Hall Junior Secondary School. We could now make final preparations for our return. The tenants at our house here were notified and I now returned to do my packing up. The required resignations to the Canadian authorities were duly sent in and arrangements were put in place with our bank to transfer our funds. In time we engaged a packing company to pack and dispatch our belongings, and at last we were ready to exit the country which had made us welcome.

Our Indian friends on the Reserve organised a big parting function for us and showered us with gifts. Among the items which they gave us was a small album from the senior part of the school, models of a tepee, a birch bark canoe, and a bow and arrow. There was also an Indian jacket and a pair of moccasins for Vinnette, all beautifully decorated and made from deerskin. A very touching moment for us at the function was the presentation of a beautiful tablecloth to us by a very poor Indian family. This family was on the lowest rung of the reserve totem pole and was always

looked down upon by their fellow Indians. We were unaware that we had
found a place in their hearts but they demonstrated it in no uncertain way.
The Indians are usually reserved and undemonstrative but our friends on
the Reserve made it very clear that they greatly appreciated our sojourn
among them and what we were able to do for them.

Then the morning came when we were to say the final goodbye to the
Lake St. Martin Reserve. It was about an hour before daylight, when we
were about ready to drive through the gate to begin our one hundred and
seventy miles drive to Winnipeg. There we would spend some days with our
Canadian 'mother', Mrs. Stewart, before boarding the plane for Jamaica.
That morning a very heart- wrenching thing happened to us. We had
become exceedingly attached to our dog 'Oddie', a very intelligent and
faithful companion and the boys' constant partner in their ramblings on the
Reserve. During our first winter on the Reserve, we had found him, a stray
dog, taking refuge in the hay which was packed around the foundation of
our trailer home. His early response to us showed that he had been badly
treated by his former owner - he was very shy, hung down his head when
we approached him and he had come wearing a close wire necklace around
his neck. Our sons were attracted to him and took charge of his restoration.
He responded very, very well and soon became a treasured member of our
family.

When we decided to leave the Reserve, we undertook to search for a
'good' Indian family which would take 'Oddie' and continue to look after
him. We eventually chose the family of a former Chief, who owned a small
ranch and who had made the point that 'Oddie' would be very useful in
helping to round up his cattle. We were satisfied and delivered 'Oddie' to
him a few days before our departure day. In our family we were all sad at
leaving 'Oddie' and prayed that he would be safe and well cared. We well
knew that it was often said that a stand-out feature of an Indian Reserve is
the multiplicity of dogs present and also that the Indian is not an endearing
dog lover and a lot of these dogs are sadly neglected. But we hoped for the
best for 'Oddie'.

Then came that departure morning; we had packed our last item in our
station wagon and would drive out in another twenty minutes. As I closed
the back hatch of the wagon and turned to walk back into the house, I spied
'Oddie' bounding across the grounds towards me. He had a short piece of
rope around his neck and he was jumping up and around me and 'telling
me' how glad he was to be back home. My heart sank. What was I to do? All
four of us looked at each other, virtually speechless. We decided to pretend
not to notice him and leave the premises as quickly as possible, for we were
in such pain. As we drove out he sat down and watched us, no doubt certain

that we would return in the evening. There was silence in the car and no one spoke until we were a couple of miles from the Reserve. We felt we had let down our trusted friend and would have to live with it.

Several months later we had word from the Reserve that 'Oddie' had stuck to the school compound and had been surviving somehow. It seemed that the former Chief, to whom we had given 'Oddie', made no attempt to coax him back and left him to his fate. Then came a distemper epidemic among the Reserve dogs and 'Oddie' disappeared, most likely a victim of the scourge. When we again settled down in Jamaica, our first dog was named 'Oddie'. He was a good dog, and dear, but not quite as intellectually gifted as the Canadian 'Oddie'. We retain fond memories of our Canadian canine friend. When we received news of his disappearance, it was as if we were saying over and over to ourselves, "Dear 'Oddie', if we were there, you would not have died".

Well, we arrived in Winnipeg where Vinnette and the boys would remain for about a week before embarking for Jamaica. I had arranged to ship my car from Montreal. In my opinion, sending it by rail to Montreal would be far too expensive and I decided to drive it from Winnipeg to Montreal and put it on the ship there. I would then board the plane there and arrive in Jamaica about two days before Vinnette and the boys did. Early one morning I said final goodbye to the city of Winnipeg and took the highway heading east for a journey of about a thousand miles. That drive from Winnipeg to Montreal was a memorable one, covering hundreds and hundreds of miles on one of Canada's main highways, through scenic countryside, on a route which was beautifully maintained. From Winnipeg I travelled up through North-West Ontaria, by Kenora and Dryden, down to Thunder Bay, along the northern and eastern shores of Lake Superior, down to Sault Ste Marie (Soo Saint Marie). From Sault Ste Marie the route continued east to Sudbury, at that time Canada's great nickel processing centre, to Sturgeon Falls, and then the route dipped south-easterly down to the federal capital of Ottawa and then easterly to Montreal.

I drove at a moderate pace, with brief stops at historical sites and well-equipped picnic parks. On the route I slept two nights in motels in Thunder Bay and Sudbury. On the third day I drove into Ottawa, sometime before midday, took a tour of Parliament Hill and had a good look at its Royal Canadian Mounted Police guards in full ceremonial regalia. I took a short walk in the immediate area around Parliament Hill, had a late lunch and then embarked on the final short leg to Montreal. I was impressed by Ottawa's quiet charm, a rather small city, clean, and with life moving at a sensible 'unhectic' pace, a great contrast to big and bustling Montreal. I drove into Montreal in late evening of the third day, secured a hotel room and settled down for the night. Early on the morrow I would locate the docks and get my car processed for shipping to Jamaica.

That night I made certain to get full information on the route to the Montreal docks. I was up early the next morning, started for the docks and had a hectic time navigating the heavy morning traffic. But I finally reached the docks and the shipping company quickly processed my car for shipping. I then had the rest of the day to see a bit of Montreal. I sauntered through a heavily French-Canadian section of the city and there I encountered the first hostility to myself on Canadian soil. I had entered a shop which seemed to have been family run, and asked for direction. The young man whom I addressed, reluctantly looked up at me, with a very uninviting countenance. He had a heavy accent and I immediately opined that he had possibly very recently arrived from French Guiana or Re'union. I had to repeat my question more than twice and he struggled to formulate an answer. He turned to his two co-workers and spoke animatedly to them in French. All three, by their body language, tone of voice, and facial expression, told me that they were annoyed and wanted to see me out of their shop. Why? Was it frustration at their language difficulty? But why take it out on this lone black whose only sin was to ask for information? Maybe they thought it was bad luck to encounter me so early in the morning. All three of them pointedly turned away from me so I walked out of the shop, very surprised and disappointed.

This did not spoil my day and I later joined a tour party from my hotel. The bus was driven by a very good-humoured driver who sang several Caribbean songs on the tour. He had a special enthusiasm for Harry Belafonte and two of his songs. Our first stop was at an Iroquois settlement on the outskirts of Montreal. Here was a progressive Indian group, well housed, and there was much for us to see. These Indians were very light-complexioned, much fairer than the Prairie groups. In fact I met individuals on this Reserve who were so fair-skinned that I would have unhesitatingly declared them white if I did not, for sure, know that they were Indian. Another interesting site we visited was a section of the St. Lawrence Seaway, a tremendous engineering feat and which was proving to be a real boon to the growth and development of Eastern Canada. After making another two stops, the tour came to an end and our tour group was taken back to the hotel. After a short period of relaxation I went to dinner, then showered and turned in to bed for a full night's sleep. Tomorrow I would bid Canada goodbye and be on my flight back home to sunny Jamaica.

I recall that on the second night of my short sojourn in Montreal, I watched a part of the evening news and it presented a short interview with Mr. Stanfield, then national leader of the Progressive-Conservative Party, and a member of the Federal Parliament in Ottawa. This memory constrains me at this point to say something on what I saw of Canadian politics. I did not become a political activist but I did faithfully vote in Federal and provincial elections and became very interested in this Canadian system. As I saw the practice of politics in Manitoba, I was impressed by its civility and common sense. There was the absence of violence and there was a greater level of cooperation between competing political groups. When I arrived in Manitoba in January 1969, Pierre Elliott Trudeau, French-Canadian from Quebec, had just recently been elected as Prime Minister of Canada. He led the Liberal Party, and I heard from so many Canadians, young and old, Liberal and non-Liberal, what a tremendous personality their Prime Minister was. He was highly educated, was a great intellect, an attractive personality and refreshingly different from the normal run of politicians. In short, no one for a long, long time was so well equipped to become the leader of that great nation. The majority of Canadians were in love with this man; also, for the many Canadians who were worried about Quebec's antics and ongoing discontent with the Federal system, Trudeau, a Quebecer and devoted to the Federal system, could be the answer to temper Quebec's separatist aspirations.

We know, of course, that Mr. Trudeau did not kill Quebec separatism. He had to deal strongly with a Quebec revolutionary group's violence in which a French-Canadian Federal Minister was kidnapped and later killed. I can well recall a cartoon at the time in a Canadian newspaper, which showed Mr. Trudeau and the two Opposition leaders in the boat "Canada". Mr. Trudeau was in the bow of the boat, gallantly fighting off the sea monster of Quebec terrorism which threatened to sink boat 'Canada', while in the back of the boat, away from the action, huddled the two Opposition leaders, busily thumbing through their rule book, trying to locate what constitutional rules the Prime Minister should be following in dealing with the crisis.

At this time, late 1960's and early 1970's, the Conservatives were strong on the Prairies and in Ontario. When I arrived in Canada, Ontario and Manitoba had Conservative governments and Alberta began a long period of Conservative rule in 1971. Then in late 1969, Manitoba's Conservatives under Walter Weir, were overthrown by the New Democratic Party, under young Ed Schreyer. This New Democratic Party stood on the Left and enacted wide-ranging social legislation in Manitoba. I recall that my son had surgery and was hospitalised and it did not cost me one dollar. Also, motor car insurance became free. Both of these services were part of the New Democratic social programme.

By this time oil had come to the forefront in Alberta, and the new Conservative Premier, Peter Lougheed, became a powerful voice on the

Prairies. There were a few colourful figures on the Canadian political scene in this early period. One was Tommy Douglas, Federal leader of the New Democrats. Stanley Knowles, also in Ottawa, was widely regarded as the expert on the rules of federal Canadian parliamentary practice. The irrepressible Joey Smallwood from Newfoundland, led that province's government and never failed to constantly voice his concern over his province's slow economic progress. W.A.C. Bennett in British Columbia held sway in that province for twenty years until 1972.

Manitoba political names come to mind. There was Werner Jorghenson from the province's deep farm belt, typical prairie Conservative legislator and very difficult to beat in his seat. Robert 'Bobby' Bend had an exceedingly short political career. I recall that he was elected as leader of the struggling Manitoba Liberals in April 1969 but failed to win a seat in the provincial legislature, in the election which came very shortly after, and he resigned forthwith, that same year. He left politics and quickly took up the position as head of a rural School Division. And, lest I forget, the old but redoubtable John Deifenbaker, former Conservative Prime Minister of Canada, was still in Ottawa, and continued to give his party brass some uncomfortable moments. I remembered that in 1958 he became Prime Minister of Canada, after winning the most massive majority in Canada's political history, up to that time. The magazine 'Readers Digest', soon after, carried an informative article on this new star from the Canadian West and compared him to a fresh new wind blowing from over the Prairies.

I think the early 1970's, when I settled down in the Canadian West, was a striking period in the region's political history. The old parties were being shaken up, as seen in the coming to power of the New Democratic Party in Manitoba, Saskatchewan and British Columbia.. The Left at last had a chance to enact long- called-for social legislation and the working man could now feel that he was getting a decent piece of the national pie. It was on my arrival in Manitoba that I first heard of a political party called the Social Credit Party, which formed the provincial governments of Alberta and British Columbia. This was a conservative, populist political movement which came out of the great hardships of the West, as a result of the Great Depression of 1929 and the 1930s. That new party, Social Credit, lost power in Alberta in 1971 and British Columbia in 1972. It had gradually lost strength in the West as the young New Democratic Party (NDP) incorporated much of its programmes and emphases.

In Canada, in former times, the political tussle had generally been between the two great traditional Parties, the Liberals and the Conservatives. They still had a strong hold on the political life of the nation but by the 1970's, there had emerged the strong third player, the democratic socialist

New Democratic Party. My family personally benefited from the Manitoba government's socialist policies but my heart was with the Conservatives. My dear Canadian friend and landlady in Winnipeg, Mrs. Stewart, was a quiet, devoted Liberal and remained faithful to her Party through all its weakness in Manitoba. I really enjoyed watching provincial and federal politics, a practice of politics which eschewed our garrison tribalism, abject voter dependence and senseless violence. At the same time, I was convinced that there was a greater will to respond to the needs of a much more literate electorate. I had seen and read much, and I returned to the Caribbean in July 1974, still a poor man, economically, but richer in a number of other areas.

Chapter Nineteen

The Morrises Return To The Tropics

I was glad to be back in sunny Jamaica. My two sons had loved the Canadian northland and just could not believe I was sane when I decided to return to Jamaica. But here we were and we had to resettle quickly. Our house in Molynes Gardens had been rented in our absence and we now had to do some amount of painting and restocking with furniture and appliances. We had our headaches associated with receiving our shipped belongings from Canada. After all the delays at Customs, the hour came when I was ready to load up and take my things home. But before I could escape from the wharf premises I had to distribute 'tips' to about four workers who claimed to have been of service to me in some way. It was as if they took time off from their duties and waited. They did not ask, but I guess they quietly held that 'the big man from Canada wid di plenty tings' must 'know how tings go and let off some dollars.' Finally, I was on my way home and the chore of unpacking would begin. As for my car, that was another story.

My car had arrived from Montreal in good time and I felt very satisfied when I viewed it in the wharf's parking lot. A few days later when I went to Newport East to pick up the custom duty assessment, I nearly jumped into the sea when I beheld it. The duty on the car was over fifteen hundred dollars, and I was shocked. How could I be paying so much money for my little Corona Wagon? I was positive it was downright wickedness. You will understand that this was 1974 and a thousand dollars was a lot of money then. How I seethed with anger at the authorities and I declared I would not pay the duty. I would let the car remain in that parking lot and in these weeks before the end of the summer holidays I would do everything in my power to get the authorities to revise the assessment. I went back to the parking lot to 'encourage' my car to sit tight for sometime longer and there I ran into a friendly custom broker who quietly advised me to give a nice 'tip' to the watchman on the parking lot, so that he would take a special interest in the continued safety of my car. I did as my custom broker friend advised and it seemed to have paid off; when I finally went to take it off the lot later, it was safe and sound and untouched. But I kept up my defiance until I remembered that the holidays would soon end and my family would need the car. About ten days before the reopening of school, I duly went down, paid the duty and went through the 'rigmarole' to get my car. In the meantime, I had written strong but respectful letters on the 'injustice', to the Ministry of Education, Ministry of Finance and a third agency which I cannot recall at this time. The matter ended nicely for me, however, as a few months later a messenger delivered a cheque to me at Shortwood College, for the full refund of the duty that I had paid. I was elated. After all, the State had a conscience, and I was grateful.

The first week of September came and our family all turned out. "Teddy", was registered at Pembroke Hall Primary School, and Paul started Fifth Form at Jamaica College. Vinnette took up duty at Pembroke Hall Junior Secondary School as Music Teacher, and I began as Lecturer on the staff of Shortwood Teachers' College. I recall that "Teddy" was very intrigued with the dialect spoken by his new classmates and he settled down very well in his new setting. In Paul's case there were two disappointments for us parents. He was expected to continue his French but for some reason he fell away from the language and dropped it after a short time. The second disappointment was in the area of athletics. In Canada he was the champion athlete in his area, but among those folks there, there was not the culture of athletics as we have in Jamaica and he could easily run away from the Indians and whites that he engaged. We thought that with proper training and guidance he would continue to do well. But that was not to be. As he confessed years later, when he turned out for the first few training sessions and noted the talent present, the necessary hard work, focus and discipline, he decided it was too steep a price to pay, and he would concentrate on his academics.

When he dropped out, we were disappointed but we came to the conclusion that he had realised he was no longer in Indian country and that he was not quite as good as he thought he was. He did devote himself to his classwork and performed creditably in his "O" Level examination later. Vinnette dug into her new job as Music Teacher at Pembroke Hall. It was her first job as a Specialist Music Education teacher and she enjoyed it immensely. I recall that she had frustrating furniture problems and had to conduct her classes on the platform of the large assembly area. She had an almost daily hunt for seating for her pupils. She maintained her enthusiasm, however, and two years later enrolled in the Jamaica School of Music for further training in School Music Education. She also rejoined her old choir, the St. Andrew Singers, under the baton of Mr. Lloyd Hall. With Church, School and Choir, she became again well integrated into the life of her community.

The Shortwood College community which I joined, was a staid, focused and hard working one. In this summer of 1974, Miss Marjorie Myers, our esteemed Principal, hired about six of us new ones. These new staff members were mostly younger, which made for a productive mix of young and older. We met there a solid, experienced teaching cohort which included Fitz Gordon in Mathematics; Myra Allen, Linden Neil and Jimmy Earle in Science; Sybil Leslie and Joyce Smith in History, Geography and Social Studies; Ethel Webber, Laurel Stewart and Miss Nicholson (Miss Nick) in English; Ivy Rhone and Madge Daye in Education, and Pearl Ashman as Internship Coordinator. The ever vigilant and perspicacious Miss Ivy White, the long-serving Vice-Principal, kept both students and junior staff in line and the staff clicked as a well-oiled unit. The student body then was possibly above three hundred and hailed from nearly every parish in the island. Discipline among the young women was good - there were sometimes quiet murmurs against the perceived heavy hand of Miss White but she never wavered in her pursuit of high standards for the entire College. Those of us who were new in this field of teacher training quickly learnt much of our craft and coped admirably with our specialist areas.

The students' Teaching Practice season was always an intriguing period. It was a time of learning for both College tutor and student teacher. The inexperienced supervisor learnt what to look for in a classroom and the assessment of instructional performance, instructional equipment and overall management of a teaching situation. To be a teacher's teacher, he or she had to learn fast and thoroughly. Students needed much guidance in planning and presenting lessons, writing up lesson plans, choosing and making instructional aids, properly writing up and hanging charts, the use of language in all this, chalkboard organisation and presentation and classroom discipline. Thus, there was so much that was involved in the proper preparation and training of the young trainee teacher and the Teachers' College tutor had to be ready, available and equipped to do his or her part in this enterprise. Part of my specialist area, Social Studies, was a relatively young subject which took its ingredients from virtually all the Social Sciences. There was much to learn here and I look back with pleasure on the expert guidance received from my Department head and the Social Studies Unit from the University of the West Indies. Dr. King, Pam Morris and Pansy Robinson were giants in this early period and did a tremendous job in establishing this subject as a pivotal area in the study of Man and his activities on Planet Earth.

This period of the 1970's also saw the operation of the Internship System where the student teacher spent two years in the College classroom and in the third year was placed in schools and closely supervised by special

Internship Supervisors. Shortwood College was assigned the parishes of Portland and St. Thomas for the placement of her student teachers or Interns. Apart from the direct Internship Supervisors, tutors in the specialist areas e.g Social Studies, Mathematics and Science, had to travel to those schools which had Interns preparing for work in Secondary Schools and provide guidance in these specialist areas. Morant Bay High, Titchfield High, Happy Grove High, Port Antonio Junior Secondary, Buff Bay Junior Secondary were the institutions where these Secondary Interns from Shortwood, were placed.

But by this time, there were strong criticisms of the Internship System, even from among the teaching profession, and the critics called for a return to the three- year in-College training. Many of us felt that the supervision of the students who were being prepared for Secondary School work could have been more thorough. The specialist tutors who supervised these students traveled out to their charges once, or at most twice per week, in some cases once per month. Sometimes the schools were quite far apart, which made covering all the schools in a day, very difficult. This meant that the job had often to be hurried, in order to get back into Kingston in good time. These said tutors had to maintain their regular in-College schedule so there was great pressure there. Some of the schools operated on the Shift System and this could pose an additional problem for the tutor traveling from Kingston. A certain tutor had student teachers at Buff Bay Secondary, Port Antonio Secondary and Titchfield High in Portland. That tutor could get only three days, at most, away from his in-College programme. Buff Bay Secondary and Port Antonio Secondary were on the Shift System and this made it more difficult for the tutor to spread his time to the best effect. Then there was that certain year when two rural girls' high schools in mid island, made special requests for Shortwood Interns to join their staffs. These two high schools were in parishes far out of Shortwood's area of operation but the College obliged and sent the Interns. As for supervision by the Shortwood tutors, we don't like to recall. It was just impossible to do much. The College would not or could not pay any mileage for travel to these far- off schools and tutors refused to use their cars to do the job. Fortunately, the Interns involved had been carefully selected and, to their credit, they worked well and their Principals gave them good reports. In time the Internship programme was closed down and the three- year in-College training returned.

1974 and 1975 were active years in the first term of Prime Minister Michael Manley. I recall that early in 1974 he paid a special visit to the College. On one particular morning he arrived, flanked by his press secretary, security and other relevant personages and proceeded to address staff and student body in the assembly area. He waxed very warm and his oratory fully bowled over his audience. However, there was one young lady staff member who seemed not very impressed and remained with a serious countenance through out all the enthusiastic applause. The Prime Minister spotted her and in his own inimitable style, he looked at her and commented, "I see a beautiful young lady over there who is not with us at all." For a few moments he continued to smile broadly at her, and then he concluded, "Don't worry, she'll in time see our point of view," and he launched into his speech again. His presentation was enthusiastically received by the audience and he must have left there very well satisfied with his foray into Shortwood. He would have seen that he had a sizeable chunk of supporters at that institution. His party and administration were very popular and he broke welcome ground in a number of areas.

But as happy as I was at Shortwood I became more and more peeved by the shortages which became more serious as the government's life wore on. Many domestic necessities could not be had and I recall that when my family and I arrived in 1974 we could not secure a tube of toothpaste in the store. Fortunately, a good family friend who had stashed away a few tubes, made a present of one to us. The shortages of vital domestic commodities became even more serious and at the same time there was a rigid clampdown on the free passage of foreign exchange out of the island. Citizens who were traveling out of Jamaica were allowed only a very tiny amount of foreign exchange to meet their needs. The Manley government was losing much support and so many of the party faithful were losing heart at what was widely seen as their party's folly road. I was really disappointed myself and I seriously questioned the motives and direction of the administration I had supported..

By this time many Jamaicans were fleeing the island and I now began to ponder if I had been wise to have returned in 1974. I thought of going back to Canada and even paid a visit to that country to test the waters. I was never a loud party man but I had deep party loyalty and so I became very worried with Manley's stewardship. I was very suspicious of the real aims of certain members of the top party hierarchy. I saw references in the press to "politburo", I distrusted the 'brigadista' programme with Cuba and I thought that an attempt to introduce Communism was a distinct possibility. Many years later, informed commentators, looking back at these years, widely agree that our Jamaican society would not have tolerated any Communist attempt, but at that time, many of us thought the threat was real. Another area which worried me was the new Public Service Commission, with its new chairman whom I personally knew to be a lower string party operative. I had grown up to regard the Public Service

Commission as almost sacred, one of those revered bodies we had inherited at Independence. I saw that body as being made heavily political and being deliberately packed.

I was also suspicious of the greatly increased attention which was now being given to Sixth Form Associations and other youth groups. And the Constitution – why were they so anxious to 'reform' our young Constitution? Oh! Those young lawyers and other over-committed souls who 'tripsed' all over the countryside trying to whip up enthusiasm for the reform of the Constitution. 'Democratic Socialism' was the term on so many lips and its virtues were extolled. I was amused by a certain popular young cleric's enthusiasm about the 'new Socialist Man', not to be found in Heaven but in the new Socialist Jamaica. And how many of our young clergy, then, were carried away by the message of Socialism. Surely, Socialism, on paper, is a glorious system, that long- looked-for answer to the world's economic and social problems. Yet, we have come to learn that its implementation is a very different kettle of fish. They told us that the new Socialist Man will take just enough for his needs, leaving the rest for his fellow men. But Man's innate greed and dishonesty have always stood in the way of realising this ideal. Hopefully, we in Jamaica learnt our lesson well. I was sure that those 'Progressives' of the governing party were bent on policies which could lead to internal turmoil and a violent eruption. I decided that when that eruption came, my family and I would not be in the country.

I had a close friend on the staff at Shortwood and he was even more worried than I was about the state of things in this country. We had many heartfelt discussions on the situation and he constantly bewailed his bitter disappointment at 'what Michael had done to the country'. We put our heads together and diligently searched for a way out of Jamaica. Should we go back to university, abroad? But then, how would we fund such a move? My friend (Willie) even got an offer from a university in the United States, but the United States Department of Labour stood in his way and there was no way around it. We continued to agonize together until a way presented itself, and we jumped at it. Willie had contacts in the Bahamas and one morning he turned up with a newspaper advertisement from a high school in Freeport, Grand Bahama. This high school had a number of teaching vacancies which it wanted filled for the next school year. Right away we sent in our applications and we settled down to wait. I was sure Willie would get a positive response as he was in Science and Mathematics, areas of great demand. I was in the Humanities, an area of much lower demand, but I kept my fingers crossed. We waited, and reported to each other every morning. Then, as we were getting a bit anxious, one particular day I was summoned from my class to take a phone call in the receptionist's room. There, on the line, was the representative of the Anglican Central Education Authority, from Nassau, the body to which we had applied and we quickly firmed up our arrangement.

I was really surprised at my getting a response before Willie but when I reported to him immediately after the phone call, I assured him that his reply would come, possibly the next day. But the next day came and there was no reply, and the next day, yet no reply. Willie was very disappointed and I endeavoured to cheer him up. The weeks passed and then we knew that that response would not come. Willie was so disappointed and I wondered how the Good Lord had been so receptive to my prayers and had answered so mightily, yet He had decreed that Willie should not leave home at this time and should wait another year. I must add here that when I reached Freeport in late August, I discovered that the school had a Science vacancy and I immediately told them of this good man in Jamaica who was available. The school immediately sent for him but by that date it was too late for him to get a release from his job. I am pleased to say that for the next school year, 1980- 81, Willie was eagerly snapped up by a prominent high school in Nassau. He had a very successful stint in the school system there and retired in the late 1990s.

When I informed my Principal, Miss Myers, of my pending resignation from Shortwood, she told me that she was not surprised as she had noticed my apparent restlessness. I verily believed that it had been whispered to her as a few staff members knew of our plans. However, she wished me well and gave me a very good recommendation. I had spent exactly five productive years at the College and I had no regrets, except that my salary remained much too low. Vinnette had completed her Music Education course at the Jamaica School of Music and had returned to her position at Pembroke Hall Junior Secondary to give them something of what she had gained on her Course. However, teaching conditions were a bit harsh there and prospects of any improvement in the foreseeable future were dim. Thus, she accepted a position as Music Teacher on the staff of the Immaculate Conception High School. She was happy there when the call to the Bahamas came and she had to bid goodbye to the Principal, Sister Maureen Clare. She had been at Immaculate Conception High for little more than a term and I felt a bit guilty for pulling her away so soon. I remember that I went in to see Sister Maureen Clare before we left and tried to explain to her.

And so Vinnette and I were hired by the Anglican Central Education Authority to teach in their high school in Freeport, Grand Bahama. Vinnette was hired as the School's Music Teacher, responsible for the Music Education programme of the School, involving planning and establishing that programme from scratch, training the school choir and entering it in the National music festivals, entering students in the British music theory examinations, as also taking charge of the musical part of the annual graduation exercises. I was hired as a History and Social Studies specialist, teaching some World History (which was really Modern European), Bahamian History and Social Studies. Later down the road I taught some West Indian History and even a little of Lower Form Mathematics was slipped in too. My younger son, "Teddy", who had been attending Jamaica College and was in Third Form, went with us to the Bahamas, and completed high school there. Paul, the older, had completed his "A" Level exams and was now employed with a Kingston accounting firm so he did not travel with us, and remained in Jamaica.

Staff, Freeport High School, Grand Bahama Island, Bahamas

Our new school, Freeport Anglican High School, was one of the several educational institutions run by the Anglican Church in the Bahamas. This school was inherited from the Grand Bahama Port Authority a short time before and was getting its first Bahamian Principal when we arrived in the summer of 1979. Several schools served the island of Grand Bahama at that time - there were the Government schools and the others run by the Catholics, the Lutherans and the Methodists. Grand Bahama's development was young and the population was just about thirty three thousand souls. But by this time, the early 1980s, Freeport had become the industrial centre of the Bahamas, with oil refining, cement manufacture and pharmaceutical production. Several other industries were there as well.

This rapid development of Grand Bahama came as a result of the 1955 Hawksbill Creek Agreement between the Bahamas Government and the Grand Bahama Port Authority. In this Agreement, the Government granted fifty thousand acres of land, with an option of an additional fifty thousand, to the Port Authority who, in return, would create a harbour and develop an industrial community. The Government also gave guarantees and wide concessions to the Company, for example, duty free import of certain items and no excise, export and stamp taxes for ninety nine years; also the guarantee of no real estate, personal property or income taxes for thirty years. So the area which is now Freeport, once covered by pine forests and largely uninhabited, was changed by this Hawksbill Creek Agreement. Today, when you visit Freeport, you will see and hear much about the man, Wallace Groves. He was the American financier who conceived the idea of a free port, and led the development of his brainchild. Of course this Agreement created a virtual "foreign domination" in Freeport, and in the early 1970s, certain sections of the Agreement were amended to bring Freeport back into the Bahamian family.

Freeport High School had a population of a little above three hundred when we arrived in 1979. The school population was quite cosmopolitan, with students from Britain, United States, Germany, Korea, Jamaica, Guyana and Barbados, with a staff of several Jamaicans and British, three Americans, one Danish, three Bahamians, including the Principal, and two Guyanese. At the end of the previous school year there had been a heavy turnover of staff and it was whispered that quite a number of the white expatriate teachers took flight when they heard of the appointment of a black Bahamian as Principal. True or false, we don't know the facts. It is to be noted that there were only three Bahamians on the staff in that year: the Principal, the Anglican Chaplain and the Physical Education instructress. It was said then that Bahamians don't bother with Teaching - they go after bigger monies.

The reception we Jamaicans received from the student body was mixed. The introduction of so many Jamaicans, at one shot, on to the staff of this once prestigious Grand Bahama Port- Authority-run school was a bit too much for some students. We could see the suspicion in their eyes and overhear pointed comments. We have to remember that Jamaicans have never been very popular throughout the Caribbean, and some of those students had never been taught by black teachers. So when so many of us arrived, about six of us, they were naturally uncertain about what to expect.

Author and his Form 3 Class

All of us Jamaican teachers had our humourous, memorable and one or two embarrassingmoments, while we settled down with our new charges. I recall the case of a young and enthusiastic Jamaican lady teacher who took over the teaching of English in a senior form. When she graded her first assignment and returned the scripts to the students, they were up in arms. They accused her of giving too low marks and implied that she did not know what she was about. Several black students openly told her that English should be taught by British teachers. This made us wonder if their former teachers had kept them happy with exaggerated grades. We surmised that these students, exposed to so many white expatriate teachers, had come to regard expertise and knowledge as the special preserve of white people - it was as if they had not been encouraged to believe in themselves. One day a middle- aged black Bahamian gardener sat a short distance from me in the courtyard of the Anglican church in Freeport. I could see, from the 'corner of my eye', that he was looking intently at me. After a time he called out to me, "You go through college?" I replied that I had, long ago. He continued, "Then you have a College degree?" Again I replied yes, and he looked at me for half a minute and half smiled.

What was he thinking? Was he amazed that this, his fellow black, from that aggressive Caribbean group, could have done so much? But we have to be understanding of his feeling. The black Bahamians had suffered long under the rule of the white Bahamians (Conky Joes) who had failed to provide sufficient educational opportunities for them. It was when the political power of the 'Conky Joes' was overthrown and the blacks took over, that black educational opportunities were opened up. This was the reason so many Caribbean expatriates were busy teaching in the Bahamas. It would take some time for the black Bahamians to catch up. One morning, a young Bahamian boy came up to me and pointedly told me that his parents had recently hired a Jamaican house maid. Another black student told me that his aunt said that Jamaicans are too pushy and they think that they know everything.

We had our interesting initial period with the white students too. A few of them seemed a bit wary of us at first, as if they were not quite sure our instruction was to be trusted. There was one American teen-aged girl who was very musical and did a lot of work in Vinnette's Music class. She was later entered in the National cultural festival, and during the period of intense practice and preparation for her event, she gave a sort of grudging cooperation to Vinnette. On the day of her event she did her piece very well. Later, when the judge came to give his decision, he gave valuable advice and helpful hints to the contestants and as he was about to announce the winner, this American girl's mother leaned over to her daughter and said to her, "But all this is just what Mrs. Morris had been telling you all along". The girl won her event, and from then on, she enthusiastically held up Vinnette's hand. She was now fully convinced.

At this time the Biology Department at the school was presided over by an English lady expatriate. She was approaching forty and had been at the school for many years. In addition, she was a real hard worker and innovator and the students revered her as 'Miss Biology'. Then, surprisingly to everyone, she got married and left the island to reside elsewhere. A Jamaican young man was brought in to succeed her and step into the shoes of this 'heroine.' He found the initial going very rough indeed. Only gradually did his new students warm towards him and he was able to settle down with them - a striking example of a situation which can arise when the shoes of 'a good man' have to be filled. But I can say that after a while we all settled down and worked beautifully with our charges, who, after the opening period of doubt, saw that we were 'good people' who wanted to do a good job and help them on as best as we could. We made some great friendships, with young, and not so young and we came to see this period in the Bahamas as a pivotal phase in our development as educators.

We settled down to life in Freeport and enjoyed the positives there. There was no income tax, nearly everything was imported from the United States but there were no shortages, good living accommodation was readily available, one travelled on excellent road surfaces and the Bahamas dollar was equivalent to the United States dollar in value. There was easy travel to and from the United States. A United States visa was more easily secured there than in Jamaica; Miami is less than one hundred miles from Freeport and the fare for a return trip was less than one hundred US dollars. One could arrive in Miami at early morning, shop all day and then return to Freeport by eight in the evening. As a Jamaican, though, you would miss the vibrant cultural scene of home - the music, drama, and the depth of the newspaper analyses and the 'sophisticated' media. Bahamian society was far less pushy and aggressive than Jamaica's and there was a greater level of civility than in our island.

And we shouldn't forget that the Bahamian economy was doing very much better than ours, which explains why so many of us Caribbean people were moving into that region of prosperity. While the Bahamian educational thrust was still young and there was not a relatively impressive record, as could be claimed for Jamaica, the school population was far more cooperative and there was the absence of severe disciplinary problems. In this period, a common feeling among us teachers was that a vast proportion of Bahamian students was uninterested in an academic education and was more wont to go after money. But whatever was his great interest he would always remain civil and friendly.

Vinnette and her Form 1 Music Class

My wife, Vinnette, in the meanwhile, was proving a great success in the Music department of the school. She had left Jamaica not very long after completing her Music Education Course, and now at Freeport High, she had the opportunity to plan and establish a fully new Music programme for the school. She had arrived in the Bahamas armed only with a Suzuki Melodian and her expertise. The school provided a new piano very soon after, and she got down to work to build her programme. She had room to innovate and implement ideas that she had garnered at the School of Music.

Her room became a centre of excellent choral work and a good measure of instrumentalization. Her regular classes were most interesting and secured the involvement of all her students. She trained many able solo voices and she was a cornerstone of the annual Music Festival movement in Grand Bahama. Large numbers were paced through, successfully, the theory examinations of the English Associated Board. I did make mention earlier, of that great biology teacher, 'Miss Biology'; here we would have to dub Vinnette as 'Mrs. Music'. Added to these were her services as co-organist at the Methodist chapel in Freeport. She made a tremendous impact on the cultural and educational life of this Bahamian community.

In these groups of Jamaicans present in Freeport, there were the teachers working at the Anglican, Methodist, Catholic, Lutheran, as well as at the government schools. There were motor mechanics. A few worked at the Bahamas Oil Refining Company (BORCO) and the Bahamas Cement Company. A number of women had become wives, married to Bahamian men and quite a number were working as domestics and in other general work areas. We were represented in the Hospitality area. There was one top electrical contractor, an insurance man and at least one top accountant. The great majority of us were on work permits and a few of the long stagers might have enjoyed 'Belongers Status', a status which allowed you to work without the hassle of securing the annual work permit. The teaching segment of this Jamaican community kept closely together and had their occasional party get-togethers. We had the impression that the Immigration authorities pricked up their ears whenever there was one of these parties; possibly they felt that there could be present even one of those Jamaicans who were illegally on the island. I recall that one young Jamaican female teacher, at whose apartment a party was held, was harried by Immigration officers about an hour after the party broke up.

There was also an amusing story we heard circulating in the Jamaican community, of Immigration officers turning up at the door of a Jamaican family sometime one night. The big-voiced mother of the family suspected that the knock came from Immigration officers and she gave out loudly and warlike: "Where is mi 'las that a spen' whole morning a sharpen? If a ever ketch a man out de, a sweep off him neck."[32] It is said that the officers beat a hasty retreat from her door. We never did find out if there were any illegal Jamaicans hiding out in her apartment but that was a glowing example of the Jamaican bravado.

Among all the Caribbean nationals working in the Bahamas, I wonder what was the rating accorded to Jamaicans, in the Immigration officers' log. Overall, we enjoyed our work in the Bahamas and never hesitated to pitch in whenever we could be of extra service, whether at school, at Church or outside in the wider community. Our distinct Jamaican accent readily advertised our nationality, but we were made welcome wherever we went. I remember an experience Vinnette had in a certain flea market in Freeport when she approached a Bahamian lady vendor to purchase an item. My wife wanted the item, enquired the price and then proceeded to 'beat down' the vendor's price. The vendor seemed very amused and laughed heartily at my wife's insistence on getting the price reduction. Our Bahamian vendor friend, still in good humour, finally agreed on the reduced price. As she collected her money, she shot out, "You Jamaican, eh? Jamaican always beat down price,"and she had another round of laughter. As Vinnette moved on, her Bahamian friend called after her, "A visiting Jamaica next summer, you know. I might see you when I come." Some Jamaicans and Guyanese at that time, would not readily identify their countries of origin when asked.. Jamaica and Guyana were the worst performing Caribbean countries then, and I guess they were a bit embarrassed. I had a Guyanese East Indian student in my class, who, whenever he was asked which was his native land, he would always say, South America.

And what did happen to my younger son "Teddy", who accompanied us to the Bahamas? He had completed high school at Freeport High and was now at the College of Arts, Science and Technology, later The University of Technology, in Jamaica. He did not boast about his academic performance but ensured that he left high school with three good subjects: English Language, with a distinction, Physics and Mathematics. We had wondered at his great insistence and persistence with that 'rather dull' subject, Physics. Nevertheless, he slogged and slogged, getting very good grades, and never failed. We never knew then, that he was heading for Electronics and Computers, fields in which he has shone brightly.

It was now the summer of 1986 and we had completed seven years in the Bahamas. We had just completed a three- year contract with the Anglicans and had signed for another three- year period. We collected our

[32] "Where is my cutlass that I spend all morning sharpening? If I ever catch a man outside that door, I'll slice off his neck."

gratuity and headed home for our summer holidays. Midway through our holidays, we had a telephone call one morning, from one of our Jamaican colleagues who was also on holidays from the Bahamas, about a 'sudden dangerous development' for us in the Bahamas. The caller who did not have much detailed information then, told of extensive firings of expatriate teachers, black and white, and there was turmoil among the expatriate community. On Grand Bahama, there were some firings but no names were known yet. Of course we were worried and we made a few calls but not much could be gathered. We sat tight for the rest of the holidays, hoping we had escaped the sweep.

When we arrived in Freeport at August end, we came face to face with a situation, which we came to realise was not surprising, if you worked as an expatriate in an area which depended heavily on expatriate labour. As the story turned out, the Bahamian minister of government under whose portfolio Immigration fell was a rather strange character and he was now determined that the part of the Immigration Law which governed the length of stay of expatriate workers in the Bahamas, should be strictly enforced. Our general information was that the law laid down that expatriate workers who had been in the Bahamas for five years would have to go back to their countries. After a certain period, maybe about two years, they could reapply to return to the Bahamas, and they would be considered. This part of the law had not been enforced over many years, apparently because of the great need for expatriate labour.

Things went on merrily for a long time, then this Minister arrived on the scene and suddenly proceeded to upset the apple cart without any notice. One can imagine the resultant confusion. Workers who had been in the country for many years, now were fired overnight and had to pack up. Some had even married Bahamians and had children. What were they to do? So many negative things were said about this Minister. How much was true, we cannot tell, but one of the stories that circulated was that he would not even renew a work permit for the Jamaican housemaid of his Prime Minister, his political boss; so weird a fellow was he. The knife did not touch our school in Freeport and we were very relieved but we now felt very uncomfortable.

Soon after we started school in September, members of the Anglican Central Education Authority made their customary annual visit to the school and had its meeting with the staff. When questioned about the Immigration situation and the future of their expatriate employees, the Director, who led the team, could supply us with little that was reassuring to us, and she left us still nervous. She kept saying that she knew very little about the new immigration policy, but she thought it to be clear that if we were there for five or more years, then we should not be surprised if our work permits were not renewed. This was wholly unsatisfactory to Vinnette and myself.

The Director's approach gave us the impression that she was insensitive to our disquiet and she did not, in our opinion, even attempt to give us a little assurance. Would the Authority be prepared to put up even a little, tiny fight for its expatriate employees? Vinnette and I remained uneasy and after about a week, we made our decision; we would complete this school year, 1986 - 87, and then return to our home in Jamaica. We communicated our decision to the school administration in good time. The acting Principal of our school urged us to reconsider. He was sure that things would level off and good sense prevail in the end. But we had made our decision and we stood by it.

Interestingly, things did level off and good sense did prevail in the end. In fact all the teachers at Freeport High School received their work permits for the next school year, 1987 - 88, uncommonly early, before they went off for the summer holidays 1987. The immigration clamour had arisen with all vengeance during the last summer. Now, one year later, it had been quietly laid aside and things were back to normal once again.

Chapter Twenty

The Trip To Europe

The end of the 1986/87 school year would see us returning home to Jamaica, after serving eight years in the Bahamas. But before we left that country there was one project we had to embark on and finish before we returned home. That project would be triply hard to handle if we left it for execution in Jamaica, hence we had to see it through before we left the Bahamas. This celebrated project was our fifteen-day package tour of six European countries, July 1 to July 16, 1987. This tour was organised by an American tour company, The American Institute for Foreign Study. Throughout the year, it conducted study tours all over the world and this particular one, Our European Heritage 111, was one of the most popular. It was not particularly expensive. It was hectic but it gave one a quick taste of these six countries that could sharpen the appetite for a full tour sometime later. The summers were packed with these tours and were aimed specially at older students, teachers and other interested adults. They took enormous organisation - lodging in hotels and other places, food, transportation and skilled guidance of the tour. The presence of linguists with the groups is another vital factor. Our tour group numbered about thirty, comprised of a group of Haitians from Nassau, led by a nun, four Bahamians, two Jamaicans in the persons of Vinnette and me and about ten teenaged American high school students, accompanied by their four teachers. We all met together in New York, then we boarded a Trans World Airways airliner and flew across the Atlantic to London. There we met our tour guide, an English young lady who spoke French fluently and guided us to our London living quarters.

The next day, July 3, we were taken on a guided tour of London, taking in St. Paul's Cathedral, the Royal Festival Hall, Buckingham Palace, the Tower of London, where we viewed the Crown Jewels, then on to Tower Bridge. I should say here that the weather was beautiful, and so warm, even hot, that when we stood outside the Palace, waiting for the Changing of the Guard, I had to sidle up behind a very tall man and stand in his shadow to get some shade. On the next, July 4, we drove past the celebrated public school, Eton, on our way to Windsor Castle, where we toured part of the Royal apartments. Ah, Windsor Castle was so awe-inspiring, the royal apartments and the magnificent furnishings, so beautiful. We were also fortunate to see the

Ghurka guards who were on guard duty at the Castle. Later, we visited Harrods store and Picadilly Circus. I was a bit disappointed with Picadilly as I had in mind a much larger place and more exciting. There were so many weirdos on show there, blatantly showing off their sillinesses. We used the rest of this day to do some shopping. These are the comments on London that I made in my travel journal at the time: "The buildings! Oh! Oh! Oh history! The Abbey, St. Paul's - magnificent, awe-inspiring, humbling. How man has built!! Behold and wonder!" I also had comments on the architecture and old grandeur as we toured the wide and narrow streets, the double deckers and passed the weirdos who paraded themselves in Picadilly Circus. London was certainly a feast. I noted in my journal then that it would take weeks to see all that the great city has to offer.

Very early next morning, Sunday, we took off from London. We were headed for Dover, and drove through Kent, through beautiful countryside with its hedged fields. We drove past Runnymede, where King John signed the Magna Carta in 1215. At Dover we boarded the ferry for the trip across the Straits of Dover to Zeebrugge in Belgium. We breakfasted on this spacious and well equipped ferry, and also had a good view of the White Cliffs of Dover. After landing at Zeebrugge, we drove on to Liege, on across the German border and tasted a little of the autobahn. We enjoyed the excellent roads and neat fields, which reminded me so much of that German discipline. We drove on by the River Rhine and also by its tributary, the Moselle. We also saw several old German castles by the Rhine. We bedded at a hotel just outside of Coblenz, and early next morning, Monday, we drove on to Boppard. From Boppard we enjoyed a short boat cruise on the Rhine, to St. Goar. Vinnette collected a pint bottle of Rhine water and lovingly preserved it for a long time after the tour. From St. Goar we motored on through the German countryside, through Bingen, on to the great city of Munich. In Munich we had fleeting looks at the BMW headquarters and Museum and the Olympic Village.

On Tuesday morning after an early and not too satisfactory breakfast, we left Munich and drove to the German-Austrian border. Passing through the border check, we motored into Austria, through great Alpine scenery, by beautiful mountain fields and quaint cottages, along a tributary of the Danube, on to lunch at picturesque Innsbruck, on through the Brenner Pass, with breathtaking scenery, the wonderful bridges and tunnels, tremendous engineering feats. It was here that my faith in Italy was restored. Italy's World War 2 record had made me think little of Italian ability, but here, I was now completely won over to her.

We then moved into Italy, through wine and fruit country. We drove into Venice and checked into the Hotel Lugano a Mestre. After dinner we made our visit to Venice's centre. We took a boat ride up the Grand Canal and under the Rialto to St. Mark's Square. We passed much decay due to some land sinking and the inroads of the waters of the canals of the city. We hoped that the engineers and restorers could arrest the city's deterioration and preserve it for posterity. Venice is too great a treasure to be lost. Our visit was all too short. We went to bed late that night and were very tired.

On Wednesday, we departed from the Hotel Lugano at nine in the morning and again drove through beautiful country with rolling cornfields, until we reached Padua. At Padua we visited the beautiful Basilica of St. Anthony. Then we went on by Ferrara and crossed the River Po. The Po Valley was very agricultural and we passed large fields of wheat, corn and sugar beet. Later we passed by Bologna, a great route centre and the home of the oldest University in Europe. We had delicious lunch just out of Bologna and then moved on through the Apennine Mountains. On this part of our route it was awesome to behold the excellent roads, the viaducts, tunnels and bridges. Here again great engineering feats were all around us. We had a short rest stop and then we headed for Perugia, capital of Umbria. From Perugia we moved on, arriving at Assisi at 12 p.m. At Assisi we toured the great Cathedral of St. Francis, ably guided by an American priest. As I stood, small, in that magnificent cathedral, I thought of the other great religious structures we had already visited. I whispered to myself in wonder, 'Look! How man has built for his God, giving Him the best of his skill and creativity.' We next stopped at the town of Trevi, had dinner there, and then headed for Rome, arriving there at 11:50 p.m.

And then, we were in Rome, the Eternal City. At 9:10 am on Thursday morning, July 9, we left our hotel for our tour of Rome. We visited the Vatican, St. Peter's Basilica and the Sistine Chapel, the old Forum and the Colosseum. We had a Roman guide, Livia, who was humourous and very knowledgeable. St. Peter's Basilica and the Sistine Chapel were enormous, stupendous, magnificent, awesome. Oh! That master, Michelangelo. In Rome, when we viewed the wonders, we wondered if it was Man in all his glory or was it that we were witnessing the most wonderful and the very best expression of Man's creativity, executed for the praise and majesty of his God. What an inspiration the 'Eternal City' was. It humbles us. We then went back to our hotel and had dinner by 7:30 p.m. Then a group of us, all Caribbean, barged into a little, quiet night club where a small band was playing. We had wine and pasta and danced away. Few young people were there but there was a fair turnout of the older adults and we were comfortable. Vinnette even sang, 'Day oh, Day oh, Day da light an me wan go home,' with the band and it was well received. It was a very enjoyable night and we returned to our hotel shortly after 12:00. By 9:30 next morning, we were on our way out of Rome, headed for Florence.

We drove for a while through Rome, along the River Tiber, navigating through some of Rome's worst traffic. By about 11:40 we arrived at Viterbo, in Latium, an old walled town. We moved on after lunch and arrived at Siena at 4:45 p.m. Siena was a picturesque town with a great tower and a pretty square. There was even a horse carnival there in July and August. From Siena, we drove through beautiful countryside, arriving in Florence at 7:30 p.m. We had to cross over the River Arno to get to our hotel and to our dinner.

We were out early on Saturday morning for our tour of Florence. On our arrival the previous night from Siena, our group was divided into two; part went to the Hotel Domini, while the other dined and slept at the Hotel Patrizia. In Florence our tour guide was an English woman named Antonia who was very good. Her explanations of art gave the impression that she was an artist herself. Vinnette remarked that 'she brought out the soul of the thing'. We visited the religious and the political centres of Florence - the Baptistry, Academy of Fine Arts, Art Gallery, city squares and Cathedrals. We saw Michelangelo's 'David', moved around with the Medicis, and saw the tombs of Michelangelo, Galileo and Rossini. We saw great leatherwork at Michelangelo's Leather and Engraving, and bought a few souvenirs there. After ice cream, we all walked back with our guide, Antonia, to the Hotel Patrizia. That was about 2:35 p.m.; we then rested and went to dinner at 7:30 p.m. On Sunday morning at 7:30, we left our hotel and drove by the River Arno and out of Florence. The traffic was very heavy but thinned out by about 8:45. We travelled through excellent country and reached Galileo's birthplace, Pisa, at 9:45. We visited the Leaning Tower and Baptistry and the Cathedral. For some unexplained reason, I did not and would not ascend the stairs up into the Tower. Vinnette blithely climbed, but I just could not. Maybe it was fear, but why? After about an hour we left Pisa and drove by Massa, with its marble works. We were now in Liguria. We drove by Genoa, then halted for lunch, then on from the outskirts of Genoa, through the heavily agricultural Po Valley, with its extensive rice fields. From the Aosta area we moved into the Alps again, to an area which fell on the borders of France, Italy and Switzerland, with its hillside villages. The people there spoke French and Italian.

We were again in the Alps and climbed up the St. Bernard Pass, passed sheer rock faces and noted the careful use of the available land with its terraces, and producing good wine. We made a halt at the town of Aosta, where was sited an old Roman army camp. We left Aosta after 5 p.m, going up and up into the Alps, past breathtaking Alpine villages, meadows, valleys and streams, and looking up at snow topped mountains. We approached the St. Bernard Tunnel at the Swiss-Italian border at 6:05 p.m and soon arrived at the town of Aigle (eagle), a wine producing centre. From there we continued up and up and arrived at Leysin at 8:10 p.m. The climb up the Alps was sometimes a bit frightening. There were the winding roads but Julian, our driver, was careful and skillful. Again, the views were breathtaking as we went up and up, passing chalets, the mountain meadows, mountain streams and cascades and snow. We bedded down at the Welcome Centre in this town of Leysin. After a good dinner of rice, chicken and bread, we went to bed at 11 p.m.

Of course, we were now in Switzerland. On Monday morning, 13th day of the month, we went to breakfast at 8:20, and left for the Diablerets Glacier by 9:10, down winding roads down to the ski lift. The more heroic of us went into the lift and were taken up to the Glacier, 10,000 ft up. The view from this height was fantastic - the snow, the Alpine view of the peaks and mountain residences. It was an amazing experience. When we finally came back down to earth and then looked back to where we had been, I ventured to ask myself a question which I had resolutely fended off while in the air: "What if anything had gone wrong and we had fallen?" Oh - h-h-h! But it was an utterly amazing experience.

We next drove to the town of Montreaux, by Lake Geneva, and had lunch there. It was a very clean and beautiful town and I recall that many of our group members cashed travellers' cheques there. At 5:15 our group gathered for a boat ride to the Castle of Chillon. Our guide, Lise, took us through the old castle, through the halls, bedrooms, weapons and chests. She also showed the dungeon where the Genevese patriot, Bonivard, was imprisoned by the Duke of Savoy. Lord Byron's famous sonnet celebrates the Castle and its courageous prisoner. We also saw Lord Byron's carved name, there. We then drove back to Leysin and checked into the Charleston Hotel and had dinner at 6:30 p.m. We had a full day, were very tired and retired soon after dinner. We rose very early next morning, Tuesday, the thirteenth day of our tour, and by 6:45 we had loaded our suitcases on the bus. By 7:35 we had breakfasted and were on our way out of Leysin and on towards Geneva. Again it was down the mountains to Aigle, then by Lake Geneva. We arrived in Geneva at 9:15. We toured the Bucherer Watch factory, and here I bought a moderate- priced Bucherer watch which is still serving me today. We did some shopping otherwise, passed the headquarters of the United Nations in Europe and had to bow to the beauty of the flower gardens we passed.

We left Geneva at 11:10, passed the source of the River Rhone and reached the Swiss-French border at 11:10. We were now in France and by 1:25 we were in the region of Burgundy. We lunched at a rest stop just after Macon, took to the road again at 2:30 and drove through great wine and cheese country, drove by Chalons on the River Saone, past Dijon, over the

Seine and entered Paris at 7:35 p.m. We put up at a small hotel and had a good dinner at 8:00. We enjoyed the dinner and the good French service. Paris was so beautiful, with wide streets, cafes, six-storey buildings and iron-railed balconies. We also drove by the 'Lady of the Revolution', the Hotel de Ville. Next day, Wednesday morning, we had breakfast at 8:00, and by 9:00 we drove out of our hotel. We crossed the Seine, passed the Eiffel Tower (984 ft. high), and past the Louvre.

Our first stop was at Notre Dame Cathedral, a wonder of Gothic architecture, with all its windows stained. We went to the Invalides, that great military museum. We saw the Tomb of Napoleon and memorials to other French military greats. We toured the Louvre Museum and gasped at the Mona Lisa. We passed under the Arc d'Triomphe and visited the Paris Military Academy, the Bastille scene, the Champ d'Elysees and a few other great sights. Oh, this beautiful city with its boulevards and multiplicity of street-side cafes and perfumery. Traffic was heavy and, surprisingly, in that centre of such sophistication, I witnessed the worst jam that I have ever seen. But Paris was just great, a wonderful city which wove its spell over all of us. We did not get the chance to visit the Eiffel Tower but our best group picture was taken with the great Tower forming a magnificent background for it. Our European tour was now almost at an end and we had to prepare for our departure from Paris on the morrow. We dined that evening at the Motte Picquat restaurant, our last big meal in Europe.

European Tour Group with Eiffel Tower in Background

And so we had come to the end of our six-country tour of Europe on this fifteenth day of July, 1987. Fittingly, it ended in Europe's most beautiful city and it left us with such great and beautiful memories. The fifteen days were really hectic and one had to live in and out of the suitcase, but everyone of us enjoyed it and we never lost our enthusiasm. It gave us a very quick look at some of the most attractive and gripping areas of Europe. How I would have liked to rent a car and do a leisurely two- month tour of most of the continent, but my meagre resources would never afford such a luxury, so I cherish the memories and remain grateful that I had the opportunity to make this tour. Even Mother Nature cooperated, insomuch that the weather was most delightful for the entire tour. There was an abundance of sunshine everywhere and when there was some rainfall, it was moderate and just sufficient. Even good old London did not show us her fog and damp. Instead, she saved the best for us. For the number of students who were in our group, I hope it was an appetizer which would be followed up by a full meal of historic Europe.

We left our hotel at 9:30 on Thursday morning, July 16, for our last drive through Paris, bound for Charles DeGaulle Airport, and then on our way to our distant homes. The Paris airport was crowded that morning and there was so much bustle to and fro. There was no queuing and our minds went back to the discipline that had so impressed us with the Germans, English and Swiss. A friend of mine had always referred to France as the most revolutionary and contentious country in the world and as I watched the airport scene that morning, I wondered if I were seeing part of the reason why. Our tour group bought some last souvenirs and then boarded the Trans World airliner for the flight to New York. After some delay, we took off at 3 p.m. and arrived in New York at 4:25 p.m. In New York, goodbyes were said all around to our travel companions as we broke up. We from the Bahamas had to wait until 7:30 p.m. to board our flight to Miami. At Miami, the final breakup took place. Vinnette and I went on to Freeport, Grand Bahama, while our Haitian and Bahamian friends went on to Nassau. We were now back on Bahamian soil but so very tired from our recent trip. It took us a few days to get fully rested and ready to prepare for our return to our home in Jamaica. We had already shipped our appliances and other bulky belongings and now we had a few last chores to attend to before our flight to Jamaica.

We bid personal goodbyes to a number of our friends there in Freeport. Our Methodist Church there, St. Paul's, bid us a touching farewell at a get-together function held in the Church hall. There, our Methodist friends at last discovered that I was not a Methodist, but a committed Moravian. Moravians, over the long ages, have been one of the most ecumenical of religious groups, and my pastors back in Jamaica would have been proud of how I adapted. There was no Moravian congregation in the Bahamas, Vinnette was a committed Methodist and I had always been a good friend of Methodism in Jamaica; hence my fruitful and enjoyable sojourn with the Methodists in Freeport. All during that quite long period, they never suspected that I was a Moravian.

Back in Jamaica, we had earlier established our residential base in the Havendale area of St. Andrew. Paul, had taken to himself a wife about two years before and both had migrated to the United States during 1986. "Teddy", was then a graduate of the College of Arts, Science and Technology (now University of Technology), and Technical Services Supervisor of a computer technology firm in Kingston. He was living in the smaller section of our house and took care of our property there. Tenants were in the larger part of the house and since we were returning to take up residence permanently, they would have to vacate. Vinnette was all a-raring to re-establish her flower garden and resume her puttering with the vegetables. She and I arrived in Jamaica in early August 1987, with the vow that this was the end of our wanderings.

Chapter Twenty One

Some Thoughts About How My Generation Saw Their Politics

At this point I have to take a few minutes to look back at a bit of the political views and attitudes of my generation, as I saw it. Earlier in this work I referred to the advent of party politics in my native part of North Manchester and the overpowering dominance of the People's National Party in that region. Whenever I hear it said over the airwaves that a certain top party operative once stated that what was good for the People's National Party is also good for Jamaica, I go back in my mind to those early years and I fully understand where that party operative 'was coming from', because, that was exactly how so many thousands of us young Jamaicans thought, politically, at the time. For us, it was just natural that what was good for the People's National Party must be good for Jamaica. If you disagreed or objected to that view, we would have looked on you as being totally misguided, unintelligent and backward. I grew up with a grandfather who was widely read and well aware of what was taking place around him, politically and otherwise. He was a great admirer of J.A.G. Smith (Barrister Smith), member of the Legislative Council, for the parish of Clarendon, and Norman Manley. Both men were eminent lawyers and my grandfather seemed to have regarded them as supreme examples of what the black Jamaican man could achieve.

He was saddened when J.A.G. Smith died, and from then on, his fond regards were centred on Norman Manley, as also Charles Archibald Reid, Member of the Legislative Council for Manchester, and Harold Egbert Allan, Member of the Legislative Council for Portland. Both Allan and Reid were named Privy Councillors later, and I recall my grandfather was delighted at their elevation. Grandpa was one of the small number of citizens who had got on the voters' list then, and he never failed to use his vote. So, as an individual who was quite politically aware, he immediately latched on to the young political movement founded by Norman Manley. To him, as to many thousands of other Jamaicans, Manley was totally honest, and a man of unquestionable integrity. He had the education and equipment to lead this country, and was a man of great intellect who had the very best interests of his country at heart.

We young people drank in all of this and Mr. Norman Manley became our hero. During my student days at Mico, the majority of the student body were sympathetic to Mr. Manley and his party. There was no political activism among us, as such, but the many loyalists were there. One of my batch mates had actually made campaign speeches in support of a certain St. Catherine member of the then House of Representatives. We never missed a Manley broadcast to the nation, we attended so many street meetings of the Party, some of us even endeavoured to pronounce certain words as Mr. Manley did. To us, Norman Manley was the natural leader for this country; how could anybody question that? When I was a student at the University of the West Indies, I had a good friend who was in the Sciences and hailed from the parish of Hanover. He was a convinced follower of Bustamante and the Jamaica Labour Party. He was a broad-minded fellow and we used to tease each other about our respective party affiliations. We had a lot of fun here, and our friendship never wavered, but I secretly thought it so unfortunate that he supported 'the wrong party'. How could such a nice fellow be so politically misguided? During my first year of Mico I had a very good friend in the Third Year batch. He was from Jones Town and was a most committed 'Labourite'. He continually questioned the rightness of my head; how could I find it possible to vote for the People's National Party? But he was the greatest human being and our friendship continued to flourish after we left Mico. In fact he was my best-man at my wedding years later. We actually had so much fun in our politics. He laughed at my Party and he laughed at his Party whenever he thought it had done something less than wise. He had no rancour and we had a whale of a time mouthing each other. He saw my side, I saw his side and we enjoyed our politics. Whenever there was a good joke on the Jamaica Labour Party, his Party, he would be the first to enjoy it and tell it.

What further did we say about the two Parties? Again, to so many thousands of Jamaicans of my generation, if you had anything progressive in you, if you had even moderate education and if you had the ambition to make something of yourself, then the natural party for you was the People's National Party. Do you wonder that in those earlier days, possibly about 80% of Jamaica's schoolteachers were Manley followers? After all, did they not have some education and were ambitious and progressive? So where would you expect them to make their political home? The top leadership of the island's Teachers' Unions provided several election candidates for that 'right political party' in General Elections. How can we forget that famous relationship between the teachers' leadership and that short, waist coated,

'B.A.' Minister of Education, from that rural parish? It was amusing too, at the time, that often the teacher who was sympathetic to the Jamaica Labour Party would be very quiet about it, for fear that his teacher colleagues would get wind of it and laugh at him. For us young 'PNPites', the 'fool, fool man' naturally chose the Labour Party, while the intelligent, thinking man chose the People's National Party.

How we swelled with pride at the People's National Party's leader when we heard him on radio or when he appeared on television or in the newspapers. How we joked about Mr. Bustamante's lack of academic achievement. Some of us really believed that Mr. Bustamante could not spell 'bread', and would with glee tell the lame story of Mr. Bustamante's spelling of 'bread' as 'bred', and when reminded that 'bread' has an 'a' in the spelling, he promptly spelt it 'breda'. Oh, ridiculous! But such was our devotion to PNPism that many believed this fictitious story. So many of us came to believe that the Jamaica Labour Party was the seat of all political skullduggery. Where corruption, dishonesty, stealing of ballot boxes, voting three or more times at an election, or violence at political meetings were concerned, the PNP was well-nigh lily white. You would have to look for those 'sins' in another certain Party.

How a certain leader of the Jamaica Labour Party was demonised. We labelled him as being ruthless, vindictive, a man of violence and an autocrat. How we lionised the top leadership of the PNP: N. N. Nethersole, Dr. Ivan Lloyd, William Seivwright, Wills Isaacs, Florizel Glasspole; then the younger tier of David Coore, Vivian Blake, the Manley sons, Carl Rattray, et al. To us, the Jamaica Labour Party's top leadership of Frank Pixley, Linden Newland, Dr. E. H. Fagan, C. M. Aitcheson, et al, and the younger tier of Edward Seaga, D. C. Tavares, Dr. Eldemire, Wilton Hill and Ken Jones, were lesser mortals when compared with the People's National Party luminaries. How our heads bled when the Jamaica Labour Party won the Independence General Elections and went on to lead Jamaica into Independence in 1962. So many of us felt that the mantle of the first Prime Minister of independent Jamaica was rightfully Norman Manley's and not Alexander Bustamante's. When that certain Jamaica Labour Party administration of the 1960s seized literature which Walter Rodney and Richard Fletcher had brought back from Cuba, we took this action as a ringing example of how backward this Labour Party government was.

We rejoiced when the People's National Party regained power in the General Election of 1972 and felt that here was a new era of greatness opening for Jamaica. We were mesmerised by Michael Manley, son of the great Norman, and new Prime Minister of Jamaica. For many years, thousands and thousands of well-thinking Jamaicans had sincerely prayed for the emergence on the Jamaica political scene, of a political leader who would be a blend of Norman Manley and Alexander Bustamante - with Bustamante's mass appeal and his understanding of the common man, and Norman Manley's intellect, his unquestionable integrity and his appeal to the middle, upper and more literate sections of the population. Michael Manley seemed the answer to this prayer and was, initially, immensely popular throughout the new nation. He was the new 'Joshua', and would lead this nation, triumphantly, to the 'Promise Land'.

The political story of the 1970s, in Jamaica, has been well documented and there is no need to repeat it here. But it was a period of great expectations, some of which were harshly disappointing; some were realised as the period saw some long-needed social legislation enacted, and the common man emerged much more politically aware than he had ever been at any time in the past. So many Jamaicans had anxiously awaited this transformation of the Jamaican society and the break-down of much of the blatant barriers between the social classes. At the same time, some saw this movement as promoting a false egalitarianism and encouraging rank indiscipline and disrespect. They saw the administration as one which would gladly cavort with any Left-leaning foreign administration, loudly trumpeting the appropriate anti-Western sentiments, and at the same time extending the 'begging bowl'.

And many, many solid and hardworking Jamaicans saw the Michael Manley administration as essentially well meaning, one which started out with a mission to improve the quality of life of the ordinary Jamaican, but, somewhere along the road it had lost its way and had now become dominated by young, rash and opportunistic Leftists. There was so much careless rhetoric, which bred distrust and suspicion. We now know that there were great exaggerations and misrepresentations of the national scene and there was a measure of deliberate undermining of programmes,'to make the government look bad'. It was a period of much that was negative, but at the same time much was achieved by the society and it was a great learning period.

I think my generation was chastened and our eyes were opened to many realities in our system. Some of us had our eyes set in the heavens, oblivious of the thorns all around us; we were rudely awakened and brought back to earth, to realise the inequalities and injustices in our midst. Many, many of my generation came out of the 1970s much wiser to the realities of politics and the evils of our blatant tribalism. Diehard political affiliation was no longer automatically acceptable and we realised that we had to be more sensible in making our political choices. When that very eminent Jamaican journalist and man of letters, also an avid supporter of the governing party, visited a few urban polling stations, at a certain General Elections, and later wrote, in sheer disgust and disappointment, 'at what he had seen his Party activists doing that morning', so many of us shook our heads in disbelief. Could we have been so blind? We had always fooled ourselves that political skull-duggery belonged in the 'other camp', not in ours. Our political education had been defective and we now had to see the world in its very real colours.

Chapter Twenty Two

We Return Home, Finally.
And My Retirement.

Vinnette and I had come back home to Jamaica, knowing this was to be the final phase of our active working life. From now on, our permanent base would be Jamaica and there would be no more extended sojourns in any foreign land. This time I did not have a car to clear at the wharf I had owned a four- year old Toyota Corolla station wagon, in excellent condition and would have brought it with me to Jamaica, but for one great snag. The Jamaica Government regulations, at the time, laid down that no car more than three years old could be imported into Jamaica. I had no intention of purchasing a new car to meet the Government requirement. In fact I could not have afforded a new car then. Many people suggested that a deal could have been quietly worked out with the Jamaican authorities so that I could have got in my beautiful car. But I would not go along that route and decided to sell the car. I would get a good price for it in Freeport and would purchase a good used car when I arrived in Jamaica. But just at that time there was a slight slump in used car sales in Grand Bahama and I was not able to get mine sold before I left. I had to leave it with a very good friend who managed to sell it at a little later date, and send on the money to me in Jamaica. Thus, for the month of September, our family was without a car and suffered the serious inconveniences of transportation to and from work, getting our groceries, and other necessary activities. Early in October I purchased a good used Toyota Corolla sedan and breathed a sigh of relief.

September 1987 saw us back in the Jamaica education service. Vinnette had landed the position of Music Education teacher at Wolmer's Girls School. She started out quite happy as she had her own Music Room and there was reasonable equipment available. Perhaps her greatest success as a Music Education Teacher was earned at this school and she had the strong support of a very good Headmistress and solid student cooperation. She re-established herself as a power on the island's Music Education scene and when hearing disability pushed her into retirement some years later, her expertise was sorely missed.

I began work on the staff of St. Joseph's Teachers' College in October 1987. I was appointed Lecturer in History and Social Studies, the same area in which I operated at Shortwood Teachers' College, in the memorable 1970s. For the month of September, I filled in for a Senior History Mistress at Wolmer's Girls School, who was on leave, and I quite enjoyed the very brief stint there. We note that this was my second experience of an all- girls' institution; St. Joseph's was my third. Later, when I retired, I did acting appointments in two other all-female institutions. So, a significant chunk of my teaching life was spent in all-female institutions. I had also worked in three all-male institutions. So it turned out that in Jamaica, after leaving the Primary classroom, I did not experience the joys of teaching co-educational classes. Nonetheless, I enjoyed my work with the ladies and have always maintained lasting good relationships with many. A good old friend of mine maintains that my temperament is so well suited to working with ladies that I would not have lasted very long in the present day all-male classroom. I know my friend to be a good judge of character and I would not attempt to argue with him on this.

St. Joseph's Teachers' College is a Roman Catholic teacher training institution. It was founded in 1897 by the Franciscan Sisters of Alleghany, and they have their headquarters in Pennsylvania, United States of America. These Sisters of Alleghany have rendered yeoman service to this country, especially in the field of education. They work very quietly, without fanfare, but they are practical people, bent on achieving very high standards. St. Joseph's is one of the smaller teacher training colleges and prepares only Early Childhood and Primary teachers. When I arrived on the staff in 1987, Sister Charlotte O'Brien, an American nun and long worker in Jamaica, was the Principal. The College, then, had a student body of about three hundred. Many years before, there seemed to have been an experiment where a few young men were admitted for training. The experiment did not last very long and it was not until sometime in the 1990s that male students were again admitted and the College really became co-educational. During my student days at Mico, St. Joseph's was exceedingly quiet and there was not a great deal of contact between the two Colleges. Today, she has shed very much of her conservatism and has placed herself in the forefront of this nation's education thrust. When I joined the staff in 1987, the College had a very experienced staff, especially in the Education Department. In that Department, all those teacher trainers, then, were people who had vast experience in the primary and early childhood classrooms and now were passing on that expertise to the young teachers. No wonder some schools specially ask for St. Joseph's graduates for their primary departments. How can we forget Father Sheehan, the College's Chaplain, Reading Specialist and a beautiful human being, Mrs Harrison, Mrs. Silma Edwards, Mrs. Beulah Johnson, the very efficient Teaching Practice Coordinator and Ms. Zona Johnson, the best in the field of creating Classroom Instructional Aids. All these people were outstanding in their special areas and the students benefitted greatly. Mrs. Joy Carter, an unrepentant disciplinarian and 'stickler' for excellence, brought lustre to the Music Department which she headed.

The Mathematics Department was ably led by Mrs. Solomon and Sister Mary Peter, a Guyanese and untiring exponent of the New Maths. Ruby Hutchinson headed the History and Social Studies Department. When I joined the staff, she was away on study leave and soon returned as Dr. Hutchinson. In her absence the Department was ably led by Geography specialist, Lil Daley. Sister Teresita and Sister Trinita Solnick did a mighty job in guiding the Religious Education programme of the College. Sister Mary Andrew was there too, a real shining light, polished, practical and wise. The other Departments, like Language Arts, Guidance, Art and Craft, Science and Physical Education, were no less productive and played their very important part in this great team effort, effectively led by Principal, Sister Charlotte, and Vice-Principal Sister Avril. This mighty team worked without ostentation but produced seeds of excellence.

In my first year at St. Joseph's, much of my teaching time was spent with a group of students who were called "Prelims". These were girls who had not yet qualified to start the regular College Course, and so were placed in a Preliminary class where they would be prepared to sit a number of General Certificate of Education subjects that they needed to qualify for entry into the College Course. If they were successful in the subjects taken, then they would begin the regular College Course. The "prelims" thus spent four years to complete their training. There were always the few students who had to struggle hard, academically, to complete the College course, but some of these went on to perform very well in the field. There was the common complaint then, that the College's primary programme was not attracting the high calibre human material that we craved, and which would result in our turning out sub-standard young teachers. Of course we did not get the brightest but year after year this College graduated many, many who have gone out and have been doing brilliant work with our young people in the schools scattered all over Jamaica.

It is a rewarding experience to witness the immense growth of individuals - growth in experience, equipment and confidence. The St. Joseph's teachers are all around and among us and we know how good they are. That first "Prelim" group that I taught in the 1987 - 88 year, was the best of the several groups that I had over those years there. They were so keen and kept with me every step of the way. When their examination results came, there were so many distinctions, and my subject with them, History, took quite a few. I recall that one of my most reliable students in that group, confessed to me that her real interest was Surveying, and not Classroom Teaching and she needed the subjects to get into the Surveying field. She implored me not to let out her secret, and I did not. As expected, she did very well in her General Certificate of Education subjects, and did not return for the new school year.

These were the young women, some of whom had enormous problems: economic and social, domestic, romantic and marital - and it is a wonder some of them survived under the various strains. I recall on one occasion that three young ladies had not handed in their assignment which I had given to their group, and in no uncertain terms I had made it clear to them that I was annoyed. Then later that same day one of these young ladies came to the staff room and asked to speak with me. There she explained to me that it was not laziness or callousness which had caused the assignment not to be done - it was simply that she just could not find the time to complete the assignment, so encircled was she with problems. Then she opened up to me about why the time could not be found. She told me of the problem of her baby and her baby's father, the problems with her aunts who lived under the same roof with her, the problems of her unemployed mother who was away in the United States and on whom she depended heavily for economic support and the problems of the measly little job that she, our student friend, had to be desperately clinging to, to ensure that her baby had food. The circumstances of each problem were more than daunting, and here was an individual, battered on nearly every side, but fighting back fiercely, not just to survive, but to succeed. By some means she held back the tears and I could only listen in silence. At the end I gave her words of understanding and encouraged her not to surrender. As she walked away, I flashed back in memory to my student days at Mico, where my economic situation was always precarious. I thought I had problems then, but this young lady's situation made me understand how much better off I had been, and how grateful I should be.

This was one of several jolting stories and they sharply remind us how much the world and times had changed. The student of the late 20th and early 21st centuries, finds himself/herself in a much more complicated and harsh world, than the student of the 1940s or 1950s. I never forget the comments of one of my tutor colleagues at Shortwood College many years before. This tutor had a brilliant student career at Shortwood in the late 1940s and had always been regarded as a model of application and hard work. In one of our conversations we touched on present day life: the changes in attitude and focus, problems and opportunities, and she made the comment, "You know, when we were in College, all we concentrated on was our studies." Today, in this high tech and very often unsympathetic world, very often this 'concentration' has to be cruelly divided. Far more opportunities are indeed present today but so many of the challenges are bitter and unyielding.

My second year at St. Joseph's started with a great, wicked bang. It was 1988 and Hurricane Gilbert came in September. I suffered a direct blow as the roof of my home was blown off. The wind lifted nearly every rafter and ripped off the zinc sheets, depositing them at various places in the neighbourhood. I can never forget Vinnette, Teddy and I, sheltering under our dining table as the winds ripped, hearing the zinc sheets being torn off and finally water pouring through the collapsed gypsum ceiling. Then this savage surge abated and we went out to view the damage. Only the 'maid's room' at the back remained intact. It was a bit strange to me that so many homes around my site had escaped damage. One or two had slab roofs but the others had the same type of roof as mine had. Was it that my roof had received the worst workmanship or that my house, unfortunately, lay smack in the direct line of the most vicious wind surge? As we stood there, bewildered, our married son's parents-in-law came over and invited us to stay with them. Their home was undamaged and lay just a stone's throw from ours. There we stayed for a few days until we could make more permanent temporary arrangements. "Teddy" went to stay with an aunt and Vinnette found refuge with a childhood friend in Valentine Gardens.

I took up residence in the 'maid's room' at the back of the house, in order to thwart, as best as I could, any attempt to loot the house. I recall that the sun was exceedingly hot on the days following the hurricane but it facilitated the quick drying of the water-soaked clothing, bedding, books and other items. Of the fruit trees in our backyard, the breadfruit tree had calmly keeled over on the approach of the first heavy blow; so had the coconut tree, which had aligned itself neatly on the ground, parallel with the back wall of the house, and had not fallen on the house, which it would have damaged. Remarkable! That coconut tree was carrying a solid crop of coconuts and on those hot days without electricity or ice water available, those jelly coconuts were a God-send. We had to wonder if that coconut tree somehow knew that 1988 would have been its last year. In previous years it would produce only some tiny nuts which we did not bother about. Then came 1988, and it carried a whopping crop of all large nuts, each filled with that cool and delicious water. Day after day, we just stepped through our back door and readily slaked our thirst from the nuts waiting on the ground. Such a blessed tree she was. And she supplied us thirsty ones with a cool drink on many a hot day after the hurricane. Our coconut friend lives on in our memory.

Then came the tremendous job of repair and restoration. Our furniture was stored in the homes of a few of our friends and we hurriedly stretched tarpaulins over the open roof to keep out the worst of the rain water. There was heavy afternoon rainfall, day after day, for a period after the hurricane and I recall that at St. Joseph's I would step out of the classroom as afternoon approached, look up in the direction of my home area, Havendale, and pray for no rain. On most of those evenings, the prayer was not answered and after classes I had to hurry home, grab my long stick and dislodge the pockets of water which had collected in the tarpaulins on the housetop. Eventually, the Insurance Company paid and we could go ahead with repairs. Our entire roof had to be re-raftered and for the first time, many of us homeowners paid attention to things like hurricane-straps. Zinc sheets were in short supply and I recall that we had to have our eyes and ears fully open for any news report or rumours or whispers re the arrival of material in the hardware store, then race down to try to procure some. On two occasions, by the time that the whisper reached me and I hurried down, the newly- arrived zinc sheets had all been sold out.

I specially remember Wood's Hardware in Cross Roads where I procured a large quantity of good quality zinc sheets. I had to personally commend the manager. It was good quality material at a reasonable price and they did not attempt to gouge the customer at this time of heavy demand. Our restoration progressed and by year end we were again safe in our castle. We had decided to stick with gypsum for our restored ceiling and we secured the services of a most efficient 'gypsum man'. It was a joy to watch him as he brought his head, hands, feet and mid body into the work and executed a job that was very neat and professional. Then there were the minor restoration jobs to be done - furniture needed to be polished and brought back home, parts replaced and various other things done for life to return to normal. But at last we were back in our home. We could now look with satisfaction on a job of restoration well done and give our grateful thanks to the Almighty who had stood with us through our peril and brought us safely home.

For so many of our people, the hurricane ravage was very traumatic and many homeowners lost everything. As a young man of twenty years, I had experienced the onslaught of Hurricane Charlie in 1951, and we had picked up the pieces very quickly. In 1951 I was in my grandfather's house, with little responsibility. In 1988 I was in my own house and laden with full responsibility. My family had received its most severe battering, up to then, but thankfully, we did not panic, and we, like so many other Jamaican families, pulled ourselves back to recovery.

One of the blots on this period of our history was the handling of some of the overseas aid which poured in during this time of national need. It was a real demonstration of the wickedness of our tribalistic political system. As was reported widely, we received donations of so much zinc roofing that we had zinc 'to stone dog'. Yet there were some devastated families who could not get one sheet of that zinc - a terrible shame. Was it true that there were handcarts in downtown Kingston, bearing some of these donated sheets for sale? But our young nation quickly recovered from the devastation, thanks to the wonderful response from so many countries abroad, who gave generously towards our rebuilding. We are eternally grateful for this help in our time of distress, and this reminds us that despite the intense competitiveness and sometimes ruthless selfishness of this our modern world, there are still great pockets of kindly concern, and the ready will to help fallen sister nations when the cry for help goes out. And the remarkable resilience of our people was so evident all through this painful period; much to the surprise of even ourselves, our country recovered quickly.

Earlier in this work I related that an unpleasant immigration situation in the Bahamas in 1987, drove our decision to return to Jamaica two years earlier than we had planned. We were annoyed at the Bahamian Administration's stance at this time, but looking back over time, we wonder if the hand of Providence was not involved here on our family's behalf. What if I had been still in Freeport when Hurricane Gilbert struck and carried off the roof of my home? How would I have dealt with this serious situation, long distance from Grand Bahama? I believe that our Good Lord had so ordered our affairs that when the big blow came I would be on spot, to face it and deal with it. I was hurt but not destroyed. Such are the blessings which must be counted..

St Joseph's had received its hurricane blow too, but the damage was not overwhelming. There was not much dislocation and the work of the College went on apace. In this period of repair and reconstruction all around us we, as a staff, worked on steadily and did not flag. Other staff members had suffered hurricane damage but they soldiered on and the College programme did not suffer. In the next few years we would witness changes in the College's infrastructure: damaged buildings were restored and there was the addition of an Audio-Visual and Teaching Demonstration facility. The new Administration and Library building was erected sometime later. We witnessed St. Joseph's gingerly entering the computer age when she acquired her first computer under the careful, mathematical eye of Sister Avril, our Vice-Principal.

There were changes on the staff: The Education Department lost one of its stalwarts, Mrs, Harrison, to cancer, and Father Sheehan, our Chaplain and Reading Specialist, moved on to another assignment. I recall that Father Sheehan's departure from St. Joseph's once again reinforced a life truth for me: do not simply accept that a man or woman is so very, very good that he or she is indispensable, is irreplaceable. That is how I felt about Father Sheehan. He was such a magnificent team member, efficient, a tremendous human being, and when I learnt that he was moving on, the first thought that came to me was: how will St. Joseph's function without him? We all went off on our Summer holidays and when College reopened for the new academic year, in September, Father Sheehan was not present. I did not hear any anguished cry for the absent Father; the College programme continued unabated and staff members were all busy getting down to work. Had they forgotten Father Sheehan? The College continued to function as beautifully as it had done before. Of course we had lost a very special staff member, but his place had to be filled and the productive life of the College had to go on.

On a more positive note, we were so happy to welcome back Ruby Hutchinson, Principal Lecturer and Head of the History and Social Studies Department, who returned with her doctorate after a period of study in the United States. Also, a little later, Nadine Scott, from the Art and Craft Department, had returned with her Doctorate which she had earned in the United States. Donna Chinn Fatt, another of our bright younger staff members, was also busy, academically, and was to earn her Doctorate sometime later. As a staff, we were proud of our sister tutors who had worked so hard in their journey to greater heights. It is necessary to repeat here: here was a very qualified staff, working quietly and most effectively, without any striking fanfare in making their contribution to that job of building this nation.

But over these years a lot of water had flowed under the bridge and I now arrived at the age of retirement. I had seen forty- eight years in the classroom, in Jamaica, Canada and the Bahamas. I was still enjoying good health but I felt it would be sensible to hang up my spikes at this point. I communicated my decision to my Principal, Sister Charlotte, who coached me well in the appropriate wording of my letter of intention to the Jamaica Ministry of Education. I was exactly sixty-five years of age when I went off on five-and-one-half months of pre-retirement leave.Officially, my retirement became effective sometime in March 1996.

Forty- eight years is a long stretch of time in one's life. How well I remember that Monday, in December 1953, as I rode in the railway coach, on the way to my home in Manchester. Three years of teacher training at the Mico had come to an end and I was now presented to an expectant society to begin my apprenticeship. The catalogue of my work and travels ranges over a wide area of time and space, and as I glance back over the years I do not harbour regrets or bitterness. Instead, I savour the joys and triumphs and those times when I literally jumped and rejoiced. I have always been convinced that when the teacher sincerely works to guide and mould that young mind, he is casting his bread upon the water and will find it after many days - often coming back to him many, many fold. This is a feeling and a pride which money cannot buy. There have been setbacks and disappointments but never have I regretted my job of helping to mould and nurture young minds. In all this I have learnt so much from the students and other individuals I have worked with: patience, open-mindedness, learning to listen and to admit when I am wrong. I have been fortunate, too, in having, for the most part, solid team leadership. I have worked with good Principals: men and women who were out in front, in terms of their knowledge of education and their commitment, their ability to motivate and keep their team firing.

I must declare here that a major plank in the satisfaction I have experienced in my teaching career has been my wife, Vinnette. So often over the years I have commented that she is the superior teacher in our home and I have the utmost respect for her skill in handling and working with young people. Children never cease to excite her and a child's progress is an inspiration for her. All along she has been a tower of strength to me and an ideal life partner. For both of us, education is life and should be available to all and we see it as a duty to do our part in opening this great world of learning to as many as possible. The great Moravian educator, John Amos Comenius, in the 17th century wrote:

> "............... *Our first wish is that all men should be educated fully, to full Humanity; not only one individual, nor a few, nor even many, but all men together and single, young and old, rich and poor, of high and lowly birth, men and women - in a word, all whose fate it is to be born human beings ; ....".*

We have entered the 21st century but Comenius' vision of education for all men has not been realised. In our island home, there are still substantial pockets of illiteracy. Surely, much greater sums are being pumped into education, there have been much improvements in infrastructure and various facilities, various reforms have been carried out in quantity and quality, but we are still a distance behind. We can recount so many of the ills which remain in our education system. But despite our continued deficiencies, as I look back and reflect on my over forty- years teaching career I see developments that give me much pleasure. I rejoice at the opening up of high school education to the urban and rural masses of this country. Professions like medicine, law and engineering are no longer virtually closed to the poor. Small farmer Jones and Miss Aggie, higgler, can now have 'lawyer sons and doctor daughters'. For my generation, this is a remarkable development. May the numbers benefiting ever expand.

Allied to this is the considerable democratisation of higher education. There are now three local universities, along with about five university colleges, serving the society - much greater numbers now have access to higher education. Even my old alma mater, Mico, has now emerged as one of the young university colleges. I beam with pride as I see her striding forward. This has also meant that more teachers have the chance to get more qualified, which is a great plus for our education thrust. A number of North American universities collaborate with certain of our tertiary institutions and conduct classes here, which adds further to our people's chances for educational improvement.

Another progressive change which has come over the last forty years is a very substantial narrowing of that great gap between academic education and technical/vocational education. Technical schools have come into their own and their graduates are finding their place in a society which is marching to become a modern technological society. The University of Technology stands supreme in the technical fields and its graduates are in great demand. The prejudice has not been fully erased but great progress has been made here.

This road over the near fifty years has been a long road, rocky in some places but also with its stretches of level, beautiful surface. We give praise and honour to the Great Almighty for giving us the strength and persistence to serve our fellow men in our particular field. Where we have opened the door to knowledge, where we have pointed the way to opportunities for good, for healthy advancement, and for a fulfilling life, we give humble thanks. All these have helped to give us a true life's purpose and have made us better human beings.

We have remained materially poor, but yet we are rich.
And we are ever thankful.